Also by Susan Gilbert Harvey

*Tea with Sister Anna: a Paris journal*

# POSTMARKS

Anna Lester
1862-1900

Edith Lester
1876-1960

# POSTMARKS
## *the summers of '98*

SUSAN GILBERT HARVEY

GOLDEN
APPLE
PRESS

Golden Apple Press
436 Broad Street, Suite 301
Rome, Georgia, 30161-3087
Telephone: (706) 291-4172
E-mail: susan@susanharvey.com
www.susanharvey.com

The author has made every effort to ensure the accuracy of information contained in this book, but she assumes no responsibility for errors, omissions, or inconsistencies regarding people or places.

Cover design, maps, and line drawings by Debbie Stubbs
Layout and typesetting by Tracy Cole

First printing 2010

ISBN 978-0-9768956-1-9

Library of Congress Control Number: 2010912772

# CONTENTS

# CHRONOLOGY

1862        Anna McNulty Lester born in Conway, South Carolina

1868        The Bannester Lester family moves to Rome, Georgia

1876        Edith Lester born in Rome, Georgia

1896-1899   Edith Lester studies music in Berlin

1897-1898   Anna Lester studies art in Paris

*1898*      *Summer travel of Anna and Edith Lester*

1900        Anna Lester dies in Rome, Georgia

1905        Edith Lester marries William Pickens Harbin, M.D.

1935        Mary Cuttino Harbin marries Warren Monroe Gilbert, M.D.

1937        Susan Cuttino Gilbert born in Rome, Georgia

1957        Susan Gilbert on Hollins Abroad-Paris program

1959        Susan Gilbert graduates from Hollins College

1959        Susan Gilbert marries David Donaldson Harvey

1959-1964   Susan and David Harvey on Okinawa and in California

1960        Edith Lester Harbin dies in Rome, Georgia

1964        The David Harvey family returns to Rome, Georgia

1972        The David Harvey family moves to 400 East Third Avenue

1985        Susan & David Harvey in Switzerland with Edith & Larry Ethridge

1987        Harveys and Ethridges in Switzerland

1991        Warren Gilbert dies in Rome, Georgia

1998        Susan Harvey goes to 9, rue Sainte-Beuve in Paris

1999        Mary Harbin Gilbert dies in Rome, Georgia

2003        Susan and David Harvey move to Forrest Place

2005        *Tea with Sister Anna: a Paris journal*

2010        *POSTMARKS: the summers of '98*

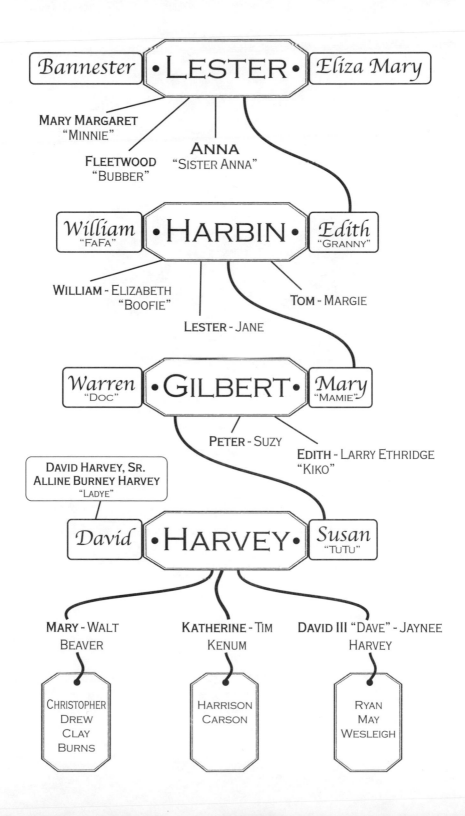

La Mer de Glace

Chamonix                    21-7-98 —

Dear Mama —        To-day we have been on a
lovely excursion. The weather was beautiful. Two
English ladies went with us. Sister rode a mule
& carried our wraps & lunch, & the rest of us walk.
We went up "Montanvert" and then had our lunch
& sent the mule back. Then we put on woolen
socks over our shoes and walked over the "Mer
de Glace" or Sea of ice. It was fine fun. I
ate a lot of beautifully clean ice that I chipped up with my stick. The way home was nice
too. The sunset on "Mont Blanc" was beautiful
to-night, but not as rosy as the night we were
in Geneva. We would like to stay a long time
here, but we have made the ordinary excursion
and leave to-morrow morning early. Came down
on the same train with a very nice party of English
people, which made it pleasanter. With love. E. Stat..

Mont Blanc is not
in this picture.

# PREFACE

*POSTMARKS: the summers of '98* is a reflective spiral in time. The first chapter begins in May 2008 on Broad Street in Rome, Georgia. In Rome's City Auditorium, I review my family's history, and I relive my escapades as a visual and performance artist. The next chapter circles back a decade to my home on East Third Avenue. In May 1998, I discarded remnants of my sculpture career, and I unpacked boxes of family memorabilia.

When I read the 1898 letters of my maternal grandmother and her sister, I entered the lives of two adventurous nineteenth-century women. During the summer of 1998, I took a vicarious journey with Edith and Anna Lester through Germany, Switzerland, and Italy. In September, I had a quiet interlude in the mountains of North Carolina.

The final chapter of *POSTMARKS* completes the book's circle. In September 2008, David Harvey and I live on Broad Street in the restored General Forrest Hotel. I have closed my art studio and have published my first book, *Tea with Sister Anna: a Paris journal.*

To braid a story from the strands of two summers, I interlaced my 1998 journal entries and dreams with the 1898 summer letters of Anna and Edith Lester. The people and places in this book are real, but scenes and dialogue are reconstructed composites. Romans contributed bits of oral history and tales of town characters. When I heard differing versions, I chose the details I liked the best. I have included a Lester family chart and a chronology of major events. The maps of Europe and Rome are for orientation and visual reference, not geographic precision.

I edited the Lester sisters' letters for length and clarity, but I did not update their spelling, grammar, or punctuation. To structure the route and chronology of their European summer, I inserted condensed entries from Anna Lester's 1898 diary. Her complete journal notes appear in *Tea with Sister Anna*. Although *POSTMARKS* is a prequel to the Paris book, it can be read as a separate memoir.

In the summer of 1898, my grandmother and her sister cruised the Rhine, hiked in the Black Forest, and crossed the Mer de Glace. Lace up your boots, grab your Alpenstock, and join me in a tramp with the Lester sisters.

Susan Gilbert Harvey
September 2010

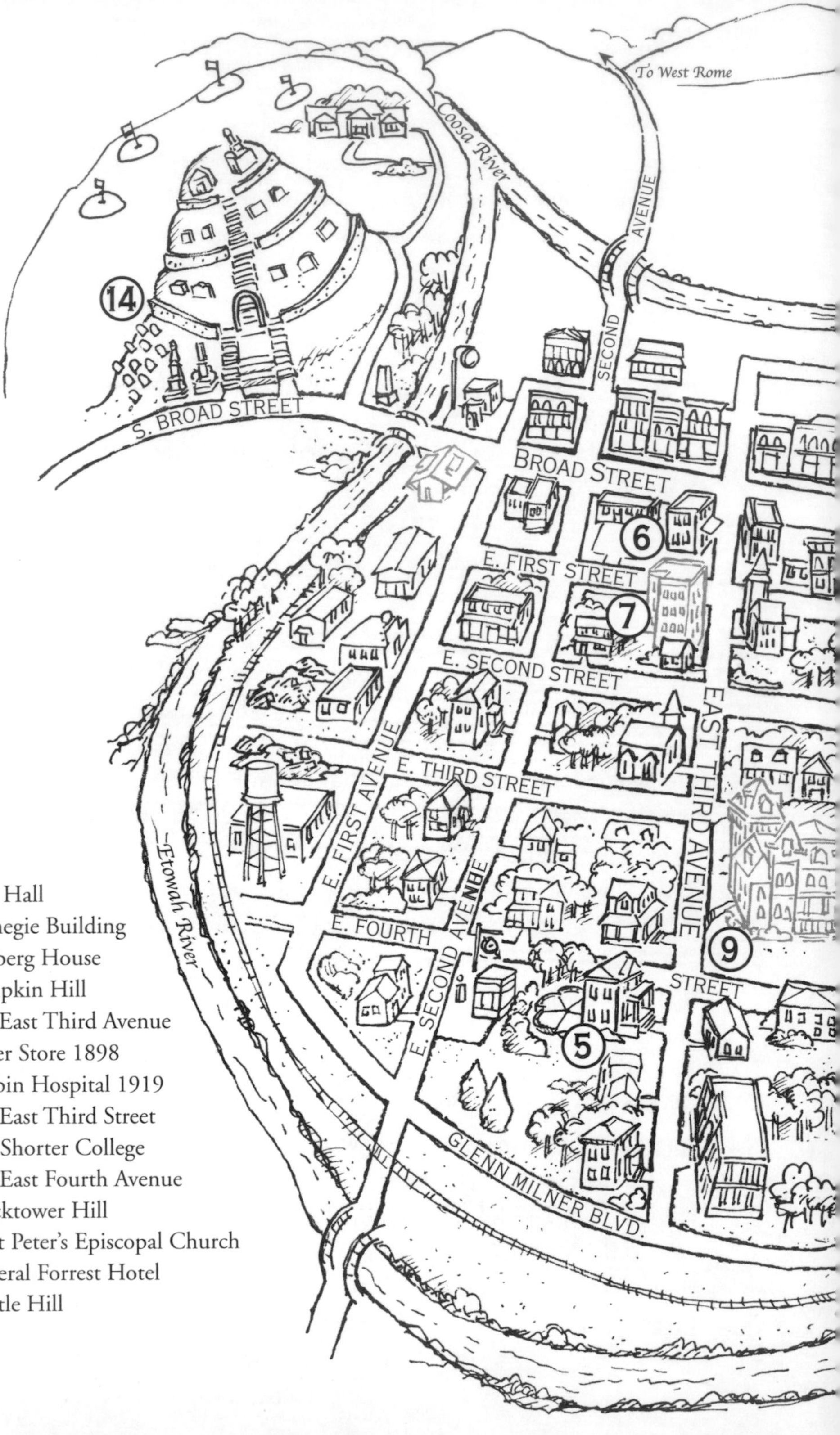

To West Rome
Coosa River
SECOND AVENUE
14
S. BROAD STREET
BROAD STREET
6
E. FIRST STREET
7
E. SECOND STREET
EAST THIRD AVENUE
E. THIRD STREET
E. FIRST AVENUE
E. SECOND AVENUE
E. FOURTH STREET
9
5
GLENN MILNER BLVD.
Etowah River

1. City Hall
2. Carnegie Building
3. Omberg House
4. Lumpkin Hill
5. 400 East Third Avenue
6. Lester Store 1898
7. Harbin Hospital 1919
8. 309 East Third Street
9. Old Shorter College
10. 311 East Fourth Avenue
11. Clocktower Hill
12. Saint Peter's Episcopal Church
13. General Forrest Hotel
14. Myrtle Hill

# Through the Rear View Mirror

*The past is never dead. It's not even past.*
William Faulkner

May 2008
City Hall, Rome, Georgia

City fathers erect monuments; city mothers mount plaques. After our town patriarchs built the monolithic City Hall of Rome, Georgia, the Daughters of the American Revolution engraved in marble what they wanted us to know about our early history.

On a spring morning in 2008, I stand in the dim vestibule of City Hall. The D.A.R. plaque carries the grime of decades. I step back to read the incised stone tablet mounted high on the wall.

A single run-on sentence describes "the coming of the first white men to the site of the present City of Rome." According to the text, "Ferdinand" DeSoto and 600 men visited this area "more than sixty years before the settlement of Jamestown and Plymouth" and found "tranquility, hospitality, and peace" among the native inhabitants of the land of "Cosa."

Our town rests on spilled blood and tears. At the other end of our main street, the D.A.R. marked the riverbank site of a 1793 Revolutionary War battle in which General John Sevier (Nolichucky Jack) defeated the Native-American leader, King Fisher. Our Cherokee predecessors fought for their ancestral earth. They won their case for nationhood in the United States Supreme Court, but President Andrew Jackson refused to enforce the ruling. The Georgia legislature perforated the Cherokee Nation into quilt pieces and re-stitched them with a surveyor's cord. The scraps of land were prizes in the Georgia Land Lottery. White settlers grabbed their winning tickets and moved into northwest Georgia. The Cherokees walked west from here on the Trail of Tears.

A plaque in downtown Rome marks the location of a spring where two men decided to found a town in 1834. According to legend, they and three others tossed prospective names into a hat; if the name "Rome" had not won the draw, we might have been Pittsburgers, Warsawians, or Hamburgers. Like ancient Rome, our city has seven hills. One of them bears the brick water tower built as the city reservoir in 1872. Our four-faced Town Clock tops the tower, and its hourly chimes give cadence to our days. Between, around, and over the hills, our founders laid out a grid of streets and avenues on either side of our aptly named Broad Street. The poetic names of Maiden Lane, Cherokee Street, and Bridge Street have given way to numerical designations: Third Avenue, First Street, and Fifth Avenue.

Because of our three rivers, you must usually cross a bridge to get to your destination, as invading Union forces learned during what gentle Southern ladies called "The Recent Unpleasantness." Our foundries and railroads made Rome a military objective, but for Romans, there was nothing "civil" about the "War of Northern Aggression." Townspeople provided makeshift hospitals for both sides of the conflict, and our cemetery mingles Union and Confederate graves. After spending a few days in Rome in 1864, General William Tecumseh Sherman left a scorched and war-weary town as he marched to the sea.

Romans like to name things for people who have passed this way. We gave DeSoto's name to a park, a township, and a movie theater. Kingfisher Circle is a residential street, named either for the bird or the slain Cherokee chief. The ferry landing of a prominent Cherokee, Major Ridge, became Ridge Ferry Park. General Sherman's name

remained associated with an oak tree under which he and his generals
sat during the occupation.

We have preserved the Cherokee river names. The Etowah and
Oostanaula converge here to form the Coosa, which flows through
Alabama to the Gulf of Mexico. You will learn these Cherokee names
and others: Notasulga, Coosawattee, Chulio, and Echota. Our litmus
test for newcomers is the name of a community north of town. You
must pronounce the invisible second "r" in Armuchee (Armurchee,
not Armoochee), or we'll know you are from "away." You may raise
your social status if your ancestors include a Colonial Dame, a
Huguenot, a Confederate general, or Pocahontas.

---

I walk out to the front steps of City Hall. The building's bricks
are the color of wholegrain mustard; in the morning's sunlight,
they have a tint of *vin rosé*. When I touch the fifty-foot Doric
columns on the front portico, I could be in the royal colonnade of
Karnac or Luxor. Purple and yellow pansies line the flagstones in
front of the building. Crêpe myrtle bushes have had their annual
pruning; they will blossom later in the summer. From the tiered
plaza, I can look down the Broad Street slope and imagine the
dirt streets that my Lester family ancestors saw when they arrived
in 1868. Carpenters and brick masons rebuilt burned buildings
and bridges. Church members reinstalled wooden pews in their
churches, which had served as stables and hospitals during the war.
Paddle-wheeled boats plied the rivers; wagons of fluffy white gold
crowded the Cotton Block on lower Broad.

Before the war, Bannester Smith Lester had been a successful
dry goods merchant in Georgetown, South Carolina; during the war,
he served in the Commissary Department. Because of the vindictive
conditions of Reconstruction, the Lesters, like many other families,
wanted to make a new start. Bannester remembered the hills of North
Georgia from his journey to the California Gold Rush in 1849. His
wife, Eliza Mary Cuttino McNulty Lester, had to yank deep roots
from the Low Country soil; her Huguenot ancestors came to South

Carolina from France in 1687. The Lester children, Mary Margaret (Minnie), Anna McNulty, and Fleetwood (Bubber) Lester left their baby sister, Alberta, buried in Prince George Winyah Church graveyard in Georgetown. When the Lester family reached the river town of Rome, they found congenial South Carolinians. Their decision to stay determined my hometown.

— ᚋ ❖ ᚌ —

If I could remove the trees from today's Broad Street, I might see the site of Bannester Lester's first store, a dry goods business similar to the one he had left in South Carolina. The Lester daughters attended the reopened Rome Female College on Lumpkin Hill, two blocks behind City Hall. Minnie had a beautiful voice; Anna had a gift for art. Fleetwood Lester went to a boys' school run by Mr. Proctor and Mr. Darlington. Although Bannester was one of the merchants who rebuilt Rome's economy, he misjudged his post-war clientele. Having served planters' wives in South Carolina, he expected similar customers in Rome, but the scruffy north Georgians did not need silk ball gowns or fine furniture on their red clay farms.

After a demoralizing bankruptcy, Bannester decided to sell groceries, but he maintained his high standards. Unlike other grocery stores, Lester's Store had screens to keep out flies. The sugar barrel had a cover, and glass jars protected candy. Butter stayed cool in a big iced box. Crocus sacks held raw coffee beans, which Bannester roasted, ground, and blended to his discriminating taste or his clients' specifications. He judged his customers by their choice of coffees.

Edith Lester was a postscript to the Lester family. Born in 1876, she was my family's first native Roman. Sixty-one years later, I was the first grandchild of Edith Lester and William Pickens Harbin, M.D.

My grandmother recalled the year of 1886, when Rome had an earthquake, a blizzard, and a "freshet" known as the Great Flood. River water inundated Broad Street, allowing rowboats, canoes, and a steamboat to travel the main thoroughfare. After the Great Flood, city officials raised the level of Broad Street, and the original storefronts became basements.

Under the sidewalk pavement, brick borders, and streetlamps of our Streetscape renovation, there is a buried Rome. As you walk our sidewalks, you might notice an underground musk rising from iron grates. Your spectral companions may be the ghosts of past Romans. Mixed with our history of ambitious bankers, wealthy cotton brokers, and innovative physicians, you will find stories of Rome women. Often denied careers in business or professions, these female Romans found power in quirks of personality. In my strolls downtown, I see their footprints on our cement.

---

I have come to Rome's City Hall with a mission: a retrospective scan of my history in this town. On the horizon of my past, I note peak years ending in the number eight. In 1958, I returned from a year in Paris on the Hollins College Abroad program. After twenty years of marriage and wonderful children, I became an exhibiting artist in 1978. During the summer of 1998, I twisted my telescope back a century to the summer of 1898 when Edith and Anna Lester traveled in Germany, Italy, and Switzerland. The postmarks on their letters and postcards became beads on my summer rosary: Chamonix. Lucerne. Pallanza. Zermatt.

I've attended many concerts and plays in the City Auditorium of City Hall. At the city clerk's office I bought a business license for my art studio. I've registered deeds to lots in Myrtle Hill Cemetery, where Old Romans value their grave plots by the cubic inch. Today, my thick-soled walking shoes squeak on the marble aggregate floor in the empty foyer; I don't slide like I did in my patent leather Mary Janes. When I pull open the wooden auditorium doors, I conjure past performances and remember the women with three names who dominated the programs. Helen Dean Rhodes raises her baton to direct the symphony that Edith Lester Harbin co-founded in 1921. Louise Arnold Hoge, concertmistress, sounds an "A" on her violin. Evelyn Torrence Harle leads the Rome Women's Chorus.

The aisles are toboggan runs down to the orchestra pit. I'm tempted to walk up onto the stage and speak into the theater's blackness like Thornton Wilder's Stage Manager, but my morning's assignment is upstairs. I want to see my life as a stage performance. The best perspective is from the balcony.

As I pass through the lobby, I crave a Coca-Cola, a Pavlovian throwback to childhood. Caffeine was forbidden on school nights, so at concert intermissions, we settled for water from the corner cooler. I splash fountain water in my mouth. The coppery taste has not changed in sixty years. In those days I assumed that as a grown-up I'd have everything I wanted to eat: Cokes at intermission and a pound of bacon with my grits. Instead of licking the Mixmaster beaters, I'd eat the whole bowl of cream cheese and powdered sugar icing. I would not have to divide my Hershey bar squares with my brother, Peter Gilbert.

Now I'd prefer organic, fair trade, anti-oxidant dark chocolate, but then I assumed that the adult Susan would be unrestricted. Atlanta, New York, Paris, and London would provide theater, music, and museums. My grandmother often recalled her time as a student in Berlin, Germany; she told me stories about European cathedrals and Wagnerian operas. She baked a rich egg custard, but I was twenty before I sat in a Paris café and cracked the burnt sugar on a *crème brûlée.*

———◦———

My mother, Mary Cuttino Harbin, also loved music and theater. She and my father, Warren Monroe Gilbert, M.D., had courted in the cheap seats at the Metropolitan Opera in the 1930s. Their New York love story combines a dropped subway nickel, a photograph, and the hand of fate. Mary, a beautiful brunette with dark brown eyes, had earned two musical degrees from Shorter College in Rome. She continued her piano studies in New York, where her brother, Lester Harbin, M.D., was an intern at St. Luke's Hospital.

After graduating from medical school in Colorado, Warren Gilbert went to New York to sell some gold mine shares. He claimed that my existence resulted from his clumsiness at a subway turnstile. He dropped his nickel, missed the train, and waited for another. On the next subway car, he saw a former teacher from the University of

Colorado. The professor urged Warren to choose St. Luke's Hospital in New York for his internship. The next year, Warren Gilbert and Lester Harbin became friends at St. Luke's.

When Warren saw a photograph of Mary Harbin on Lester's desk, he asked for an introduction. Lester was not sure he wanted the mountain man to know, or date, his May Queen sister. Warren was persistent. He had grown up climbing steep Colorado peaks, but his riskiest gambit was asking the popular Southern woman to marry him. Mary's big leap was marrying outside her tribe.

The Gilbert family was much like Mary's own; the men were physicians, and the women were cultural leaders. Warren practiced medicine with his father, a tuberculosis specialist in Boulder, Colorado. Mary attended musical and literary events with her mother-in-law. Many doctors left Boulder during the Great Depression. Warren accepted his father-in-law's invitation to join the Harbin Hospital staff in Rome. My mother

*Mary and Warren Gilbert*

could again have picnics on lush green grass instead of arid red rocks. Though he missed the snow-capped mountains, my dad said moving to Rome was the best decision he ever made.

I was born at the Harbin Hospital in 1937; my brother Peter followed in 1939. After our father returned from World War II, we celebrated the arrival of our sister, Edith, in 1947. Although she had the Lester family red hair, Edith's middle name was Kirkbride from my father's English grandparents. We called her "E-E." Pete and I had the harder-to-pronounce Huguenot middle names of Gaillard and Cuttino. I was "TuTu." He was "Bubber."

My grandfather, Dr. William Harbin, was a bald man with round glasses whose adoring patients called him "Dr. Will." I called him "FaFa." In my memory, he whistles "Listen to the Mockingbird" on trips to the Harbin country farmhouse. He took me with him on house calls to treat the visionary Miss Martha Berry at her Oak Hill estate north of Rome. After Dr. Will died, Edith Lester Harbin never dropped a stitch from her knitting or missed a student's music lesson. She extended her post-Civil War thrift into our World War II era; she saved string, tin foil, and rubber bands. She bought corsets but softened them by soaking in water. She removed the whalebone stays and used the strips as straight edges to draw lines for music staffs. She reminded her grandchildren that every person has the same twenty-four hours in a day. No whining about not having time to practice the scales or fill in the blanks on musical theory quizzes.

On our overnight visits to 309 East Third Street, we saw a more relaxed grandmother. She fed us bacon, grits cakes, and homemade blackberry jelly. After supper she read us stories from *The Saturday Evening Post*. She often told us about her sisters. "Sister Minnie" had died when Granny was two, but "Sister Anna" was a beloved benefactor and role model. On Saturday morning trips to the dusty attic, we saw two steamer trunks. One held Minnie Lester Brower's trousseau; the other contained Anna Lester's souvenirs from Paris.

---

A gray marble staircase leads to the second floor of City Hall. I used to skip up these steps, but this morning, I take them one at a time and grasp the smooth wooden cables of the handrail. The staircase railings are low for me, perhaps gauged to the height of my grandmother's contemporaries. With each step, I chant the musical names I remember from Granny's front porch: Alida Printup. Beulah Cunyus. Addie Lou Lay. Ida Belle Teat.

More stairs lead to the auditorium balcony. On the second row, my grandmother lined up her oldest grandchildren to hear musical programs. Granny wore concert dresses of navy faille or printed voile.

Her laced black oxfords were from Dr. Locke. Her cleavage always had a dusting of Johnson's Baby Powder and a handkerchief for sniffles.

Harbin children learned concert rules: never sit under the balcony where the sound is muffled, never clap between symphony movements, and always stand for the "Hallelujah Chorus." Edith Lester Harbin embodied the word "concert": harmony or accord in purpose or action. Brother Pete and cousin Banny Harbin were in accord with scuffling but not in harmony with sitting still. Granny pinched knees and gave stern looks when they fidgeted. Along with Harbin cousins Betsy, Mary Shelor, and Helen, I crossed my feet at the ankles. The boys sprawled in their seats, rocked the creaky veneered chair bottoms, and thwanged the wire hat holders underneath.

We children dozed to the melodies of Schubert and Brahms. We snapped straight during "The 1812 Overture." We giggled when fire trucks roared out from the basement fire station. Their sirens were less disruptive when the Valkyries were riding than when Hansel prayed to his fourteen angels. At intermission, Granny pulled out a roll of Life Savers and passed the candy package down the row. We slid off the paper cylinder, tugged the red string to tear the foil package, and distributed the sticky circles. I wanted the green ones.

---

In the new plush seats of the renovated City Auditorium, I inventory my childhood ambitions. My grandmother taught me piano, and my good ear helped me fake proficiency at recitals, but my math-phobic mind never comprehended thirty-second notes. Although I was too tall to be a professional ballerina, I loved dance class. I stuffed my toe shoes with fluffy lambswool and braided the pink satin ribbons around my ankles. My teacher during high school, Anita Chapman Davis, confided to me that, even as a wife and mother, she "had to dance" and started her studio. Her apology for breaking Rome's housewife rules forecast my decision to "be an artist" twenty-five years later.

From the balcony, my memory spotlight illuminates my senior dance recital. In the wings, a phonograph plays "In my Sweet Little

Alice Blue Gown." I spin onto the stage in an eyelet-embroidered organdy dress tied with a wide blue satin sash. Anita Davis had commandeered David Harvey to steady me as I twirled on one point. He declined to wear tights.

For the last fifty years, David has been my pole star axis and support beam as I've rotated through motherhood, art, performance, and writing. He (and his proper mother) thought he dated and married a ladylike girl in an organdy dress. I turned out to be more like the iconoclastic Alice Roosevelt Longworth, for whom the color "Alice Blue" was named. Over the decades, my wardrobe devolved into sweatpants and turtlenecks; ankle-twisting toe shoes gave way to black shoes or boots with treads.

I walk down the steps to the balcony rim and look over the vertiginous overhang to the orchestra seats below. My spotlight moves to my high school senior play. I played Nana, a gray-wigged old woman in a rocking chair. Perhaps the director cast me as a grandmother because I was a serious student, voted "most likely to succeed." Ingénue roles went to girls voted "most popular," or "most beautiful," or "best personality." In the final scene, I jumped up from the rocking chair to dance a jig. The role was prophetic: as a grandmother, I would not be rocker-bound.

The Harbin bloodstream mingled music and theater. Granny's attic provided costumes for Christmas Eve skits and for the operettas my mother staged for the Junior Music Lovers' Club. We dressed as red birds, pumpkins, flowers, elves, and fairy queens. During the 1980s, using costumed characters, I harrowed my theatrical roots in a visual narrative I titled *Rôle Call*. This morning I see the linked genetic chain from my grandmother's costume trunk to my performance art to my grandchildren who dress up as Superman and Wonder Woman. I am the fulcrum of a five-generation seesaw. While I can still teeter-totter, I want to record my memories.

———◈———

Patriarchy was not a word known to Harbin grandchildren, but in our world, Doctor equaled King. A hospital emergency trumped any family plans. While our fathers saved lives, we waited in the hot car outside the hospital. Our picnic lunches were packed for delay. Tomato slices in waxed paper sacks waited to be inserted between Merita bread slices at the picnic site. Stuffed eggs sat on a chunk of ice chipped from a larger block from the icehouse. With no cell phones, pagers, or answering machines, our dads were off duty only beyond the city limits.

*Elizabeth, Jane, Margie, and Mary*

During the week, while their husbands removed tumors, delivered babies, and dilated eyes, the Harbin women and my Gilbert mother were daylight activists. Edith Lester Harbin held state and regional offices in musical organizations and started two orchestras. Mary Harbin Gilbert taught piano for decades and belonged to the PTA, Garden Club, and the Junior Service League. Combining vision with her charm, she spearheaded the historic preservation movement in Rome as the first female board member of the Chamber of Commerce. She helped found Chieftains Museum and was a charter member of the Georgia Trust for Historic Preservation.

Elizabeth Warner Harbin (Aunt Beth, later "Boofie") had studied dance in New York. She gave private dance lessons when she wasn't rubbing Jergen's Lotion on Uncle William's bald head or bleaching the shoestrings of her four daughters' Keds. Each spring she placed a magnolia blossom on the hall pedestal table; every summer she rolled up the rugs and pulled white slipcovers onto her furniture. She closed the shutters after lunch for rest time. She and Aunt Jane taught us the correct pronunciation of the French words *lingerie, foyer,* and *chaise longue.*

Jane Goodwin Harbin took son Banny to nursery school on her bicycle handlebars during World War II. Although she and Uncle

Lester had five children, Aunt Jane chaired civic organizations and was the first woman on the Rome Board of Education. As president of the Junior Service League in the late 1940s, she electrified the City Auditorium with a bump-and-grind mock strip tease in the League Follies.

Margaret Troutman Harbin instructed pilots in the Link Trainer flight simulator during the war years, but Uncle Tom did not want her to have a paying job after their marriage. In addition to raising five sons, Aunt Margie was the first female on the vestry of St. Peter's Episcopal Church; in 1953 she was women's golf champion at the Coosa Country Club. Margie took every science course offered by Shorter College, but she was always home by noon. After Uncle Tom hired an efficiency expert to revamp his office and Margie's kitchen, he installed a private phone line to alert Margie of his arrival for lunch. By the time he walked in the back door, his crustless sandwich had to be quartered and accompanied by nine potato chips and two olives. After an eighteen-minute nap, he returned to his ophthalmology office.

Late on summer afternoons, the women changed into fresh frocks. The dinner, prepared during the cool morning, waited to be reheated: fried chicken, rice, gravy, and garden vegetables. Cocktail hour began when the men came home from their air-conditioned offices. We Gilberts had moved from West Rome to a farm named Fieldwood in the early 1950s, and my parents sipped bourbon and branch water in Adirondack chairs as they watched the sun set over the pasture. In their Georgian home bordering the Coosa Country Club golf course, Aunt Beth mixed Uncle William's martini to his precise prescription: four parts Gordon's gin, one part Martini and Rossi extra dry vermouth, served on the rocks. Aunt Beth's father, Charles Jacques Warner, sat in the paneled den. When his glass ran dry, "Papa" gave one of his granddaughters a dime to take his drink to be "freshened." He only drank white lightning, not "that old brown stuff."

Two houses down on Virginia Circle, Aunt Jane catered to Uncle Lester. She spoke of the Golden Stethoscope Syndrome. In the operating room, "Dr. Lester" opened his hand and expected a scalpel to appear. At home, he wanted his drink poured and his soup scalding hot. When dissecting a turkey or hen, he abhorred a sticky carving knife or fork. Although she often corrected the grammar of the newspaper editor, Jane coddled her surgeon husband: "Now, Lovey…" "Now, Sweetie…"

---

Because he was male and of the house and lineage of both Harbin and Gilbert, my brother Peter was destined to be a physician; for three generations, every male in his gene pool had been in medicine. Careers for females included secretary, nurse, librarian, or teacher.

"Get a college education," they told us. "You will be a better wife and mother. You can converse with your husband's business associates at dinner parties, and you will raise intelligent children."

My female cousins and I took typing in the summers so we would be prepared in case "something" happened to our husbands. As part of their marketing plans, our mothers burnished our exteriors. Noxzema cream cured blemishes. Orthodontia corralled buckteeth. Fifty strokes with a natural bristle hairbrush made hair glisten. At The Shop for Beauty, Marie Roberts curled my limp hair with permanent waves; she urged me to buy theatrical mustache wax to tame my unruly (Gilbert) eyebrows. Dorothy Parker taunted us about "girls who wear glasses," so I was the first person to receive contact lenses from the Harbin Clinic Optical Department.

---

Before my senior year at Rome High School, I had completed all the required courses and electives, including chemistry. I wanted to learn how mechanical things work, but only boys could take physics. They also took mechanical drawing in a side room off the gym. Their drawing instruments were seductive successors to the compass and protractor from my geometry class. I liked to draw floor plans for houses, but I did not know that the architecture field was more male-dominated than medicine.

My crinoline petticoat rustled under my cotton skirt when I went to the office of Mr. J. B. Maddox, our high school principal. He sat behind his desk, next to the iron safe where he kept school records and petty cash. I could see the top of his head and the valiant wisps of gray hair that didn't cover his baldness. His suit was as shiny as his bald pate.

"Excuse me, Mr. Maddox, but I'd like to take physics and mechanical drawing next year."

Mr. Maddox raised his owl eyebrows above the rim of his glasses.

"Oh now, honey, you don't want to be in classes with all those boys. You'll never need to know those things. You should take Miss Sue's home economics and learn to sew and cook."

Miss Sue Griffith taught girls to make aprons and baking powder biscuits. The final exam required a lumpless white sauce and hardboiled egg whites. Grated egg yolks dotted the top of Goldenrod Eggs.

Mr. Maddox dismissed me with a flick of his long fingers.

"You just go on back to class now."

My cheeks reddened. If I'd known how to make the blasted Goldenrod Eggs, I might have thrown them in his face, but male family members and school officials did not tolerate anger. To me, the rebuke was personal; women would not learn gender discrimination vocabulary for another twenty years.

I refused to take home economics. My grandmother taught me to sew on her pedal-powered Singer machine. Like Sabrina, I made a cheese soufflé in Paris. At Hollins College, my Harbin genes helped me ace Biology with a perfect frog dissection. I never took physics.

———◆———

My dad liked art museums; my mother loved historic houses. I can smell the nutty boxwood gardens at Mount Vernon and the trumpet vine perfume in the Venetian courtyard of Isabella Gardner's museum. At Hollins College, I took all the courses offered in the history of architecture. Women could not design or construct buildings, but we could name the parts: architraves, triglyphs, metopes, and plinths. By graduation I knew Flemish bond brick patterns, egg and dart molding, and the Compostella pilgrimage churches. With my Hollins Abroad classmates, I stood in Agamemnon's beehive tomb and on the parapets of Chartres Cathedral.

Dr. Frances Niederer was my mentor at Hollins. Her classes inspired my love for contemporary spaces and three-dimensional design. We studied the Seagram building in New York, Philip Johnson's glass house in Connecticut, and Frank Lloyd Wright's new Guggenheim Museum. Despite her PhD, she was always "Miss" Niederer and lucky to have a job in male world of Art History. She encouraged me to apply for graduate school fellowships, but she warned me that she had faced discrimination. Princeton did not admit women. In some classes, Yale women had to sit in the balcony, not on the main floor with the male students. Art history teaching posts for women often required a pledge not to marry.

———————

Hollins Abroad started my addiction to Europe. The blood of Paris entered my veins and has never left. With only a few weeks left on the continent, I squeezed in a ski trip to Austria over the Christmas break from the Sorbonne. I then went to Vienna to celebrate the new year of 1958 with my cousin, Martha Moseley. Martha is the granddaughter of Fleetwood (Bubber) Lester. She and I had followed the example of Anna and Edith Lester by studying abroad. On January 1, 1958, I wrote my resolutions for the coming year. My stimulating year in Europe was ending. With resignation, I told myself: "Decide on rest of life. Settle down, the fun's over."

My liberal arts education prompted my resolve to develop "a working and living philosophy." I planned to get a masters degree, a scholarship, and go back to Europe. I set priorities: "get good grades, read French and German, don't waste time, be friendly, be tolerant, kind, compassionate and understanding, be alive and interesting, be tidy."

My social mother would have approved my resolve to "be friendly." David would have liked the word "tidy." The last resolution echoed my Rome, Georgia, childhood and my Virginia education. Using capital letters and double underlining, I wrote: "be a LADY."

Six weeks after I wrote my Vienna resolutions, the ship carrying our Hollins Abroad group docked in New York City. My mother saved articles from the *Rome News-Tribune*. In her flowery words, our Society Editor, Miss Isabel Martin Gammon, reported my return from France with her trademark uppercase letters:

*SUSAN GILBERT IS BEING WARMLY WELCOMED BY A HOST OF FRIENDS, RELATIVES. SHE REACHED HOME FRIDAY AFTER A YEAR'S ABSENCE, STUDYING, SEEING PARIS, OTHER EUROPEAN CAPITALS* with Hollins College classmates. Besides the thrill of seeing New York's skyline come into view from the deck of the Mauritania she had the keen pleasure of spying *DAVID HARVEY, A FRIEND OF YEARS STANDING ON THE PIER TO GREET, WELCOME HER.* There were only hours for this Rome twosome to do New York but they managed to get about, see the sights—before boarding a Sonstelation [Lockheed Constellation flown by Eastern Airlines] for Atlanta, Rome.

When my classmates and I returned from our year in Paris, we knew the Métro system, the subjunctive mood, and how to use a bidet. Our sophistication met society's code: a bachelor's degree was fine; bagging an eligible bachelor was better. In summer school that year at the University of Colorado, I sought to balance my French and Art courses with practical knowledge. Because wifehood simmered on the horizon, I enrolled in a Home Management course. The 1940s textbook showed smiling women in frilly, winged aprons crimping apple pie crusts. After two tedious classes on household budgets, I sprinted to the registrar and transferred to Russian History.

In the spring of 1959, I had to tell Miss Niederer that hormones and a diamond ring had triumphed over my graduate school ambitions.

With our engagement, I entered the social bailiwick of Miss Isabel Gammon. She announced our "upcoming nuptials" with this headline: "Gilbert-Harvey Engagement Climaxes Lifelong Friendship." We thought she might have chosen a less suggestive verb.

Isabel Gammon had been a teacher and school principal, but as Society Editor she devised her own grammar rules. She substituted commas for conjunctions and stacked adjectives to precarious heights. In the best southern tradition, Miss Isabel perfected the passive voice: guests were greeted, tea was poured, petit fours were passed, dance cards were filled, and wedding vows were exchanged.

Rome's social arbiter could make or break the reputation of a hostess, and she persecuted ladies who did not divulge every social detail. If a wedding announcement stated only bare facts, Miss Isabel sputtered, "That won't do!" She embellished the report to suit her superior taste. A bride with auburn hair was a "Titian beauty." A tall bride was "statuesque." A petite young bride might be "winsome." One bride had a saucy "retroussé" nose.

Miss Isabel was a dervish who whirled into a hostess's house before guests arrived. She could not report with authority unless she had personally observed the golden chrysanthemums in a bronze compote, the Apple Blossom sasanquas in a crystal prism epergne, the gleaming tapers in the candelabra, or the "highly-polished bare inlaid mahogany table."

 Miss Isabel called our house to ask what I was wearing to bridal parties. My mother made a detailed list of my trousseau and accessories. She was prepared for Miss Isabel's brisk demands.

"Mary! This is Isabel. What's Susan wearing to the luncheon tomorrow?"

"Let's see. She's wearing a cocoa silk shirtwaist, beige suede shoes, and a Bettmar Derby hat."

"Didn't she wear that last week in Marietta?"

"Yes, but…"

"I'll just add a lace collar and change the shoes. I'll make it sound different."

Click. Miss Isabel hung up to make her deadline. My mother collapsed onto her bed and shut her eyes after conversations with Miss Isabel.

*David and Susan Harvey*

David Harvey and I married in October 1959, four months after my Hollins graduation. Instead of joining classmates in Greenwich Village and getting a master's degree at N.Y.U., I trusted David when he promised me a sea cruise to his duty station in Hawaii. The Navy decreed otherwise. A few weeks before the wedding, he received orders to the U.S. Protectorate of Okinawa, the tailbone island of the Japanese archipelago. My southern belle mother took to her bed. In November, David and I took to the road on a weeklong drive to California.

We had our first marital fight in Texas when I did not correctly refold the road map. David, a recent graduate of the U.S. Navy navigational training, had great respect for the proper care of maps and charts. I, of the immediate expediency school, had folded and creased the Texas map to showcase the day's drive. At his vehement insistence, I refolded the map but missed an important exit sign, a worse navigational sin. Faced with his anger, I weighed my response. I could get out of the car and take a long bus ride to Georgia, but how would Miss Isabel report my marital defection?

I decided to honor my vows for better or for worse. I had lost my virginity, my embossed Crane's notepaper had my new monogram, and I owed hundreds of thank you notes. Besides, I loved this man. We pressed on to California and Okinawa, but our ten-day-old marriage wobbled during the tense map moments on the Houston bypass.

We spent six weeks in a rented room behind a preschool in Coronado, California. David survived the Navy's Survival Training. When he was not flying, he practiced Wife Training. One night he called from the bathroom.

"TuTu, you put the toilet paper on the holder backwards."

I couldn't see his face. Was he joking? Maybe Home Economics women knew the correct way to install a toilet paper roll.

"Oh?"

"It's supposed to come over the top!"

My future flashed: I was about to fly across the Pacific Ocean and spend the rest of my life with a map-folding man to whom it mattered how the toilet paper rolled off its cardboard tube.

———⊷⊷———

On Christmas Eve 1959, we spent twenty-four-hours aboard a vibrating, propeller-driven plane. I dressed for travel in lady clothes: a belted striped knit dress, a girdle, stockings, black kid heels, and a hat. In Hawaii, ukuleles played "Silent Night" in the humid air before we flew into the Pacific night. After we reached Naha, Okinawa, I would not touch U.S. soil or talk to my parents by telephone for two and a half years.

The metal dog tags around my neck stated truths: my blood type was "A" and my status was "Dependent." Military authority topped any other I had experienced. A Navy wife told me: If the Navy had wanted David to have a wife, they would have issued him one.

On Okinawa, I told the toilet paper story to my new friend Marcy Lockhart, also a recent bride. "Yeah," she laughed, "at our first breakfast, Chuck told me I had put the butter on the wrong side of the toast. And I was a Home Ec major!"

Other officers' wives gave me helpful hints. Charlotte Colburn taught me her mother's trick: throw an onion in a hot oven, and your aviator husband will think you've been cooking all afternoon instead of playing bridge. Bunky Gallaher told me to add extra gelatin to my congealed fruit salads to combat the East China Sea humidity.

We wives had no control over our husbands' schedules. I knew David was coming home when I heard the overhead drone of his P2V aircraft as it approached Naha air base. I tied on a chiffon scarf to keep my pin-curled hairdo from frizzing in the unrelenting wind.

White-rimmed dark glasses cut the setting sun's glare as I drove our 1959 Chevrolet at 35 mph down Highway One (and Only). I dodged ox carts, squatting mamasans with swaddled babies, and papasans in conical hats. At the Naha base, we wives stood behind chain-linked fences to watch our warriors deplane. Their flight suits smelled of adrenaline sweat, a potent aphrodisiac. We had brief honeymoons until the next duty roster was posted. David's ditty bag sometimes contained books banned in America but printed illegally in Taiwan. Reading Henry Miller's uncensored *Tropic of Cancer* was as risqué as a new wife could get in base housing.

The U.S. Navy reinforced David's mother's training in obsessive neatness. "Ship shape" and "orderly" were his operative words. He was the Captain of our household, and I was his Executive Officer. A month before our daughter Mary was born, David wrote my dad, "Susan is a good wife. She runs a taut ship and a taut ship is a happy ship." He had no suspicion of the lax and messy art I would make after Junk Woman eclipsed my Southern Belle and Good Navy Wife personae.

One afternoon, I was bored. I had picked pimientos out of some olives to decorate a tuna noodle casserole. David's dress white uniform waited for starch and the iron, but my fingers itched to make something. I thought of Alexander Calder and decided to make a mobile. From white notebook paper I cut out snowflakes and hung them from sewing thread. Dry strands of spaghetti became my support sticks. I suspended the snowflakes, hung my mobile creation over the table, and blew on it to make it rotate. By the time David got home, the humid sea air had collapsed the dry spaghetti into dangling limp noodles.

Before typhoons arrived, the men took the airplanes to safety in Taiwan or the Philippines, where they ate fresh strawberries and played golf. Talented young Asian women walked barefoot on our husbands' backs to massage and relax their vertebrae. Confined to our leaky cement-block houses and rusty Quonset huts, we dependent wives leaned our vertebrae against Navy-issue rattan headboards and ate peanut butter and soggy crackers by candlelight. I survived fifteen typhoons with a mop, a bucket, a Sterno stove, and a flashlight. With daughter Mary Gilbert Harvey in my womb, and later on my hip, I waded in ankle-deep water through our dark house while the banshee winds howled. The men returned from their refreshing "fly-aways" with dozens of pineapples and fifty pound bags of rice as compensatory gifts. We wives would have preferred industrial ShopVacs to suck up typhoon water, but they had not been invented.

David clung to his vision of my domestication; he brought me a small sewing machine from Hong Kong. After we got base housing, I bought sixty yards of silk at ten cents a yard, and Marcy and I made curtains for the huge louvered windows. I took weekly courses in Japanese flower arrangement and collected traditional and contemporary containers. The spare flower arrangements of Ikebana introduced me to the three-dimensional design world I would later inhabit.

In addition to Japanese dancing, singing, and language classes, I took a Red Cross childcare course. Liberal-arts-educated Miss Susan knew nothing about birthin' babies. Our Okinawan live-in maids knew even less. Sachiko panicked and disappeared the day we brought Mary home from the Kadena Army hospital. I released Ayiko after she put embroidery scissors in Mary's wicker bassinet "to kill evil spirits, Okusan." Mariko starched David's underwear and polished my silver-plated candlesticks with a Brillo pad. She read no English, so she confused a small jar of horseradish with the Gerber baby food on the refrigerator shelf.

"Okusan! Maydy no like this!"

Red-faced little Mary spluttered the horseradish across the kitchen.

Mary called each successive maid "Kiko." When we returned to the States in July 1962, two-year-old Mary transferred the name Kiko to my sister. Her teenaged Aunt Edith was the same size as the Okinawan girls we had left behind.

---

Our next duty station was the Naval Air Station in Coronado, California. On a late October day in 1962, we moved into a rental house near the Pacific Ocean. In the Atlantic Ocean, Russian ships steamed toward Cuba, loaded with missiles. I unpacked boxes and stacked brick and plank bookshelves through labor contractions and nuclear holocaust panic. Would my mother and Mary be blown up while I was in the maternity ward?

David's flight crew was on high alert, but grounded due to bad weather. He navigated us through fog to the Coronado Hospital minutes before Katherine Burney Harvey's birth. The Russians backed down, and I came home with our second daughter.

After our years on tropical Okinawa and in sunny California, we missed our families and the seasons of winter, spring, and fall. David resigned from the Navy in 1964. We returned to Rome, and David started his career with Northwestern Mutual Life Insurance Company. We bought a new house in a North Rome subdivision, not far from my parents' Fieldwood home.

---

The Rome Way of Life replaced the Navy Way of Life. I knew the Rome Lady Rules: Bobby Wyatt should decorate your house, Ransom's should arrange your flowers, and Daniel's Funeral Home would bury you in Myrtle Hill Cemetery. I should (if invited) join the Junior Service League, a garden club, and the North Rome School PTA. To serve on the Altar Guild of St. Peter's Episcopal Church, I would require approval from dowager chairman Sara Joyce Cooper; she sanctioned membership with a steel hand in a white glove.

David played golf at the Coosa Country Club. He bought his dream car: a Riverside Red 1963 Corvette Sting Ray. When he joined the Rotary Club and the Jaycees, I could claim auxiliary status as a Rotary Ann or a Jaycette. As in our Navy days, my status was Parenthetical Wife.

For supper club parties, we stirred onion soup mix into sour cream and poured pepper jelly over cream cheese slabs. After dinner, the husbands hunkered in paneled dens paved with shag from area carpet mills. In addition to sports, they discussed local politics. In 1968, David was one of The Dedicated Eight, a group of seven men and one woman who ran as Republicans for the Rome City Commission. David and two other men were elected, thus opening Rome to two-party politics. After the Jaycees sponsored a referendum to legalize liquor sales, Rome women lost their status as rum-runners. In an unwritten contract, wives could buy what they wanted at Rich's in Atlanta as long as they stopped at Pearson's Liquor Store on the way home. Some women went to a less-trafficked liquor store to avoid bumping into members of their church. For years, contraband whiskey had gurgled in brown sacks in our car trunks, but no lady was arrested crossing the dry Floyd County line.

At social events, we wives gathered in living rooms to admire the crewel-embroidered wing chairs from Wyatt's store. We exchanged recipes for chicken divan and hamburger stroganoff. We discussed babysitters, carpools, and bake sales. I smiled through the mind-numbing chatter, but my depression was as rampant as the honeysuckle vines I yanked from the red clay back yard of our North Hills house.

I had not yet learned that stifled creativity could lead to melancholia. I coped by making draperies for all the windows in our new house. I vacuumed the avocado green carpet. The girls and I painted and folded paper. I hung a makeshift stage curtain between two pine trees for my daughters' costume shows. On the Fourth of July they had parades with flags and drums. To amuse the kids, I took a mixing bowl out the back door to pick "clouds" for cheese soufflés. I gathered fresh "grasshoppers" for Grasshopper Pie. I loved being near my family in Rome, but an inner voice nudged:

"Aren't you supposed to be in New York or Paris?"

———— ⊗ ————

Rescue from parenthetical status came through Aunt Margie Harbin. She and I joined a design class at Shorter College. Our teacher, Virginia Dudley, was a gaunt-faced compulsive dynamo. My still life paintings and landscapes at Hollins had been static two-dimensional rectangles. Virginia exploded the flat picture plane into assemblages and constructions. A flash bulb electrified my brain when I looked at an artwork from six directions.

Our class climbed scrap piles behind a cabinetmaker's shop to find wood for our projects. We watched Virginia weld metal scraps into fanciful animals. We salvaged yarn from north Georgia carpet mills for hooked tapestries. I sharpened broomsticks into five-foot knitting needles to knit loopy wall hangings. David might have preferred argyle socks. As members of the Georgia Designer-Craftsmen, some of us exhibited our tapestries and tie-dyed hangings at the High Museum in Atlanta.

While I made art at Shorter, I also staged a flower show for the Green Thumb Garden Club and designed the interiors for the North Heights Elementary School. I danced a soft-shoe routine in the Follies in a strapless, purple, elasticized gown and plumed picture hat. Our son, David Donaldson Harvey III, arrived in 1969. He and I chanted nursery rhymes in my Oldsmobile Vista Cruiser as we drove the girls to cheerleader camps, music lessons, birthday parties, Brownies, and swim meets. I was a green clay Gumby figure stretched between the worlds of service and creativity. I tried to do it all.

—⊷—⊜—⊶—

My Hollins professors had ignored the Abstract Expressionists who pitched paint in New York in the 1950s; our modern art courses ended with Cézanne and Picasso. There were no women artists in the Hollins art history textbook, so we heard nothing about Cassatt, O'Keefe, or Frankenthaler. To catch up, I audited Dr. Tommy Mew's Modern Art Seminar at Berry College, just north of Rome. New York feminist artists Hannah Wilke and Harmony Hammond came to speak to students. On escape trips to New York, I saw the assemblages of Louise Nevelson, Lee Bontecou, Joseph Cornell, and Robert Rauschenberg. Man Ray's tack-studded flatiron was a revelation. Edward Weston's iconic peppers were epiphanies. In an Atlanta lecture, Lucy Lippard connected prehistoric Irish earth structures like New Grange to Robert Smithson's *Spiral Jetty* in the Great Salt Lake. I heard of the Guerilla Girls who protested the paucity of women artists in museums, textbooks, and galleries.

The mother bird of the art universe swooped into Rome with tidbits for my beak. When earth artist Nancy Holt spoke at Berry College, she showed photos of her installation in the Utah desert. For *Sun Tunnels*, Holt aligned huge concrete pipes to solar directions. Holes pierced in the concrete cylinders created constellation patterns on the shaded interior walls. I drove home, walked into my house, cleaned up the pizza scraps from my kids' supper, and sat down in stunned shock: Nancy Holt lived my dream. She had flatbed trucks and cranes and the earth's surface to play on. She joined my female artist pantheon.

In 1971, Gloria Steinem started *Ms.* magazine. The U.S. Congress passed the Equal Rights Amendment in 1972, but Phyllis Schafly muddied the simple language of "equality of rights under the law" with her irrational ravings about unisex bathrooms and women in military service. She made a career for herself by urging other women to stay at home. Alice Paul, author of the Equal Rights Amendment, died in 1977 at the age of 92, without seeing her amendment ratified by the states.

The Women's Movement seeped south to Georgia, but like a good southern girl, I wanted an authority to give me permission to "unleash my inner artist." I sought guidance for depression. Physicians prescribed drugs. Counselors suggested handiwork therapy: découpage, needlepoint, or Tole painting. I did not want a hobby; I wanted to make ART. In 1978, at age forty-one, I wrote my own prescription and permission slip. I said, "To hell with taking courses, I want to BE an artist." Tommy Mew had encouraged my art and had included my work in a show called "Five Women Artists." I called him and said: "Give me a date for a solo show in the Moon Gallery."

———————

After my commitment, artwork ideas deluged my brain. I scoured the flea markets and scrap yards of Rome for assemblage materials. Two small oxygen tanks became child victims of the Jim Jones Kool-aid massacre; silver saltshakers represented the SALT Treaty talks. Well pulleys and fire tongs were persecution tools used on seventeenth-century French Protestants. The graphic rendition of our Huguenot heritage puzzled my mother. My mortified mother-in-law said: "I'm so embarrassed. Can't you make some nice little watercolors of magnolia blossoms?"

The words "nice" and "little" rarely applied to my art. I used shipping crates, rusted industrial gears, cast-off furniture, and medical instruments. Military hardware from WWII, ammunition crates, and the burned carcass of a grand piano became materials for my installations. In 1982, I mourned the Georgia Legislature's defeat of the ERA with a small sculpture: I screwed a woman's wooden foot to a block of wood. The backdrop song was, "Good Night, Ladies." Scored for male quartet.

Yes, my sculpture themes had roots in my youth: medicine, music, and the military. And yes, I was angry. I tallied my decades. For the first twenty years of my life, I did what my parents and family expected: piano lessons, college, and study abroad. I followed David during my second twenty years, while he served our country, established his business, and ran community organizations.

Fissures of liberation opened when I turned forty and read Virginia Woolf and Charlotte Gilman. David saw the scratch marks on the wallpaper. He suggested that I take the next decade to see what I could do with my art. The decade meter started humming at the Harvey house, and I never looked back. For twenty years, I exhibited my sculpture and lectured in galleries and art centers. I experimented with poetry, essays, and offbeat performance scripts.

My *Rôle Call* narrative evolved as a way to share my work without driving a truck. I interspersed my sculpture images with photos of Susan Harvey in costumes. "Southern Belle" wore my hoop-skirted ball gown from the Chattanooga Cotton Ball and sported a hard hat from the Southern Bell Company. From a phone booth, she emerged as "Junk Woman," the activist crusader for women's rights. In a gold plastic milk bottle helmet and a hooded navy cape, Junk Woman wielded a Civil War sword and a trashcan lid shield. When weary, she retired to a white room as "Monk Woman." This white-robed introvert wrote poetry, meditated, and observed solar events. After a few years in seclusion, Monk Woman abandoned her cocoon and burst forth as the frolicking "Lunatic Moth." Dressed in hot pink wings, glittered antennae, and pink basketball shoes, the Lunatic Moth appeared on the top of Rome's City Clock on the Spring Equinox and later at the Empire State Building. One of the last *Rôle Call* shows was on the City Auditorium stage when I told my fellow Romans about Junk Woman's subversive adventures. As I tromp down the steps from the Auditorium balcony, I remember their surprised laughter.

Outside, the sunshine is bright after the dark auditorium. From City Hall plaza, I walk to the intersection of Broad Street and East Sixth Avenue. This corner was the scene of one of Junk Woman's mischievous spoofs. In my travels, I had noticed that society often honors prominent males with phallic obelisks. My alter-ego developed a playful hobby: Junk Woman started "measuring" the monuments erected to great men. A Washington friend photographed Junk Woman in cape and helmet as she measured the obelisk of George Washington. That day, the police were arresting the anti-Ku Klux Klan rioters

F.N. WELLS

*Junk Woman in Washington, D.C.*

who smashed windows on the streets of our nation's capital. Security guards ignored Junk Woman and her yardstick.

Back in Rome, Junk Woman and I saw that Rome had its own version of male valor. On the corner of City Hall lawn, a stubby obelisk honors pioneer gynecologist, Dr. Robert Battey. In addition to treating tuberculosis and clubfeet, Dr. Battey founded a Rome sanitarium for the treatment of women's disorders. In 1872, he performed the first normal oophorectomy, when he removed healthy ovaries from his patient, Julia Omberg. During the experimental surgery, a group of Romans and Rome doctors formed "indignation groups" across the street from the Nicolas Omberg house. They planned to lynch Dr. Battey if Julia died. Both surgeon and patient were fortunate. Julia lived another fifty years and died of heart failure.

When the Seventh District Medical Society dedicated Dr. Battey's granite obelisk in 1921, physicians posed on City Hall lawn. One photo caption read: "Doctors honor Rome surgeon with shaft." My great-uncle, Dr. Robert Harbin, chose the words for the base of the obelisk: Originality, Modesty, Fidelity, Courage. After the monument dedication, the (male) doctors "repaired to the Coosa Country Club for barbeque."

In a feminist bookstore in Washington, I found a pamphlet with a description of Dr. Battey's operation. According to the text, the surgeon sometimes removed healthy ovaries for psychological reasons (manias). The booklet listed symptomatic indicators like "a troublesomeness, erotic tendencies, eating like a ploughman, persecution mania, and simple cussedness." Dr. Robert Battey gained worldwide recognition for his innovative surgery. "Battey's Operation" became so popular that, at medical meetings, surgeons flaunted platters of ovary trophies.

With my consciousness raised, I saw Dr. Battey's obelisk as a pointed scalpel aimed at women's reproductive organs. Junk Woman whipped out her trusty yardstick and tape measure and calculated the length and girth of the famous doctor's shaft. Four spherical bushes surrounded the base of Dr. Battey's monument. I photographed the suggestive arrangement. A few weeks later, the round bushes disappeared. Perhaps an overzealous city gardener chopped them down. I like to think that Dr. Battey's former patients came at midnight with surgical shears to perform a tit-for-tat castration of Dr. Battey.

*Junk Woman in Rome, Georgia*

Behind Dr. Battey's monument, in the midst of Japanese cherry trees, mistletoe festoons a large oak tree. To the ancient Druids, mistletoe berries represented the semen of Zeus. Druid priests cut the parasite out of a sacred oak before their sexual orgies. The symbolism felt appropriate for Dr. Battey's neighborhood, and once I saw these related images, they stuck to my cranium and became part of the *Rôle Call* saga.

In Dr. Battey's era, my monument-measuring antics might have qualified for a symptom list under "obstreperousness." When I pointed out naked Emperors and their suggestive monuments, a photographer added legitimacy to my antics. One dignified woman told me, "Susan! I saw you dancing barefoot with a parasol in the middle of East Fourth Street. I thought you had finally lost your mind, but then I saw the photographer, so I knew it was all right."

—————

Sexual symbolism at City Hall does not end with Dr. Battey's obelisk. When the City Commission meets on the second floor, a female activist named Serpentfoot often appears. Serpentfoot founded the Church of Nudists, Natives and Naturalists with a Mission. She lobbies for recognition of Cherokee Chief John Ross; the city built a football stadium and a medical center on this Native-American's land. According to public records, Serpentfoot has staged "nude protests" to emphasize her points. Police personnel are prepared for "indecent exposure." They know to have blankets handy on the nights that Serpentfoot is on the agenda.

We also have nudity on the City Hall front plaza, where sunshine warms the bare bottoms of Romulus and Remus. The two naked bronze babies sit beneath the multi-breasted Capitoline Wolf. We Romans are used to seeing wolf teats and baby penises as we arrive for performances in the Auditorium, but in the early days, to appease prudish elements of the city, Rome officials diapered the babies with handkerchiefs during civic events. Pranksters often put brassieres on the wolf's breasts.

Romans know the story of the mythical Romulus. Nurtured by wolf milk, he survived river and forest to found the city of Rome, Italy. When an Italian rayon mill (Chatillon) opened here in 1929, the government of Benito Mussolini gave New Rome the Etruscan statue replica "in forecast of prosperity and glory." During World War II, anti-Fascist sentiment prompted prudent City Fathers to hide the statue in an undisclosed location. In 1952, art patrons led by Virginia (Dickie) Culbreath Barron fought to get the wolf and babies returned to their marble pedestal.

Mussolini's name remains on the statue base near the *fasces*, a bundle of rods that symbolized the magistrates of ancient Rome. The rods surround an axe, similar to the fake tomahawks now brandished at our Rome Braves baseball games.

---

I shake off my symbolic connections and walk next door to the Carnegie Building, the empress building next to our imperial City Hall. I have history in this neo-classical brick building, Andrew Carnegie's gift to the city in 1911. The sumptuous smell of magnolia blossoms returns me to childhood. Here I read Nancy Drew mysteries and the biographies of Clara Barton, Florence Nightingale, and Harriet Beecher Stowe. In the decade of the 1990s, I had my art studio in the former Bookmobile garage. Ropes of wisteria vine cover the back wall of the building. The door to my former studio is locked, but I remember good creative times.

When the new library computerized its collection in the 1990s, I salvaged hundreds of catalog index cards to make ornaments and bookmarks. I assembled vignettes in the discarded drawers of the card catalog cases for a 1991 exhibit in the restored Carnegie lobby. Exploring the concept of The Parenthetical Wife, I wrote a series of poems about the second-hand power of famous men's wives: "The Wet Blanket by Mrs. Noah," "The Saline Solution by Mrs. Lot," and "Return to Cinder by

*Mrs. Dewey*
*Decimates the System*

Mrs. Nero." These poems led to the humorous performance I called, "Mrs. Dewey Decimates the System."

In my monologue, I portrayed the wife of über-librarian Melvil Dewey. This time-conscious thrifty man would have loved texting on a cell phone; to conserve letters, he spelled his name DUI. After he categorized all of human knowledge into ten classifications, he (like my Uncle Tom) hyper-organized his household. In the finale of my monologue, Annie Dewey grabs a carving knife and decimates Melvil's lunch sausage into ten precise classifications, including Ancient History. Wearing Aunt Margie Harbin's pink hat and white gloves, I premiered "Mrs. Dewey" here in the Carnegie building basement and later in the stacks of our new library. Any resemblance between Mr. Dewey's obsessions and those of my orderly husband was purely coincidental.

---

Vestiges of Junk Woman's antics and Mrs. Dewey's rebellion cling to my back as I cross the parking lot to West First Street to face the Nicolas Omberg House. When Julia Omberg lay on the wooden kitchen table awaiting Dr. Battey's knife, she could not have known that her surgery would garner a plaque for her house, now listed on the National Register of Historic Places. She might be surprised to know that the wooden table became a Battey family heirloom; one half sits in the home of Aunt Margie Harbin, Dr. Battey's great-granddaughter.

---

The Omberg House is only a block from Lumpkin Hill, one of Rome's seven hills. This East Eighth Avenue site reconnects me with my Lester kinswomen. After the Lesters moved here from South Carolina, Anna and Mary Margaret Lester attended school on this hill. Pictures of the Rome Female College show a two-story brick building with double porches and a cupola on the roof. Students could push open a wrought iron entrance gate to stroll serpentine garden pathways between classes. The College Circular of 1880 promised a pleasant healthful atmosphere and strict adherence to rules. The college required lady-like conduct on all occasions: promptness, punctuality, neatness, and good order. Things prohibited included boisterous noise, loud talking on the street, games of chance, and throwing anything from the windows. The Reverend S.E. Axson (father of a future First Lady) lectured on Moral Science. A few years after his famous operation, Dr. Robert Battey taught Hygiene to the young ladies.

Although the stated goal of the college was to make "earnest, thinking women, not automata," the administrators invited the Reverend Dr. David Wills, Chaplain of the U.S. Army, to speak at graduation in June 1881. According to a Rome newspaper, his subject was "The Ideal Woman." He exhorted each young woman not to assume duties beyond her "true sphere as a ministering angel around the hearth stone." She should not "go to the polls with the vulgar crowd," but should "lay her hand to the spindle" and be the "tutelary saint of a happy home circle." He claimed: "Fat women are the hope of the nation."

Anna Lester and Ellen Lou Axson exhibited their paintings during the 1881 graduation exercises, but they ignored Chaplain Wills' avuncular advice. Anna followed her RFC art teacher, Miss Helen Fairchild, to the Augusta Female Institute in Staunton, Virginia. Anna's business school degree was in bookkeeping; she also received a gold medal in drawing and painting. In October 1884, Anna Lester and Ellen Lou Axson went to New York City to enroll in The Art Students' League. At this prestigious school, talent, not gender, determined acceptance, and a few instructors used nude models for life drawing classes.

Ellen Lou Axson suspended her art training to marry Woodrow Wilson. While he was in the White House, she became our first activist First Lady by advocating slum clearance in the District of Columbia. In the summers, she resumed painting and studied with William Merritt Chase, a leading American Impressionist. Anna Lester taught art at Shorter College in Rome and at the Augusta Female Institute, later Mary Baldwin Seminary. In 1897 she took another leap out of woman's "true sphere." She went to Paris to draw from life.

The Rome Female College closed in 1890, and the building became a hospital. Later, David's maternal grandfather bought the property on Lumpkin Hill. The iron college gate led to Albert Sidney Burney's columned Greek Revival home. He bragged that, from his elevated windows, he could see the Burney lot in Myrtle Hill Cemetery. A Broad Street merchant, Mr. Burney had six daughters from his two marriages. Alline Burney, David's mother, was number five. Alline's life expectations came from the elegant Burney home. On New Year's Day, the butler shucked a barrel of oysters on the back porch. "Mammy" Lizzie McWillis tended the little children, and servants starched and ironed the Burney girls' petticoats. Dust never settled on mahogany tables. Sterling silver never drifted into tarnish.

In the 1950s, developers demolished the Burney home and leveled the top of Lumpkin Hill to build car dealerships and a hotel. The scrolled iron gate of the Rome Female College moved to a downtown garden on East Fourth Avenue.

During her years at the Rome Female College, Anna Lester had pushed open the swivel gate to study art. Three decades later, Alline Burney and her five sisters played on the swinging gate before dining on Irish linen tablecloths.

In the summer of 1998, in my home on East Third Avenue, I had artifacts from both eras. Anna McNulty Lester's watercolors and Alline Burney Harvey's finger bowls were part of my legacy from Lumpkin Hill.

*What's past is prologue.*
William Shakespeare

# 400 East Third Avenue

*To be rooted is perhaps the most important*
*and least recognized need of the human soul.*

Simone Weil

May 1998

Our house at 400 East Third Avenue was the hub of a history wheel. This street had been my familial artery for four generations. Since 1972, the Harvey house had witnessed our children's school years and their graduations. Here, we hosted our daughters' weddings and our grandsons' baptisms. We lived at an intersection, and in the spring of 1998, my life was at a crossroads.

On a May afternoon, I waited on my front porch for a young man named Anthony Raines. He would help me pitch wooden crates and iron scraps from my backyard. While Anthony tossed these remnants of my sculpture, I planned to unpack family mementoes from storage boxes. The seedpods of my future were in the memorabilia of Anna and Edith Lester. Their summer of 1898 would meld with mine.

━━ ⊗ ━━

Third Avenue begins near the Oostanaula River. After crossing Broad Street, it passes the capped underground spring where the city of Rome was conceived. In 1898, my great-grandfather's grocery store occupied the northwest corner of East First Street and East Third

*Bannester Lester's Grocery Store*

Avenue. The façade has changed little since that tine, so it's easy to imagine white-bearded Bannester Lester standing in the doorway. His grocery clerks pose among wooden crates and tin canisters. A stalk of bananas hangs by the door. An advertisement for Chase and Sanborn coffee touts availability at Lester's Store. Bannester Lester maintains his courtly South Carolina manners; he gives each lady customer a tuberose and a geranium leaf as she leaves with her custom-ground coffee and fine tea.

*The Lester Home*
*309 East Third Street*

In my mind, I follow my great-grandfather as he walks up Third Avenue. He passes the First Presbyterian Church, where Woodrow Wilson first saw his future bride. After another block, Bannester turns up the steep hill onto East

Third Street, formerly Alpine Street. He is glad he bought this high land after the Great Flood of 1886. The ten-year-old Lester house overlooks downtown church steeples. In the distance are Myrtle Hill, Mount Alto, John's Mountain, and Lavender Mountain. On the hill across the street, the brick towers of Shorter College are the architectural peaks of Rome's skyline.

At age sixty-eight, Bannester may be out of breath when he sits in a rocking chair on the vine-shaded verandah at number 309. He pets Edith's dogs, Dickens and Danny, and pours some cream from the store for Moses, Anna's female cat. After dinner he may enjoy a cigar on the porch. Through the summer, he will read his daughters' letters, postmarked from Germany, Italy, and Switzerland. Eliza Mary Lester will save the letters.

---

In 1898, Bannester and Eliza Mary lived alone with their housekeeper, Miss Beall. Their oldest daughter, Minnie Lester Brower, had died in childbirth in 1878. The Lesters had helped raise Minnie's son, LeFoy Brower, who was a student at Princeton University. Fleetwood (Bubber) was the Lesters' only son. Less ambitious than his sisters, he spent time in California and now worked as a hardware salesman in Texas. Anna McNulty Lester had been a well-paid teacher at Mary Baldwin Seminary in Virginia. In 1897, at age thirty-five, she quit her job. Her savings and investments funded her art study in Paris. Twenty-one-year-old Edith Lester had studied music in Berlin since 1896, thanks to a generous loan from Sister Anna's savings accounts.

Anna Lester returned from Paris in December 1898. Edith Lester came back to America in 1899 and taught music at Agnes Scott Institute in Decatur, Georgia. After Anna died in 1900, Edith moved to Rome to live with her parents. In 1905, she married Dr. William Pickens Harbin, and they lived in the Lester house until their deaths. Edith might have preferred a house of her own, but she and Dr. Will committed all their earnings to building his Harbin Hospital. The Harbin home at 309 East Third Street welcomed four

children, seventeen grandchildren, distant relatives, and celebrities
of the music world.

⸺⸺◆⸺⸺

When David and I bought our Third Avenue house, we returned
to the familiar sidewalk grid surrounding my grandmother's house.
I had spent many nights on Granny's sleeping porch, so I knew the
cooing whispers of downtown pigeons. I had crunched Third Avenue
acorns when I walked to Rome High School at the end of the street. I
grew up in West Rome, but David was an urban kid. His mother still
lived in her yellow frame house on the north slope of Clocktower Hill.

While we traveled with the U.S. Navy, real estate agents
had gentrified "Central Rome" into the "Between the Rivers
Historic District." Shouldered by two of our three rivers,
our neighborhood is a peninsula of columned mansions
and one-story cottages. Rome's City Clock is a beacon on
its central hill. Built as a water reservoir only four years
after the Lesters arrived in Rome, the cylindrical brick base has the
crenellated battlements of a Venetian fortress. The white lattice clock
housing resembles a Chippendale chef's hat. I call it a "Tick Toque."

City officials expect protests at City Hall if they change the
nighttime volume of the clock's chimes. The City Clock unites
downtown residents, but occasional squabbles erupt in our shaded
streets. Neighbors might disagree about fence heights, encroaching
limbs, or barking dogs. House additions or gaudy paint colors
prompt cries of "Architecturally Inappropriate!" or "Just Plain Tacky!"

Old Romans like to claim they were born "in the shadow of
the clock tower." For most people, this means the delivery room
of my grandfather's Harbin Hospital. Dr. William Harbin and Dr.
Robert Harbin built their modern facility on the corner of East
Third Avenue, across East First Street from the Lester store site. Dr.
Will retraced Bannester's steps up the East Third Street hill to eat my
grandmother's vegetable soup. Edith Lester Harbin taught music in
the afternoons. In the mornings she made biscuits, cornbread, and
mayonnaise. Before her sons came to lunch, she refilled the crystal

saltcellars that sat at each person's place at the dining room table. Salt, sugar, and heavy cream were staples on East Third Street, harbingers of the cardiovascular diseases that followed.

On June 26, 1937, I backed out of my mother's womb to join the Harbin clan; my first jewelry was a pink bead bracelet in the Harbin Hospital nursery. In that day's edition of the Rome newspaper, along with my birth announcement, a headline reported the appeasement of Hitler and Il Duce. My grandfather would die of a heart attack at his hospital desk before the Allies defeated the Axis powers.

———————

Doctors William and Robert Harbin completed their six-story hospital in 1919, but over the years, they met magnolia steel when they tried to expand their property up East Third Avenue. Miss Carrie Beysiegel lived in a small house adjacent to the hospital. She refused to sell her home to the Harbin brothers. When the hospital became the Harbin Clinic and moved to a larger location, the deserted building was demolished. With camera and tape recorder, I documented the destruction of my birthplace and my grandfather's dream.

For two weeks in 1979, a determined wrecking ball beat the former hospital into rubble. Demolition experts urged Miss Beysiegel to move to a safe motel, away from the dust and falling bricks. I photographed the bird-boned Miss Carrie as she confronted the workmen. Wearing a navy shirtwaist dress, a blue cardigan sweater, and pearl button earrings, she banged her cane on her gravel driveway and raised her other hand in an arthritic fist.

"I'm not leaving!" she screeched. "I was here when the building went up. I'll be here when the building comes down!"

Molecules of female obstinacy may lurk in our downtown water pipes, because Third Avenue women can be feisty. Miss Carrie outlasted my grandfather, his brother, and their classic building. From the hospital trash pile, Junk Woman liberated sections of Miss Beysiegel's iron fence along with limestone blocks from the hospital façade. These fragments migrated over the hill to my Third Avenue home.

———————

The highest point of Third Avenue is on the western flank of Old Shorter Hill. The Harvey house was on the downhill run as the street slopes south to commercial buildings along the Etowah River. A gray Queen Anne Victorian house, built by Thomas Fahy, looked down onto our roof. For almost a century, the family operated the Fahy Store on Broad Street. President Woodrow Wilson stopped for breakfast with the Fahys en route to his wife's funeral in 1914. Margaret Mitchell often visited Miss Agnes Fahy.

When we moved to Third Avenue, Miss Janie Fahy invited me to tea in her cavernous home. A petite wisp of gentility, Miss Janie was one of my grandmother's first music pupils. She played the piano for my grandparents' wedding. One morning in 1986, Miss Janie walked her normal route over the Third Avenue hill to shop downtown. A mugger snatched her purse and pushed the fragile lady into a stone retaining wall. She died from her injuries.

Miss Mary Lee (Polly) Sullivan had been our next-door neighbor at number 402. When Polly razed the childhood home of Ellen Lou Axson Wilson to build her contemporary home, she incited Historic Frenzy at Rome's bridge tables. Into the narrow lot, she squeezed a gray shoebox house, at right angles to our historic street.

Polly was a compulsive catalog shopper. Every day the UPS truck delivered timesaving gadgets, humorous door signs, or tartan sweaters for her miniature poodles. After Polly died, we missed the click of mahjong tiles and the falsetto barks of TouToun and FonFon. I often wore the souvenir necklace Polly brought me from her cruise down the Amazon River. The beads, nuts, and animal teeth were not Between the Rivers pearls, but for years I had led an unladylike existence in my neighborhood.

By May of 1998, newcomers lived in the historic Fahy mansion, and other corner neighbors had died. Rome's patriarch, Mr. Wilson "Squire" Hardy, no longer backed into Third Avenue from his limited-sight driveway. Mr. Albert "Reddy" Fahy now greeted customers in a celestial Fahy Store. By default and longevity, David and I were the senior Old Romans at our crossroads.

My porch was warm as I waited for Anthony. For years, he had cleaned and painted boxes and crates for my exhibits. I left telephone messages at his house, but mental telepathy was often more effective. I concentrated a plea: "Anthony, this is Mrs. Harvey. I need you!"

My stomach churned in a classic southern woman's dilemma. When our husbands and sons are not at work, they are in season: football, basketball, golf, quail, deer, or dove. Our seasons of pansy, sultana, mum, and poinsettia required hired help. As my frustration mounted, I morphed into an old woman with blue-rinsed hair. My afternoon frock smelled of lilac cologne. My walking stick had a monogrammed gold handle. I didn't have a name for this emerging crone, but she tapped her fingernails on the arm of my chair: "Where *is* that Anthony?"

I had the proper two-story brick house for such a grande dame. On the corners of my porch, between limestone fragments from the Harbin Hospital, coral impatiens spilled from the cement urns placed by the original owners. Corinthian columns supported the portico; leaded glass windows flanked the front door. Genteel cracks rippled the light taupe paint on the French door mullions. The iron furniture needed a wire brush and paint. Rust from the chair legs stained the marble squares of the porch floor.

Mr. and Mrs. John Glover had built our house in the 1920s. My mother had known the family. She told me, "Those were our rich friends." Mr. Glover's Rome Oil Mill pressed oil from cottonseeds. The local newspaper noted one of his feats: John Glover was the first Roman to drive to Atlanta and return to Rome on the same day.

Bobby Wyatt, Mr. Glover's nephew, told me a story about his aunt. Mattie Wall Glover had decorated her fine new home with care and taste. One afternoon she called young Bobby over to see her final touch: new Chinese vases placed behind the sofa. She told him, "I have everything my heart desires; my life is complete." Mrs. Glover died that night. She was thirty-four.

Bobby said the statement impressed his nine-year-old mind; as an interior decorator, he never finished acquiring beautiful things. During my frustrating summer, I pondered Mrs. Glover's final words.

From my porch, I could see the maple trees along the sidewalk. Some Third Avenue trees had crew cuts; almost all had concave spaces threaded with power lines. Rena Patton, my friend at the top of the hill, warned me when orange trucks roared over the hill brandishing their buckets. We became sidewalk sentries while the hard hats elevated their cherry pickers to eviscerate our trees.

"That's enough!" we yelled over the roar. If we'd had canes, we would have thrashed the truck fenders. When we saved a tree from a frontal lobotomy, Rena and I invoked the name of our arboreal heroine, Rosalind Burns Gammon.

In the 1890s, Mrs. Gammon lived in the last house at the foot of Third Avenue. Her home faced a magnificent elm tree across the street. When a telephone lineman came to trim some limbs for wires, Mrs. Gammon begged him to spare the tree. Unmoved, the workman returned with a saw. He found tall, auburn-haired Rosalind Gammon seated beneath the elm with a double-barreled shotgun in her lap. She won that battle.

Mrs. Gammon's elm tree stood for years on the grounds of Rome High School. Although our school had moved down from buildings on Old Shorter Hill, we remained the Hilltoppers. The building later became part of our junior college, but if you listen, you may hear our pep rally cheers in the restored auditorium. Our chant is a Between the Rivers mantra:

"Roman born and Roman bred,
 And when I die I'll be a Roman dead…"

When I stood up, I could see Ethel Toles Smith in her yard across the street. Her Tudoresque house and our Georgian home were the only brick houses in the 400 block. This energetic lady and her yardman, L.D. Raines, tended the lawn and flowers. Mrs. Smith's dogwoods and pink azaleas were traffic-stoppers in the spring.

L.D. Raines was the father of my helper, Anthony. I called to him as he walked up the sidewalk.

"L.D., do you know where Anthony is? I left a message for him to come help me today."

L.D. gave me a meandering synopsis of his life, every sentence punctured with "druther" and ending with "Miz Harvey, ma'm": Their phone may have been shut off, his wife was doing poorly, and his shoes were wearing out. He thought Anthony might be over at the Solid Rock Church on the Kingston Road.

L.D. drifted around the corner to East Fourth Street, but his non-stop patter replayed in my mind after he was out of sight. His perseverations were as much a part of our neighborhood soundtrack as the sixty daily trains that rumbled on the tracks across the river.

———⚬———

To stretch my legs, I walked to the corner to look for Anthony. As I stepped off the curb, someone honked twice. I jumped back. The driver lowered her car window. Sherrie Bacon and I shared memories of Old Rome ladies, so she laughed when I said, "You startled me. I thought you were Madeline Kuttner."

Rome's best-known domineering woman had ruled with one hand on her steering wheel and one on the horn. The Kuttner brothers, Max and Sam, operated the Kuttner family store on Broad Street. Sam was phobic about germs and dirty money; he always wore gloves. A chauffeur drove the brothers from their Fourth Avenue home to the Kuttner store, three blocks away.

Madeline Kuttner had her own form of cruise control. Once mobile, she never parked her baby blue Cadillac. She idled in the right lane of Broad Street in front of Kuttner's and honked until a salesperson came out with her face powder or gloves. When summoned by the familiar horn, the shoe shop owner ran to the car window, took Mrs. Kuttner's shoes, repaired them, and returned them to the waiting car. Grocery store clerks as well as Rome's finest lawyers went to Madeline's car to deliver food or legal papers. She honked; they trotted. Children called her "Mrs. Toot Toot Kuttner." In Atlanta, Mrs. Kuttner got curb service on Peachtree Street. If she honked long enough in front of Thompson Boland-Lee, a salesman brought shoes to her car.

Two destinations required Mrs. Kuttner to park. When she had her hair crimped and dyed red-orange at The Shop for Beauty, Madeline sat in her slip under the beehive dryer. While she blotted her bosom with a hand towel, her booming voice summoned the receptionist: "Honey! Run next door to Enloe's and get me a Coke." At matinees at the DeSoto Theater, Madeline would grab a kid as he walked up the balcony steps: "Honey! Here's a nickel. Go down to the concessions and get me a Hershey bar."

Some people say that Madeline Kuttner was the last person rescued from the fire that destroyed the Coosa Country Club in 1959. After a Christmas tree ignited the fire-resistant draperies, plate-glass windows exploded, and the clubhouse blazed. A valiant fireman found Mrs. Kuttner, trapped in a ladies room stall. The overheated Madeline probably said, "Honey! Go get me a Coke."

I reminded Sherrie of a site sculpture I'd created on Clocktower Hill, across the street from the former Kuttner house. I had recorded Madeline stories, accompanied by blasts from my Vista Cruiser horn. Background music was a Mozart horn concerto. We laughed about other good times we'd had at the base of the City Clock. On the spring equinox in 1985, Sherrie and I went to the clocktower steps to balance eggs on end. Our "Standing Ovation" became a Rome tradition.

As Sherrie drove up the Third Avenue hill, she honked a Kuttner double toot.

---

Madeline Kuttner was not the only eccentric driver in our neighborhood. Lola Newberry Legg was an artist who had lived on East Fourth Street in a house worthy of the Addams family. Dirty dishes were tectonic plates in her kitchen sink; dead celery stalks were fossilized palm trees. Neighbors reported that she gardened in her slip, or her pantyhose, or less.

Lola drove a battered DeSoto. She mastered the push button gearshift, but never the art of parallel parking. When she abandoned the car in mid-street, we eased around the DeSoto, hoping its brakes would hold. Sometimes the car rolled across Fourth Avenue into a neighbor's yard. Downtown children knew to jump out of the street if they saw or heard Mrs. Legg coming.

Both Lola and her dog had frowzled peachy-sandy hair. While Lola roared through our corner stop sign, the emaciated dog yapped from a broken back window. When legal custodians took away Lola's car keys, she swiped a Big Star shopping cart and rattled it down the middle of the street to do her errands. Her dog yipped from the prow of the basket, its sea-siren hair tousled by the wind.

Linseed oil and turpentine may have driven Lola to senility, because she was a compulsive painter. When removed to a nursing home, she may have mourned the end of her art making, just as I was doing in 1998. During my art career, I had my own obsessions. I drove my high-decibel Junkmobile to dusty flea markets to search for iron tools. I wandered through an abandoned stove foundry to collect pattern molds. I breathed the acrid smoke of burning rubber in Rome's scrap yards.

———— ⊗ ————

The streets were clear as I walked to the center of my intersection. I looked up and down Third Avenue and east and west on East Fourth Street for Anthony's lanky silhouette. I was a modern day Hecate, the Greek goddess of crossroads. I knew that Hecate helps people let go of the familiar and travel to the unknown. As I balanced the past, present, and future, I needed the guidance of this goddess.

Greek goddess archetypes were familiar to me from my *Rôle Call* narrative. Southern Belle echoed Hera as a pattern of conformity and wifely support. Junk Woman drew on the warrior Athena. Clara Bow and Arrow was my huntress character, based on the goddess Artemis. When I carted casseroles to the sick, I was Florence Day and Nightingale; she referenced the "ministering angel of the hearth." Monk Woman was the introspective Hestia who craved solitude. When I emerged from Monk Woman's cocoon as The Lunatic Moth, I wore the frivolous hot pink of a young Persephone.

———— ⊗ ————

I did not have a Greek archetype for my matron persona, but my patience with Anthony had expired. I would start my projects without him. I gathered my dust mask and work gloves, squeezed the spring latch of the side gate, and stepped into my backyard, the matrix for my summer's work. Like most Rome women, I had known to paint my garden gate Karl Dance Green, the color preferred by Rome's premier ironworker. The gate once had the requisite proportions of Viridian Green, umber, and black, but sun had faded the paint. The clanging latch recalled decades of openings and closings for children, grandchildren, and dogs. Square stepping-stones made a path between patches of ragged liriope groundcover. A peek-a-boo brick wall ran parallel to the sidewalk and around three sides of the backyard. At one corner, a wooden barn-type gate led to a former driveway. Supporting the gate, square brick columns held egg-shaped limestone finials from the Harbin Hospital.

Along with memorabilia, my family hands down trees. Under our bedroom window, a spindly white peach tree was a second-generation descendant of a tree I had climbed in my Westmore Road backyard. A Japanese maple sapling from daughter Mary's garden in Charlotte grew between hemlocks planted for daughter Katherine's wedding. Our multiple-personality peach tree was a horticultural anomaly. This hybrid hatched from tree hanky-panky when my white peach tree cross-pollinated with a fuchsia peach planted by the previous owner. The volunteer offspring sprouted limbs with white, pink, fuchsia, and candy-striped blossoms. A tree doctor pronounced that the schizophrenic tree was "circling the drain," but each spring its limbs reached over the wall to spill multicolored confetti on the sidewalk. We postponed pulling its plug.

Beneath the peach, we had planted two gingko seedlings, orphans of a female gingko that once stood beside the General Forrest Hotel on Broad Street. The city executed that tree for the crime of dropping odiferous fruit on the Fifth Avenue sidewalk. Perhaps Dr. Robert Battey inspired this punishment for obstreperous fecundity. My tree-loving husband had protested the slaughter, and after the tree was sawdust, a garden club lady brought us gingko seedlings rooted

in paper cups. We planted the two-inch saplings under our dying
schizoid peach. We thought one seedling might fill the space when
the old tree succumbed. By 1998 the two gingkoes had grown thirty
feet to daylight through the old peach tree branches.

⊷⊷⊷

Because our back yard turf had turned to mud during Mary and
Walt Beaver's wedding reception in 1984, we paved the center of
the yard six weeks before Katherine's wedding in 1990. A landscape
designer drew a scalloped flower pattern whose five pie segments
resembled a gothic rose window. I wanted to incorporate a surface
sundial into the scalloped patio. I supplied the measurements and
angles needed for a flat analemmatic sundial, including the latitude
and longitude of Rome, Georgia. The elliptical dial in the northern
scallop was as site specific as we novices could devise.

Brick masons used a sextant to form a brick axis on the south
to north line; this line marked the Harvey Prime Meridian. After

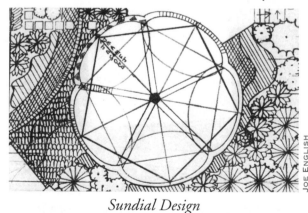

Katherine's wedding
to Tim Kenum, I
planned to align
myself with the
North Star and
celebrate the yearly
cycles of the sun.
Ronald Cescutti,
Rome's gifted
stonemason, cut

*Sundial Design*

a marble pentagon for the center crossing. A monument company
sandblasted numerals into marble triangles for my hour markers.

A lightning rod was my gnomon. From solstice to solstice, I
would move this vertical marker on the meridian as the sun traveled
higher or lower in the sky. After the brick masons completed the
north-south line, we took a break in the shade. The air was calm
when a pair of gray doves fluttered into the yard and landed on the
row of bricks. They traversed the meridian like tightrope walkers.

They cooed. I shivered. I knew that doves were messengers between oracle sites in the Mediterranean. I welcomed this good omen for the wedding patio we were building. Later, in a book about Egypt, I found a hieroglyph of two doves facing an omphalos, the conical stone that marked Delphi as the center of the Greek world. The dove-omphalos glyph represented the laying out of meridians. In the spring of 1990, two oracular doves used their innate antennae to bless the Harvey Meridian.

Rain fell during the wedding ceremony, but the patio drained in three minutes. Katherine's scalloped silk gown echoed the scallops of the patio. We served scallops at the wedding luncheon. After Mary and Walt's wedding, all I had were new bathroom faucets and muddy leather pumps. Katherine and Tim's wedding left us with a sacred space oriented to Polaris. Harvey grandchildren soon appropriated the circular patio as a racetrack for bikes, scooters, and Big Wheels.

By May 1998, our Japanese stone lantern from Okinawa was a corner accent among towering hemlock trees. The poured concrete of the wedding patio had poisoned the roots of our large maple tree. In its place, a weeping willow now flailed its tentacles against the pierced brick wall.

My first large assemblage leaned against the wall behind the willow tree. For my solo show at Berry College in 1979, I backed five oxygen tanks into a wooden crate and braced them with a dump truck gear. *Resurrection* represented the medieval wheel of judgment as well as my birth as a visual artist. Once, when we loaded the sculpture onto a truck, dozens of butterflies rose from the bushes and circled the crate in a resurrection blessing. After I retired *Resurrection* to our back yard, the crate rotted. Anthony would haul the splintered wood to the gutter. The toothed truck gear leaned against the wall awaiting its return to a foundry scrap heap. The oxygen tanks that portrayed resuscitated bodies stood by the back gate for recycling. The willow wept along with me over my dismantled artwork. My phoenix days were over.

We'd had no rain for weeks, and the rhododendrons and hemlocks would need pine straw mulch to survive the summer. The cement patio exhaled the heat absorbed from the morning sun. Plastic tape peeled from cardboard boxes warped by years of storage in my mother's attic. Architectural fragments from demolished Rome buildings stood around the yard. My sister-in-law, Ludie Harvey White, had dubbed them "archifrags." The word made me smile.

---

To make a worktable, I dragged two sawhorses under the back porch overhang. I could have used Anthony's help in lifting a large sheet of plywood onto the base. My afternoon equipment included plastic containers from the Super Discount Store. I had Borax to sprinkle in the boxes to kill the mustiness from generations of aging paper. In addition to molds, "musts" surrounded me, the things my ancestors thought vital to save.

The first cardboard box revealed the Lester family in the nineteenth century. I found photos of Bannester's store, the Lester house on East Third Street, and Bannester and Eliza Mary Lester in their Sunday clothes. Mary Margaret (Minnie) Lester is regal in

*Edith Lester and Dickens*

a buttoned silk gown. Anna Lester is shown in profile wearing cameo earrings. A young Edith Lester sits in front of a photographer's backdrop of trees and flowers. She looks uncomfortable in her taffeta suit and lace collar. She holds a straw hat. Dickens, her favorite dog, rests on a hay-strewn floor. His fur is as unruly as Edith's hair.

A small scrapbook held souvenirs from Edith's childhood: invitations to parties with friends, pressed flowers from a picnic at Silver Creek, holiday cards for Valentine's Day, Christmas, and Halloween.

Wedged in the memory book was a piece of lined notebook paper. Folded into a small square, the paper had a list written in Edith Lester's schoolgirl script. I laughed as I read the twenty-five rules prescribed for Baptist Sunday School girls. Like the rules at the Rome Female College, the list was a litany for female behavior. I pictured my young grandmother reading these twenty-five instructions once a week:

A girl should learn to sew, to cook, to mend, to be gentle, to value time, to dress neatly, to keep a secret. She should also be self-reliant, avoid idleness, mind the baby, darn stockings, and respect old age. A girl should make good bread, keep a house tidy, control her temper, and be above gossiping. In addition, she should make a home happy, take care of the sick, marry a man for his worth, be a helpmate to a husband, take plenty of active exercise, read some books besides novels, and see a mouse without screaming.

I applauded the final two items: a girl should be light-hearted and fleet-footed, and she should wear shoes that won't cramp the feet. I wiggled my toes in my old tennis shoes. Edith's Sunday School list had reminded me of Baptist constriction in my youth.

⁃⟐⁃

At the First Baptist Church, we did not make "A girl should" lists. Our salvation was mathematically calculated. We received points for bringing our Bible, memorizing a verse, staying for church, making an offering, being saved, and joining the church. The last two items made me an outcast: I had never heard a booming voice from the clouds, and I was not going to fake a conversion. Each Sunday, I was the black sheep who kept my department from one-hundred-percent salvation. The singsong hymns piled hot coals of hell on my pre-teen head:

"I was sinking deep in sin, far from the peaceful shore.

Very deeply stained within, sinking to rise no more."

After several humiliating years, I took my unwashed soul across Fourth Avenue to Saint Peter's Episcopal Church, where my Harbin aunts, Elizabeth and Margie, attended. The Reverend Russell Daniel sprinkled me at the baptismal font near windows dedicated to Mary Margaret Brower and Anna McNulty Lester. The Anglican hymns were less graphic: "Come ye faithful, raise the strain, of triumphant gladness."

My school friend, Ludie Harvey, taught me vocabulary: intinction, chasuble, canticle, vespers, and alb. Ludie's brother, David Harvey, was the sexiest crucifer on the acolyte team. Our youth group sponsored the weekly coffee hour. David and I fell in love while spicing the tomato juice. That Tabasco sauce has had a fifty-year half-life.

Another friend told me that the Saint Peter's ladies were forming a Junior Auto Guild. We were all learning to drive, but why did the church ladies want to help? Being a neophyte, I did not understand that she meant a Junior *Altar* Guild. I had much to learn about silver polish, fair linens, and Alberta Hight's scuppernong wine.

At Saint Peter's, the vestry was a self-perpetuating group of men. There were no female acolytes and no female priests. Women exercised their limited authority in the ecclesiastical fiefdoms of Altar Guild, Thrift Shop, and Cook Book. Some Saint Peter's ladies foreshadowed the autocratic woman who percolated in my psyche.

———— ❦ ————

Not long after I crossed the street, I slipped into a pew halfway up the center aisle. After kneeling to pray, I eased back onto the varnished seat, avoiding the splinters that could pierce panty girdles. A cane rapped three times on the end of the pew, and a heavy-breathing presence loomed in the aisle. A kind person seated behind me leaned forward and hissed, "Susan, move over! You're in Miss Rosa's seat." I slid to the far end of the bench. Miss Rosa O'Neill did not tolerate interlopers in her pew; she was as rigid as the marble altar where the O'Neill name was chiseled in stone. When a fellow parishioner admired her feathered hat, Miss Rosa sniffed, "I do not care for personal comments."

Josephine Walraven asserted her female power in fancy clothing and territorial audacity. She favored floaty purple gowns and large lavender-flowered hats: "My husband likes to see me dressed up." Josephine held her patent leather purse like an Amazon shield when she marched a reluctant Mr. Walraven across the South Broad Bridge to attend church. Stained glass windows made rainbows on her back pew, but Josephine had already appropriated the violet end of the spectrum. She declared that every church service was open to the public; she attended all weddings, engraved invitation or not. One mother of the bride looked at her daughter's wedding pictures in shock: Mrs. Walraven and her purple hat had insinuated themselves into the family group photographs.

Esther Watson Tipple was a straight-laced intellectual. She was a petite, upright woman with a Boston accent and prep school manners from Dana Hall, but she often covered her severe gray hair with a fancy hat from Rome milliner, Miss Mildred Galloway. Mrs. Tipple's New England breeding contrasted with Mrs. Walraven's flamboyant South Rome style. They sat at diagonal corners of the church.

One hot Sunday morning, the fragile Mrs. Tipple toppled in her front pew. She mistrusted medicines, so she refused the smelling salts kept in the choir loft. She declined a ride to the hospital. Lying supine on the pew, she clenched her teeth: "I'm not moving. I'm not leaving until Mrs. Walraven has left the church. I will *not* have her see me carried out on a stretcher."

Mrs. Tipple wrote a book on international harmonic standards and the Frye-Tipple tuning fork bears her name. Because she lectured on the history of the telephone, we knew her father was Thomas A. Watson to whom Alexander Graham Bell spoke, "Mr. Watson, come here, I want to see you." Esther Watson Tipple died on the one-hundredth anniversary of that first telephone call.

One winter morning, my mother and I sat together in church. David sang in the choir, and my dad was on the golf course. Mamie and I snuggled close for warmth in our Chesterfield coats and kid gloves. Into the pew in front of us stepped Dr. Emma Lewis Lipps, the brilliant Shorter College biologist who supervised the Marshall Forest. Unlike the veiled, gloved ladies of Saint Peter's, Dr. Lipps had dressed for the weather in hiking boots, striped socks, slacks, a puffy jacket, and earmuffs. I thought: Someday, I want to be liberated enough to wear my down jacket to church.

In my backyard, I whispered, "Free at last, free at last." My wardrobe had long ago descended, or ascended, to Dr. Lipps' standards.

———※———

Digging deeper into the cardboard box, I found pictures of Edith Lester during her Berlin years. When she celebrated the Fourth of July with friends at a sidewalk café, beer steins littered the outdoor table.

Another photo showed Edith and two friends wearing full skirts and sailor hats to rent bicycles outside Berlin's city limits. I was excited to see a photo of my grandmother wearing a costume on New Year's Eve in 1897. For festivities in her boarding house, she dressed as a Tyrolean flower girl in a laced corselet.

My mother had bound some letters with a rubber band around Granny's

*Edith Lester, Berlin 1897*

photo. She marked the envelopes: "Edith and Susan, Read! Granny drinks Champagne in Berlin!" In a letter to her parents, Edith confessed that she drank Champagne and smoked a cigarette on New Year's Eve. I was glad my young grandmother enjoyed the effervescent continental life.

In later years, my parents, aunts, and uncles had to sneak sips from a silver flask on the way to Christmas Eve parties at the dry Harbin house.

———※———

"Miz Harvey, Miz Harvey." Anthony Raines loped around the open back gate. "My birthday's coming up soon." For about twenty years, Anthony had reminded me of his day; this year he really wanted a boom box. I pulled out the garden hose, and Anthony scrubbed twenty years of dust from my hinged ammunition crates. The damp wood smelled of varnish, and the wet hemp handles reminded me of childhood rope swings. The run-off water from the hose perked up the wilted hosta plants bordering the patio. In my anti-war artwork phase in the 1980s, I had merged ammunition cartridges, bullets, and war medals with militant Christian music. The crates would return to the flea market where I bought them. I hummed the tune to "Onward, Christian Soldiers."

Anthony shared his father's repetitive speech patterns. To the scratchy rhythm of his scrub brush, he told me that his preacher had warned him about the Y2K bug about to invade the earth. We were living in perilous times. Would this Y2K bug bite him? Were we in the last days, the end times like the Bible predicted? Anthony's nattering had been a sidebar during the years we had worked together. I refused to adopt his panic. He scrubbed. I shuffled boxes.

—— ❦ ——

The next cardboard carton revealed a copy of my grandmother's family memories. I sat on a Karl Dance iron bench and opened the blue-bound paper booklet I had first seen when I returned from Paris in 1958. While I was in Europe, Edith Lester Harbin had hired a typist to transfer onto onionskin paper her handwritten memories of her Lester siblings, parents, and grandparents. At eighty-one, Granny was bedridden from a stroke, but she made genealogical charts for each of her grandchildren. Her memories had seemed old-fashioned and distant in 1958 because I had graduate school on my agenda. Forty years later, in a memoir stage of my own, her accounts sucked me into a centennial vortex.

In August 1897, Edith Lester had come to Antwerp to meet Anna Lester's ship from America. They traveled for several weeks in Germany before Anna went to Paris to study art. Edith wrote:

> As Sister's boat docked quite late at night, I didn't try
> to go to meet her, but the porter did it nicely and had no

trouble locating her. Before we went to bed, she had a bad coughing spell, and I immediately thought of T.B. She hooted at the idea. "It's just a cold," she said.

When we got to Berlin, I had a doctor examine Sister. I was under the impression that if a person had T.B. the germ would be in the sputum, but they couldn't find it, so she went on to Paris and worked hard at her art. I went to Paris for two weeks at Christmas, and I had another doctor see Sister with the same results. I knew nothing then of the places in Switzerland where so many are cured.

Edith also wrote a brief account of their summer of 1898 travels:

We wanted to take a walking trip in the Black Forest, so we went to a little town on the train and started to walk from there. The guidebook said the descending view of the valley was the prettiest. Well, we were ascending the valley, which was beautiful. A man came along in a wagon, and I asked him if we could ride. He said yes, so we climbed in and hung our feet over the back end, so we went up the valley but got a descending view.

We took a bus to Zermatt. One day we took a walking trip up one of the lower Alps. We had to go slowly so as not to tire Sister. In fact, as I look back on all we did in Switzerland, I wonder how we did it. The mountain air must have been good for her. We had lunch on the top of the Rifle Alp. Coming down, I saw some edelweiss growing in the snow, so I picked a little mess.

I *owned* that "little mess" of edelweiss. After my grandmother picked the flowers from the snow, she had pressed the soft gray blossoms onto black velvet. The framed edelweiss hung in her music studio as a reminder of Zermatt. After Granny died, the flowers went to my mother's house. In 1998, they sat in Granny's secretary in my Third Avenue living room.

I closed my eyes and remembered the summer afternoon when my sister Edith and I found Zermatt letters in my mother's bedroom closet.

Our mother had remained in her Fieldwood home for several years after our father died. Bedridden from small strokes and Alzheimer's disease, she required twenty-four-hour care. While Edith was visiting from Kentucky, we went to Fieldwood to clean out one closet, anything to simulate closure to our mother's sad condition.

Sunlight entered Mamie's Delft blue bedroom through a bay window framed by damask draperies. Under the window, a wooden chest was locked with a key. Green yarn looped through the skeleton key with a note attached: "Important! Valuable family history!" We laughed because many items in Mamie's house had similar tags: "Save! Read!" More than one tag said, "Oldest thing we've got!"

We opened the accordion closet doors. Our mother would never again wear the plaid Tanner shirtwaist dresses from The Town House or the enameled dogwood earrings in the leatherette jewelry box.

"TuTu, where do we start?" Edith whispered.

"Let's save the blue silk Doncaster dress for her funeral. She wore it to Mary's wedding in 1984 and to the big fiftieth-anniversary party in 1985."

"Should we save one pair of shoes?"

"Kiko, she's not going to need shoes again until she gets dem golden slippers."

Edith and I started singing, "Oh dem golden slippers, golden slippers I'm gwine a wear to walk the golden streets."

We went over to Mamie's hospital bed and held her stiff hands. Through tears, we sang some more. Perhaps she heard our voices from her distant limbo. If she had any consciousness, she'd be longing for the golden streets. I returned to the closet.

"Kiko, can you reach that hatbox on the top shelf?"

Edith climbed the step stool and brought down the box and its silted dust. Under the lid was Mamie's note: "Kiko and Susan, read these letters about Granny and Sister Anna in Europe!"

We spread the letters on the wooden chest by the window. The envelopes were addressed to Mr. and Mrs. Bannester Lester in Rome,

Georgia. The postmarks were from Switzerland, Germany, and Italy. The dates were June, July, and August of 1898.

"Zermatt!" Edith grabbed a letter from her favorite Alpine town.

"Here's a postcard from Rigi. I had no idea they went to Rigi. Remember that view we had in 1987?" I asked.

"A spooky place. We could hardly breathe watching the sun rise."

"Kiko, you and I should figure out Granny and Sister Anna's summer route. In 1998 we could make a centennial pilgrimage to Zermatt. Mamie should be settled in Myrtle Hill by then."

"TuTu, I feel one of your projects coming on."

We stood by our mother's bed. "Thank you, Mamie, for all you have done for us. You can rest now."

Mamie's face was a house façade with the shades drawn. She opened one bleary eye, and then closed her lids.

Edith bundled the clothes for the Salvation Army. I set the hatbox of letters by the back door to go home with me. All that remained in the closet were wire hangers with hospital gowns and a pink chenille robe with embroidered roses on the pocket. I pulled two gray bobby pins from a crack in the vanity drawer and closed the closet door.

———————

After our afternoon in Fieldwood, I filed Edith and Anna Lester's summer letters in my office. Since then, we had moved our mother to a nursing facility. I still dreamed of a sister trip, but Edith had summer school, and the Harvey finances discouraged any transatlantic crossing, even one of centennial import. David's income covered our living expenses. My past income had paid for my artwork materials, studio rent, and some travel, but in the summer of 1998, there was no meaty shinbone in Mother Hubbard-Harvey's cupboard.

———————

"Miz Harvey!" Anthony interrupted my reverie. He had been muttering in the background about his birthday boom box and the Y2K bug. He pointed to a truck out in the street.

"O.K., Anthony, that's the men from the oxygen company. They've come to get my tanks. Put two on the dolly. Let's roll them out to the street."

I used the royal "Let's." Anthony did the rolling.

My collection of oxygen tanks dated to 1979 when I had seen the rusted cylinders as humans, depleted of oxygen. Their single eyes stared at me from trucks and loading docks. In my first show, I reclined two tanks in a wooden shipping crate; they became Adam and Eve at their funeral. I put war medals on Adam, and my Navy dog tags rested on Eve's torso. The metal tags were imprinted, "Protestant," and in that show, I protested war, injustice, and religious persecution.

My rough theatrical work was never marketable. I'd always known that these oxygen tanks were in my custody for a short time, but parting with them stung. Strapped to the side of the lumbering truck, the cylinders stared at me with Cyclops eyes. As my old friends clanged down East Fourth Street, I heard their muffled voices: Please don't ship us to Dachau.

These tanks were my repertory troupe. We had traveled by truck to Atlanta and Washington for exhibits. I severed bonds to my cast of characters. I was striking the set.

<hr/>

Anthony and I leaned the damp ammunition crates against the patio furniture to dry. While he hauled the wood scraps from my *Resurrection* crate to the gutter, I lifted the flap of another box. Mounted on cardboard were colored photographs of Zermatt and Nuremberg. Souvenir cards showed the New Bridge in Lucerne. A bright red accordion book from Frankfurt, Germany, had city views. My grandmother's book about Rhine River legends rested on a piece of coffee brown newspaper.

I lifted out *The Rome Georgian* of April 16, 1898. The newspaper, scorched from attic heat, was as brittle as phyllo pastry. The Rome Lesters must have sent this paper to Edith in Berlin because the newspaper's musical correspondent brags about two graduates of the

Southern Conservatory of Music who are studying in Germany. They had to be Edith Lester and her friend, Frances Snell. The article also praised the violin artistry of Roman Miss Alida Printup.

Holding the fragile paper, I read what Romans were doing in the spring of 1898. Alla Holmes Cheney's column was titled "The Demands of Modern Civilization on Women." A small blurb announced a new book, *The War of the Worlds* by H.G. Wells. Rome girls learned that HRH the Prince of Wales had taken up the bicycle. The recipe column included beaten biscuits, chicken salad for thirty, and Roman Punch (Santa Cruz rum, two gills of sherry, one pint of Champagne with lemon juice and crushed pineapple). Under "Superstitions" were health tips: rub a stye with a black cat's tail; cure shingles with blood from a black chicken. J. Kuttner offered dry goods, notions, shoes, and hats.

This was the Rome world that Anna and Edith Lester left to study and travel in Europe. The newspaper broke at every crease. The edges crumbled like ashes.

---

The phone rang in the downstairs playroom. I stepped over puddles from the dribbling faucet and walked around the theater seats I had rescued from the Rome City Auditorium renovation. Scrolled white roof brackets from Madeline Kuttner's house leaned against the brick foundation wall next to the iron rails of Miss Beysiegel's fence. The screened door whacked behind me.

Sister Edith reported from Kentucky. She had received her summer school schedule. For professional and financial reasons, she could not consider a trip to Europe to trace Anna and Edith Lester's route. The vision of a centennial journey with my sister dissolved on the dingy playroom carpet.

Edith was my preferred companion for any research adventure. In 1997 we sold some rental property and went to England to celebrate our sixty-fifty birthdays. We wedged three weeks of travel between my son Dave's wedding and Edith's summer classes. That length of travel now seemed as impossible as Anna and Edith Lester's two-month jaunt. In June, we planned to visit our female Gilbert cousins in Pennsylvania before Edith finished her training as a low vision specialist. I would meet her in Atlanta after her final exam. Travel with my sister was always fun, but Bucks County was not the Alps. Atlanta was not Lucerne.

I would have to follow the Lester sisters in spirit, alone.

---

I gave Anthony his money and some extra for his birthday boom box. I reassured him that the Y2K bug would only bite computers and elevators. I did not stress him with the possible collapse of the Russian ruble. He declined a Coca-Cola because it made his face break out. He headed for Mr. Purdy's service station to get a Sprite. I held the gate open and watched him saunter to the bottom of the East Fourth Street hill. I'd known Anthony since he was seven. Now he was over six feet and the only helper I'd had.

As an artist, my fantasy had been to have a crew of cute young men in hard hats, cleated boots, and leather tool belts. They would have unloaded my sculpture with skill and good humor. Instead, I'd had Anthony and whatever men I could coerce into loading heavy objects onto trucks. Not many men helped me twice.

I once saw my dream staff in New York City. As I left the Whitney Museum on Madison Avenue, a flatbed truck bearing Mark di Suvero's sculpture pulled up at the curb. His rusted I-beams stretched half a block. His crew had ponytails. I stood on the museum drawbridge to watch Mark di Suvero rise from the Whitney garden moat on a hoisted I-beam. I wanted to straddle that I-beam in jeans and a hard hat. I lusted for that crane and those brawny men. Like a serf at the castle gate, I held the door open for Mark di Suvero to enter the Whitney Museum.

---

While I lingered at my back gate, Anthony reached the foot of the hill. On the opposite corner of East Fourth Street stood the "Lady in Red." Part of the peripheral street scene of downtown

Rome, this woman wore only red: dress, hat, gloves, patent leather purse, lipstick, stockings, and heels. In hot weather, she wore scarlet satin shorts and a halter. A ruffled red parasol protected her rouged cheeks from the sun. We never knew if she was waiting for the bus or for someone to pick her up. This woman was gutsier in her red satin than I had been in hot pink wings and a sequined tube top on the Empire State Building observation deck. In New York City, no one noticed the Lunatic

*The Lunatic Moth 1988*

MARY BEAVER

Moth. After my adventures, I could recede into the bricks and bric-a-brac of downtown Rome. The Lady in Red was a continuing exhibition. She was the exclamation point of East Second Avenue.

After I closed the back gate, I sat at our iron mesh picnic table, the site of many family meals. In 1990, our first two Beaver grandsons spent a week with us while Mary and Walt went to Hawaii. I had served the boys pizza at the backyard table. I gave Christopher the first slice, and then I cut a wedge for Drew, aged two. He looked at his older brother's portion.

"Moo Moo! Christopher got too much. I don't got too much. I want too much!"

David and I had laughed at this classic portion envy, and our family uses Drew's words when we feel deprived. When my siblings and I divided our mother's belongings, I sometimes looked at their stacks with envy: "I don't got too much."

With my stuffed basement, the covered area under the porch, the new plastic boxes filled with papers and photographs, I told myself, "Moo Moo, you *do* got too much."

With a giggle, I snapped my dirty latex gloves into the trashcan and hung my faded hat on the iron trellis. I scuffed paint flakes of Karl Dance Green as I climbed the back steps to the kitchen door. I wanted a Coca-Cola with lots of ice and a wedge of lemon, the classic drink of dewy southern ladies coming in from an afternoon of garden work.

Instead of picking hollyhocks or parsley, I had hoed and raked memorabilia in my "back forty." The dandelion weeds I pitched were scraps of metal and wood. If my inheritance had been vegetables, I'd have put them up in Mason jars. Scrapbooks and tape recorders were inadequate for the letters, photos, and ephemera from Edith and Anna Lester.

During our summer dialogue, I hoped to find inspiration from their freewheeling adventures. I wanted to link myself to the past, but I also wanted to catapult my discoveries into a future orbit.

The Coke fizzled my nostrils in a down-home taste from childhood.

Good. So good.

*Arrange whatever pieces come your way.*
Virginia Woolf

# The Junes of '98

*With one eye, observe the external world*
*With the other, look deep into oneself*
Amedeo Modigliani

June 1, 1998 Rome, Georgia

*Dream: David is riding in an inner tube in a suit and tie. I dream of a large egg. I'm being shown how to inject it to fertilize it.*

While David ate his Raisin Bran and read the newspaper, I thought about my dreams. Were we going down the tubes? The Russian stock market shuddered, and our basement chaos echoed the depression of the financial world. The large dream egg might be the gelatinous mess of my inheritance. Only I could fertilize my family history, but the weight of it pulled on us both. David's job was to keep our family's inner tube afloat. He polished his shoes, picked up his briefcase, and drove to his office. My commute was shorter. I climbed one flight of stairs.

After our children left home for college and marriage, I had taken over the upstairs bedrooms. One, a former sleeping porch, had casement windows on two sides. I painted the room white and used it as an alternative bedroom when I had ideas to write down at midnight or dawn. I furnished my sanctuary with the white hospital bed I had used in my installation titled *Dream House Complex*. I had a white metal chair, two white tables, cotton sheets and blankets.

SUSAN HARVEY

*The White Room*

The White Room was refuge and dream place. The full moon rose between branches of the dogwood tree outside the east window. I tracked the first moment of sunrise from solstice to equinox to solstice.

Across the hall, another bedroom had become my office. I chose pumpkin orange for the walls; slatted bamboo blinds covered the windows behind a rickety daybed used for lightweight guests. The desk and bookcases were cheap wood, and two stuffed file cabinets held poems and manuscripts for performance pieces. Stacks of papers sat in box tops on two rolling carts. I alone knew the geology of my jumbled terrain.

Anna and Edith Lester's summer letters from 1898 waited in two large three-ring binders until I could organize them by date and decipher the faded script. Edith's handwriting was larger and more legible than Anna's, even though Anna taught penmanship at one of her colleges.

My Lester Harbin cousins had inherited Anna Lester's *Handbook for Travellers* by Karl Baedeker. They lent me the book, just in time for my summer research. When I opened the cover, the first page said, "The Rhine." From experience, I knew that my great-aunt left whiffs of spirit in her books, so I was not surprised when my neck warmed, just above my collar. Anna used a purple pencil to mark the date: August 14, 1897. She bought the book a few days after her transatlantic ship docked in Antwerp.

Anna had covered the guidebook in black silk taffeta. She folded the cloth into precise corners, hemmed and fortified with black thread. The Baedeker red leather binding peeked from under the black fabric. The page edges were marbleized scallops of blue, brown, and tan. A tape bookmark remained brilliant forest green after one hundred years. Anna left it on page 289, in a section on the town of Strassburg (Strasbourg).

Foldout maps showed successive segments of the Rhine, names of hotels in each city, plus advice for boat, rail, and carriage travel. With her purple pencil, Anna underlined their hotels and the sites they visited.

I also had my grandmother's book titled, *The Legends of the Rhine from Basle to Rotterdam.* Her faint pencil inscription told me that she bought the book on August 18, 1897. I didn't know how much of the Rhine the sisters had seen that year, but they studied these books before their summer travels in 1898.

---

My plan was to follow Anna and Edith day by day through the summer. Their letters, maps, and guidebooks would provide the route. With encyclopedias and the Internet, I could research the cities, rivers, and mountains that they saw.

Along with my narrative, and as counterpoint to their travel reports, my journal would track my twentieth-century days. I would record the dreams that punctuated my nights. I didn't know where this descant would take me, but I knew the dialogue was the next circuit on my labyrinth.

---

I raised the bamboo blinds to let eastern light into my office. The daybed under the window had a view of my front yard cherry tree. Propped up on pillows and armed with a magnifying glass and sticky notes, I joined Anna and Edith in their preparations. At age thirty-six, Anna had the fluttery jitters of a pre-menopausal woman. Edith was twenty-two. Though matured by her two years in Germany, she corresponded with young Rome friends from her teenage years.

In May 1898, Anna Lester was completing eight months of work at the Académie Colarossi in Paris. She wanted to sketch outdoors, and her card from the Prefect of the Seine gave her legal permission

to draw in the parks. In Berlin, Edith Lester had finished two years
of study with top musicians. The sisters exchanged letters as they
planned their two-month vacation. They assured their parents
that the Spanish-American War was no deterrent to their itinerary.
Thomas Cook and Son Travel Agency was their primary resource for
timetables, tickets, and the forwarding of letters. Letters and postcards
were the only forms of communication.

Other than Herr Baedeker, Mr. Cook, and the railroad agents,
Edith and Anna had no male advisors. When they needed money,
they had to remind their father to send bank drafts from Anna's

*Bannester and Eliza Mary Lester*

savings accounts in
America. Perhaps
Bannester resented
his daughters'
independence, or
passive-aggression
made him forget.

Anna may have
looked at this photo
of her parents as
she wrote to them
from Madame Bazin's boarding house at the corner of Boulevard
Montparnasse and rue Léopold-Robert. She used the formal
"Mother" and "Father."

May 15, 1898 Paris, France
My dear Mother and Father,

On Thursday I went up town in the morning to the Bank
and to Cooks to see about my ticket, then to the Louvre,
then to the Studio all the afternoon. It rained while I was on
my way back from the Studio and although I stopped in a
doorway and waited until it stopped, I got my feet wet and
had to change my shoes and stockings when I came in—and
made a little fire. Friday I worked until 5 P.M. then went to
Mary's. [Mary Young was Anna's friend from Rome, Georgia.]

I left a note for we want to go and see Sarah Bernhardt this week sometime. Saturday it poured *all day all night* and has been nearly all of today. Such weather! Not one day since I got my [permission] card have I been able to go out an half hour in safety. That will not do for sketching, will it?

I can get a round trip ticket from here to Geneva, Lausanne, Berne, Interlaken, Lucerne, Zurich, Munich, Nuremberg, Frankfort, Heidelberg, Strassburg, Paris! 2nd class—good for 2 months for 206.40 francs. Now I am going to see what one will be from here to Geneva 2nd class and the estimate from there 3rd class. If it is cheaper, I will perhaps do that and not get a round trip as I cannot tell, now the war is on, just what to do. I do hope Peace will be declared very soon, don't you? If France should go against us, which I do not think she will do, I would stay in Germany next winter. I am skittish about Italy, riots go on there so much—I might not like a whole winter at once though I should hate to come back to America without seeing as much of Italy as possible. All the pictures—they are lovely.

Madame Bazin says I can leave my trunk here all summer in her storeroom, then I will only take a few things. I am only going to take old things. I guess Edith will scold but I am fat enough now to stand that. I cannot be bothered with things. I did not wish to go so many places but in getting a round trip, he said I *could* stop off at any of those I wished, that is about $41.50 which I do not think is much to pay to see so many places in Switzerland and Germany. I am waiting though to hear what Edith has to say on the subject.

I dream nearly every third night that I am back in the Studio at Shorter. All sorts of dreams about the store, the knife, and any *little* thing I used to think about comes back. I am wondering if the mind does rest when people dream. Does it?

I will tell you [my plans] as soon as I know. How I wish you could go in my stead, Mother, and let me stay here and work. If you both could come, I would be so glad. Can you manage it and leave Miss Beall in charge at home and Ed at the store? If so, use half of what I have invested and come by way of Atlantic Transport Line to England. That is good and cheaper. I am going home that way. If I had only been here longer I would come the first week in June and no mistake.

I am so glad the flowers are doing well. Love to my "little darling" [Moses, Anna's cat] and kiss her and squeeze her for me. Love to Miss Beall, tell her to keep you both well *for me.* With much love, a whole heartful for each and plenty of kisses as many as you will take.

Your loving child,
Anna M. Lester

I was surprised that Anna and Edith signed their full names on family letters. Anna's "M." stood for McNulty. Edith had no middle name. Edith's letters came from the pension of Frau Welle on Potsdammerstrasse in Berlin. From my childhood conversations with my grandmother, I knew she accented the second syllable of her parents' familial names: "Mamah" and "Papah."

May 31, 1898 Berlin, Germany
My own dear Mama and Papa,

This week I have succeeded in starting my letter "on time." Yours of the seventeenth came Monday, also the paper, and all were enjoyed immensely.

I will probably leave here on June the twenty-fourth unless Sister changes her mind about when and where she wants me to meet her. I mentioned some time ago that I would need a check the first part of June and last time I asked you please not to fail to send it. I certainly hope it will arrive in time. If you still haven't sent it when you receive this it will have to be telegraphed. I have about enough to pay for my board and lessons of June. You see when the last check came I was almost entirely out, owing to my spring

dress. This month too I had to get a skirt and a few little
things, so I will have no money left over for my ticket. If
we get our return tickets in Köln, Sister's too will have to be
paid for in German money. Of course, French money is used
in Switzerland, but as I said last week a good part of the time
will be spent in Germany. I hope it will not inconvenience
you sending it on such short notice, but to be on time I
must have it by June the twentieth.

I suppose I will take my steamer trunk this summer,
for I couldn't very well carry enough for two months in my
hands. I have had my blue skirt shortened to my shoe tops
and bloomers of blue satin made for walking this summer,
mountain climbing, and the few times I may ride [a bicycle]. I
told Sister to do the same. Skirts are a nuisance on a mountain.

Papa must give my love to all the boys that ask after me.
I appreciate their asking after me. I will write them whenever
I find the time. Love to Miss Beall and a whole heart full for
my Mama and Papa from their devoted baby.

Edith Lester

———————

In early June 1998, I had to leave Anna and Edith Lester for a few
days. While they packed and corresponded, my sister, Edith Ethridge,
and I flew to Pennsylvania to meet our female Gilbert first cousins.

Our common great-grandparents were George and Jane Horn
Kirkbride, who left England in 1878 to search for gold in America.
En route to the mines of California, the Kirkbrides visited friends in
Gold Hill, Colorado. After a scary ride to the mountaintop mining
town, Jane Kirkbride refused to go back down the precipitous road.
Her stubbornness determined our Rocky Mountain roots.

We cousins were the granddaughters of George and Jane's
daughter, Agnes Kirkbride Gilbert. We gathered in cousin Jean
Meade's art-filled home in the country outside of Pottstown. The
majestic blue spruce trees and the indigo sky reminded us of Colorado.

June 6, 1998 Pottstown, Pennsylvania
*Dream: I've built a labyrinth in my back yard in an area that I'm not*
*familiar with. I've laid it out and the grass is growing two-toned—*
*green and paler green. The labyrinth is on an inverted Glastonbury*
*Tor—a ridged bowl in the ground; the design is square, but the paths*
*curl. Water fills the container and the grasses sway under the water like*
*seaweed. The water is clear enough to see the bottom where there's a*
*drain, which may be stopped up. We need to let the water drain before*
*we can walk the labyrinth.*

At five o'clock in the morning, a crow cawed outside the window
of the bedroom where Edith and I slept. We've often conjectured
that our dad's spirit totem is a crow. Perhaps "Doc" was glad that his
Gilbert daughters and nieces were together.

My dad's siblings had scattered across the country, so we cousins
had not known each other as children; this was the first adult
gathering of our generation's females. Edith and I sat down with
Janie, Karen, Jean, and Mary Anne. Gaynor was traveling in England;
Lee lived nearby and joined us for dinner. We learned that four of
us are artists. We all love art, antiques, and good things to eat. My
dad and Uncle Howard were dead. Our aunts, Rachel, Dorothy, and
Barbara, were the last living children of Agnes and Oscar Gilbert.

Aunt Barbara brought Agnes Kirkbride Gilbert's gold-filigreed
white china for us to use at dinner. She left quickly, evading our
questions. We wanted to know which great-grandmother hid her
beat-up cooking pots and pans under the mattress when company
came. Did Uncle Johnny Kirkbride and his geriatric lady friend drive
off the cliff on Sunshine Canyon Road?

When our parents died, we would be blood-linked orphans, but we
would not know the family secrets. Some cousins had stronger Colorado
memories because they lived closer to our grandparents in Boulder.
Cousin Karen recalled that a dictionary sat beside the Oscar Gilbert dining
room table. Word arguments could be settled before dessert.

Dr. Oscar Gilbert, like my Harbin grandfather, died during World
War II, while his sons, Howard and Warren, were overseas. To my

mother, Agnes was "Mother Gilbert," and we called her "Grandmother Gilbert." Other cousins had used the more intimate "Gamo."

I remembered a wiry woman with waved grey hair and sparkling blue Kirkbride eyes. Her squealing hearing aid was a barrier to conversation, but when she sang "Johnny Sands" and "Sweet Coral Bells," we heard the lilt of Cumbrian hills. At age eighty, Agnes wrote down every song and poem she knew by heart; they ranged from nursery rhymes and Scottish ballads to King James and Shakespeare. My mother, the archivist, bound the collected memories of Agnes into a one-inch thick book for all the cousins.

June 7, 1998 Bucks County, Pennsylvania

Edith and I hugged our cousins and drove to Bucks County. We were not in Europe with Anna and Edith Lester, but we looked for clues that they were with us. We grinned when we saw the Swiss flag flying over the door of the Barley Sheaf Inn. During our naps in twin iron beds, the tinkling bells of sheep were an Alpine echo. After a dinner of Italian sole with lemon butter, I read Edith our grandmother's letter of June eighth. Edith Lester enjoyed stories of Rome's townspeople, but quickly defended a school friend named Mary. We dubbed the letter "Meddling Romans and a Pedaling Granny."

June 8, 1898 Berlin, Germany
My dear Papa and Mama,

I started out with a new pen tonight in hopes my letter would look a little more respectable, but so far it doesn't look much better. I enjoyed your letter of May the twenty-fifth immensely. I laughed so over the report about Dr. Hoyt and Miss Kate Jones that Frances [Snell, from Rome] and Frau Welle wanted to know what the matter was. When anyone knows those two at home and thinks of them marrying it is enough to send one off in convulsions. He better think twice before he leaps for he might at any moment find some of his precious papers dumped into the trash barrel. As for Miss Kate, if she is thinking of marrying

such an old thin widower, what is she tormenting poor
Mary for? She can be a holy terror!

Mama says it's rumored that Mary's engagement is
broken. Will the Romans never cease to let other people's
affairs alone and tend to their own business? It makes me
*mad*, for Mary has never done any thing out of the way
and doesn't deserve to be talked about so. Suppose she is
engaged or not engaged, what difference does that make
to outsiders?

Early Sunday morning while we were eating breakfast,
here came Mr. Turner on his wheel [bicycle] and had
brought Mrs. Hanson's with him. He wanted us to rent
another wheel, go for a little ride, and then go out there
for dinner. I told him if he could wait until I finished my
coffee and got on my riggings I would go with him. We rode
all the way to Hundekehle, one of the favorite suburbs of
Berlin and there got something to eat. Then after resting a
while under the big trees in the cool shade we rode to West
End to the Hansons. She had a nice dinner that I enjoyed
very much, and *delightful* American ice cream (not the kind
Frau Welle makes) for dessert. We got home just in time for
supper and I had had a perfectly lovely day.

I hope you will not disapprove of bicycling on a Sunday.
Had I thought it any harm I would not have gone. As I
saw no harm in it, I went and enjoyed myself very much.
I am quite sure I was no worse morally after the ride, and
physically it did me much good. Sister is delighted that I
have learned for she knows it is just what is good for me.
Sitting still for eight hours every day is rather tiring and
walking on the hot pavements is worse tiring, so you see my
exercise is very limited. Mr. Boise [Edith's teacher] says I
should go for a ride every day and I would be delighted to,
but have neither the time or the money to rent a wheel so
often. As we have been to no concerts during May and June,
I think I can afford a ride or two.

I am very glad that I have only two more weeks of work. The Theory isn't bad, but it's warm practicing and I have been at it pretty steady since the first of September. Berlin has agreed with me splendidly, and I have been able to work almost every working day.

It's a great pleasure to know that you both are so well and happy, and I hope you will stay so. Go out a lot and enjoy the summer. Love to Miss Beall and oceans of it for you two, also hugs and kisses.

Devotedly,
E. Lester

*Edith Lester and Friends*
*Berlin 1898*

Over the next few days in Pennsylvania, Sister Edith and I assumed our travel routine. She drove, while I read the maps and watched for signs. When David and I travel, he carries the bags and tips the cab drivers. I carry the routes, reservations, boarding passes, and the heavy task of making the right decisions.

My sister's personality is as lively as her red hair and brown eyes. We travel with lightness and see wrong turns as providential. We get hungry at the same time and pick the same menu items, usually a crayfish bisque or a fish with almonds and *beurre blanc*.

With no husbands to appease, we stopped at every antique shop. When we had lunch overlooking a waterfall at the Cuttalossa

Inn, we didn't yet know how many waterfalls Anna and Edith Lester would visit during their summer together. On the last night, in Lambertville, we watched television for the first time in days. The world had survived without us, but the fall of the Japanese yen had rattled Wall Street.

June 14, 1998 Rome, Georgia

Coming home from vacation was difficult, although David had stacked the newspapers and mail in chronological order, the unused kitchen was neat, and his Oriental rug fringe lay in military rows. He muted the television and said there was water in our basement from a clogged drainpipe. Sounded like my labyrinth dream.

June 15, 1998 Rome, Georgia

*Dream: There is a war with airplanes nose diving and flying over our house. In another dream I'm packing to go to Europe, to Paris, or on Hollins Abroad. How little can I pack? I do have my passport. The brakes don't work on my Junkmobile, and I'm yelling.*

I was glad to wake up in my own bed after the dreams of war and panic. As he shaved, David whistled a snatch of opera. My mind caught the refrain, and we spent breakfast guessing the source. *Tosca? La Traviata? Il Trovatore?*

Upstairs in my office, I reunited with Anna and Edith Lester in Paris and Berlin. The travel arrangements made Anna tired and indecisive, so she abdicated to Edith for their final route. The ladies packed their summer clothes in small trunks. Their belted suitcases were called "straps."

In addition to trains and lake steamboats they would travel by diligence, a European public stagecoach pulled by four or six horses. According to Baededker, the average speed of a diligence was five English miles per hour.

I liked the idea of diligent travel. I learned the French origin. *Faire diligence* means to hurry. A *carrosse de diligence* was a coach of diligence or a fast coach. As Anna and Edith rode through mountain passes, I would visualize the persistent, hurrying coach. Posthaste.

*Diligence*

June 16, 1898 Paris, France
My dear Edith,

   I mailed you a letter on my way to the Studio this A.M. Baedeker says there are schools and a Palace at Karlsruhe, but I think we both want to see the Black Forest. At Strassburg you know is the cathedral and clock we have heard so much of. Maybe we could go to Karlsruhe to the place you know for a week and take a side trip over to Strassburg. That I think would be better for we will be ready to stop a week at K. and if you can give me some idea of the time we will be there I will give that address to Madame for my letters, which will come two days after I leave.

   Now this is all I can find in Baedeker. From Göschenen to Airolo *over* the St. Gotthard is 22 miles. There is a Diligence to Andermatt twice a day—1 hour. To Haspenthal twice a day. *No* Diligence from Haspenthal *over* the St. Gotthard. Carriage and one horse from Göschenen to Haspenthal. St. Gotthard has been deserted for the Simplon Pass. Those who wish can walk.

   Baedeker does not say turkey about Interlaken from here as far as I can see. Get the ticket any way that suits you, stop any place you like. I do not mind. When I begin to think of it my head feels like a *boil* and hurts to touch. It makes no difference to me where we go but we better arrange to stop a week when we do halt so as to get board cheap. Only be sure that you have in all the places *you* want—so as not to regret after we get there.

And by *all* means don't forget to get in a [train] car with three or four people. A girl was almost murdered only two days ago in one alone. Traveled from Dresden to Berlin— you know, with a side aisle. She rang the bell however and they caught the man. I am as much afraid of one woman as one man. So have a *number.*

Third class is just as good in Italy as Germany but on the boats second class they say is not good. I do not know how we will manage unless we go and pay a little more after getting on. I have been told to do that way.

I am going to mail this for I do not know anything more about what I ought to know than a *cat.* Just drop me a postal where to meet you in Köln and if we get my ticket then and there, why can't we start Monday A.M. on the Rhine? Good bye until next week Saturday.

Much love,
Anna M. Lester

Baedeker says a *whole lot* about that *tunnel* but who wants to go in there?

## June 17, 1998 Rome, Georgia
*Dreams: my car runs out of gas, we buy a new house in the country, and I am lost on an unfamiliar street.*

Outside the casement window of my quiet white room, the dogwood tree hosted green leaves after the white blossoms of the spring. A squirrel jumped from a branch onto the windowsill and stared at me through the window. His greedy black pea eyes warned: store up nuts and berries for the winter.

During the spring, I'd lost my passion for most things. David and I wandered in the same swamp. I thought we had already had our midlife crises, but age sixty was a crisis of its own dimensions.

A few things made me feel alive. I loved planning a trip, especially to Europe. Travel quests satisfied my detective need for research and discovery. I liked waking up with a spark of inspiration about a sculpture, poem, or monologue. Working with my hands was satisfying, especially if I had grandsons to share the scissors and glue.

Prehistoric rock alignments had been my passion for several years. In 1997, Sister Edith and I had bought copper dowsing rods at the Avebury stone circle in England. We walked ancient turf mazes. With some crop circle fanatics, we breaststroked through a yellow rape field to absorb rainbow energy from a fresh crop circle. When we dowsed the stone circle of Long Meg and her Daughters, we learned that such circles came with warnings to wayward women: Don't misbehave, dance on Sunday, or become a witch. You might solidify into a monolithic pillar.

In the summer solstice twilight, when we dowsed the Castlerigg circle in northern England, I had wondered if my solar obsessions dated to my British Isle forebears. At every stone circle, Edith and I taught people to dowse for energy

*Edith Ethridge*
*Long Meg 1997*

lines. One frustrated man shook his head as he returned our copper rods: "I guess I just don't have the boobies."

⚊⚊⚊◈⚊⚊⚊

In 1998, I trolled depressing anchors through the summer sea. My beautiful mother huddled in frozen bones between non-death and non-life. Our aging house was a snail shell that no longer fit our shapes. Two dear friends, Rena Patton and Mildred Greear,

were moving from Rome; their departure sucked air from my lungs.
David was in pre-retirement inertia, and the financial world rumbled
trouble. My basement held generational strata. To spin my straw into
gold, I needed to be my own alchemical Rumpelstiltskin.

For my artwork in the 1980s, I had researched potent fairytale
characters like the Frog Prince, Rapunzel, and Snow White. I had
learned that in German, Rumpelstiltskin means "crumpled foreskin."
Perhaps a Teutonic curse on dirty old men.

---

While I ran errands in the stifling heat, my new hormones
kept hot flashes just below my gritty skin, but a steamy aura formed
around my body. Anthony and I potted the wilting sultana that the
yard crew had neglected to plant. He wondered if he should buy a
flashlight for the Y2K blackout.

I dashed for water solace at my brother Pete's swimming pool.
Behind their East Fourth Avenue home, the Gilberts' enclosed garden
had become Provence under the tutelage of Suzy's green fingers. Vines
crawled on the cement wall and iron fences. Verbena and strawflowers
bloomed. Purple lantana, my mother's favorite plant, attracted
small yellow butterflies. Limestone finials from the Harbin Hospital
ambulance entrance were disappearing under ascending fig vine. I
could smell basil and rosemary as I floated across the small pool.
Because I was reading *Under the Tuscan Sun*, I fantasized that I was
looking at the Mediterranean blue sky.

June 21, 1998 Rome, Georgia

At 10 o'clock on the summer solstice, I went down to my
backyard to adjust my sundial gnomon. On the longest day of the
year, the sun is highest in the sky and the shadows are shortest. I
dragged the lightning rod gnomon close to the noon marker of my
dial and stepped back onto the Harvey Meridian to ground myself on
the north-south line.

Before the winter solstice, I would stand on the brass meridian
on the floor of Saint Sulpice church in Paris. Until then, the sun and I
had to track our way through summer and fall.

June 22, 1998 Rome, Georgia
*Dream: I'm in a toilet stall, and I've started to bleed.*

Dreams have no propriety filters, so I noted details no lady
would mention in the front parlor. Bladder and uterine dream
images echoed my body's state, but I looked deeper. In aviation, a
"stall" is prelude to a crash. Parts of me were slowing down, and as I
ended my art making, my female parts grieved along with my spirit.
I recognized old friends: Frustration, Irritation, and Resentment. I
pictured them as snake-haired Furies etched by Albrecht Dürer, but
the underlying emotion was anger.

In society's lexicon, women can be annoyed, miffed, peeved,
peckish, or vexed. In the early 1990s, I had identified a subspecies of
female anger, not yet coded as a psychological disorder. The "Pissed
Princess Syndrome" described some affluent women I'd observed,
including the woman I glimpsed in my gilt-framed mirror.

I started writing a fairytale called *The Pissed Princess.* In my story,
the Princess stamps her feet and pouts. As a supportive medieval wife,
she has embroidered crewel tapestries to put her husband through
the Knight-in-Shining-Armor Academy; she deserves to be a carefree
Queen in a turreted castle. The Prince-Husband is a victim of economic
outsourcing and has lost his job to mercenary jousters from an offshore
island. When the heroine's King-Father dies, he leaves penny stocks
and dollar debts. Custodial care devours the income from the Queen-
Mother's scrawny livestock. The Princess is royally pissed when her
inheritance is a single golden apple from the Queen's stunted orchard.

The Princess wants to rescue her parents, her husband, and her
children. Her own fantasy is a royal coach ticket to Paris.

I saw princess prototypes in fiction, on television, and at the
country club. When I described the syndrome to David, he recalled
princesses he had met in his work as a financial advisor.

———⊷⊷⊷———

One summer night in 1996, I asked David to read what I'd
written about the Pissed Princess. Smart prince, he caught the blatant
message and looked up from my manuscript.

"I guess I'd better take you to Paris."

I reeled him in: "Wouldn't you like to see the D-Day beaches?"

As we brainstormed an October anniversary celebration in Normandy, I told David about an empty envelope that I had seen in my grandmother's souvenirs. The envelope was addressed to Anna M. Lester, but the unfamiliar Paris street name had puzzled me.

"I'd really like to find that street where Sister Anna lived in Paris. Saint Beef, or a female saint I never heard of."

With Paris a possibility, I dug out the letter from my grandmother's scrapbook. A magnifying glass helped me find the one-block rue Sainte-Beuve on a Paris street map. A serendipitous glance through a hotel guidebook gave me a shock: a small hotel occupied number 9, rue Sainte-Beuve, Anna Lester's address in 1898.

After visiting Normandy, David and I spent two nights on the fifth floor of the Hotel le Sainte-Beuve. I learned that Charles Augustin Sainte-Beuve (1804—1869) was a major figure in French literary history and had lived in the neighborhood.

On our last morning at the hotel, I walked down the spiral staircase to the ground floor. Sister Anna and her trunk had come down the same steps in 1898. The mystery envelope led me to rue Sainte-Beuve in 1996. Sister Anna had twirled the wheel of my future.

———

Like my morning dream, the Pissed Princess project and I were stalled. I hadn't devised a way to get to Europe with the Lester sisters. My moss-covered castle needed power washing. I was angry that the art world had not anointed my sculpture.

"No *Art in America* cover for *you*, young lady!"

"The Venice Biennale? Are you kidding?"

———

The telephone interrupted my musings. Barbara Knott, a friend from the C.G. Jung Society in Atlanta, wanted to come to Rome to research a book she was writing. I had described the Pissed Princess

Syndrome to Barbara, and she had told Rosemary Daniell, her writing mentor. Rosemary, a flamboyant expert on southern women's lives, wanted to know more.

Taking one concrete step, I vowed to mail *The Pissed Princess* manuscript to Barbara to give to Rosemary.

—⧓—

June 23, 1898 Paris, France
Dear Mother and Father,

This A.M. I finished the binding on my skirt, cleaned my studs, the silver ones, went to the laundry for my shirtwaist. Then an old man came from Monroe's for my trunk. I got that off and then had lunch. After lunch—I had a few things to fix.

I am all ready to leave now. This afternoon Mme. Bazin came in with your letters and the paper. The Munsey *[Munsey's Magazine]* has not come yet, I suppose will tomorrow. How nice it was to send them a few days earlier so I would have them before I left—I did enjoy them so much—some will take to Edith—think of seeing Edith in the morning! If we *all* could only be here for three months— it would be charming.

Neither of you mentioned receiving the letter I enclosed to Mlle Ballu on 31st May or if she had sent you her address. I hope it is all right. I cannot imagine what became of that other letter of mine. Can you? What could have gone wrong? I must say good-bye for Paris—almost dinnertime— will finish and mail in Köln—I get there ten minutes before Edith in the morning. I will kiss her for you both—and would give anything under the sun to come and stay two minutes at home and kiss you.

Anna M. Lester

I am very naughty to worry you with all my disappointments—I did not realize what I was doing.

Anna's catalog from Mary Baldwin Seminary lists Mademoiselle Henriette Ballu as a teacher of French, German, Italian, and Spanish for the 1896-1897 session. Anna left the school after the spring of 1897. Mlle Ballu may also have left Mary Baldwin for a new address.

I didn't know what disappointments Anna had confessed to her parents. In April, she had written to her mother: "All I have to show for my time in Paris are these charcoal nudes, and I suppose the people in Rome would be too modest to look at them."

Anna drew naked studio models, male and female. She knew that professional artists had to master the human form in order to paint portraits and historical scenes. Like all art students, she wanted critical praise from her professors. The ultimate reward was acceptance by the Paris Salon jury.

My ambition had been to have a New York gallery exhibit of my sculpture, but on a bitter cold day, I met Reality on a slushy Soho street corner. Tears and sleet dampened my portfolio of plastic slide sheets. The Big Apple rejected the Junk Woman of Rome. Maybe I gave up too soon.

Anna and I had wanted approval from our townspeople, but we chose mediums outside propriety's fence. She drew from nude models; I made graphic sculpture. By contrast, Edith Lester's profession was non-controversial. In Berlin, she basked in praise from her piano instructors and hoped to command a good salary in a fine college. My kinswomen had the adrenaline to keep them at the piano, organ, easel, and canvas.

Anna's disappointments came from her inflated ambitions, but also from her parents' expectations. Someone must have pushed Minnie Lester to sing, Anna to paint, and Edith to play. Their mother, Eliza Mary Cuttino McNulty Lester, had studied for four years at Miss Sherwood's School in Danbury, Connecticut. Perhaps her dreams dissolved in an early marriage, the birth of two babies during the Civil War, and the family's move to Rome after the war. While Anna and Edith followed their career paths, Eliza Mary read the popular *Munsey's Magazine* articles about art and literature before she forwarded them to her daughters. She followed international news reports and traced her daughters' travel route on a map.

I didn't have letters from the senior Lesters, but I could imagine the questions they encountered on Rome sidewalks:

"Your daughters are *still* in Europe?"

"Miss Anna is drawing those nude models in Paris?"

"When are they coming home?"

"Any marriage prospects?"

June 23, 1998 Rome, Georgia
*Dream: I'm driving down a street in Atlanta with daughter Katherine and a load of kids. I see the kind of house I want, and we stop. The house is a combination of old and new, traditional and contemporary. Roof levels have been changed and windows put in interesting places.*

During the month of June, I wrote an essay about the quintessential tomato sandwich. I planned to read it at Poetry Night in Schroeder's New Deli courtyard on the twenty-eighth. In the essay, I described my mother-in-law's kitchen.

For Alline Burney Harvey, assembling a tomato sandwich required as much ritual as setting the altar for Holy Communion. First, the celebrant centered a square of paper towel on the enameled kitchen table. Next, she spread two slices of Merita "light" bread with Durkee's Famous Sauce and homemade mayonnaise. For minor feast days, she substituted Hellmann's mayonnaise but added a few drops of lemon juice. The incarnation required the piercing, peeling, and slicing of a blood-red Big Boy. Tomato juice dripping from white bread was a Dixie Goddess sacrament.

---

Alline Harvey's life was a case study for the Pissed Princess Syndrome. Her southern belle mold shattered when David's father died in a car crash in 1941. She had to find employment and support two small children. Despite financial hardships, Alline was ersatz royalty in her small house on East First Street.

She created a stage set: flowered chintz draperies framed the windows and French doors. Claw-footed wing chairs and mahogany piecrust tables rested on the worn burgundy carpet. Silver teapots and a coffee urn from the Burney home on Lumpkin Hill sat on the dining room sideboard, and glass bobeches caught candle drippings on the girandoles. When her grandchildren arrived, Alline chose her own grandmother name. She was to be called, "Ladye."

Alline had salved her Princess anger by creating a costumed persona: a curly white wig, blue-framed glasses, and fur-trimmed suits. Diamonds only left her fingers to be cleaned and polished. In the hospital for psychosomatic "illnesses," she wore frilly negligées, a pearl choker, quarter-sized button earrings, and her Hamilton watch. After filling her need for royal attention, she got "well." The exhausted nurses were happy to roll Ladye out the door to my Oldsmobile station wagon.

Ouch! I felt the pinch of insight. Maybe I had hidden my own Princess anger in costumes. Junk Woman's sword had pierced male stereotypes with pointed, wicked humor. In her pink picture hat and white gloves, Mrs. Dewey decimated Mr. Dewey's sausage with costumed impunity. I garnered attention by making outrageous art and telling ribald stories. I'd like to claim that I saw what I was doing.

———— ❦ ————

I proofread my tomato essay and set it aside for Poetry Night. For lunch I fixed a nostalgic dish, my mother's version of a tomato sandwich. Mamie spread bleu cheese and mayonnaise on Holland Rusk toast. She topped a slice of ripe tomato with hard-boiled eggs and crumbles of bacon. She poured rémoulade sauce over the open-faced sandwich.

While I crunched my mother's delicacy, Anna and Edith Lester were about to start their summer adventure. The Lester work ethic was evident. Edith was afraid of losing her musical technique during a summer of travel. Anna wished her mother could go around Europe with Edith so she could stay in Paris and paint.

———— ❦ ————

Anna wrote brief notes in her journal during the summer. Her letters home were more detailed.

June 25, 1898 Anna M. Lester journal
Köln. Got here at 8 A.M. We went to Hotel St. Paul. Got my round trip ticket after all. For 104.90 and will have to come back here in two months! So cool and nice.

June 26, 1898 AML journal
Today we went to the dear Cathedral. After service we spent until one o'clock in the museum. Have decided that this is a very good way to spend one's time on Sunday. One forgets the disagreeable things and admires the beautiful! Edith says she hates to think of going back to America.

June 26,1898 Köln, Germany
My dear Mother and Father,
      Yesterday I got here five minutes before Edith, waited in the station as a lady nearby told me the train would not be in for half an hour. I sat down behind the door for a few minutes rest and in "two minutes and a 1/2" here Edith came and looked behind the door—she saw my bag—and thought nothing but bags were behind there—but looked to see! This Hotel is not but one block from the Station, and *just* in front of the Cathedral! A lovely place to be. How I wish you all were as cool and comfortable as we are this afternoon. Edith looks well and is strong. She says to tell you she is deep in Baedeker so cannot write today but will send a postal this week. Baedeker you know is our very best friend and guide. He tells what one wants to do and how to do it— so has to be studied. I got my ticket just like Edith's round trip—so after we leave Nürnberg, she goes to Berlin. I come back here.
      After dinner we mended some of Edith's things—she her stockings and I her bicycle skirt. Then took a nap and when I waked up, Edith said it had turned out to be a

beautiful afternoon and sure enough the sun was out, bright
sky blue—a nice breeze—so I dressed and so did she—and
while we were doing so it grew a little cloudy and by the
time we got our hats on was a *steady rain!* After supper it
had stopped raining so we walked round the cathedral.
Then came up and went to bed.

Sunday

This morning, after breakfast, we went to Mass at
9.30—marched in as if we were Catholics, took seats, as the
old man in a red cloak did not send us out—they do, you
know, if one talks and does not behave. After service, we
went to the museum and saw again that beautiful picture of
Queen Louise—and others—then we hunted up our little
old apple woman—got some cherries—and a few apricots—
Edith says to tell you she is "eating cherries by the *pound*." I
do not like them, you know. Came here to dinner and really
ate so much—I could not take the strawberries at the last—
came up here and *had* to go to sleep—I do not like dinner
midday—I cannot do anything the whole afternoon.

In this I enclose a letter to Mlle Ballu. You did not say if
the others had been received. I do hope so though, and that
they were sent to her soon. I hope it is no trouble to you. I
may know her address before time to send another. I enjoyed
your letters so much Friday, and the Munseys came as I was
going down to get in the cab.

We will write often—if not so long and keep you posted
in all we do. This is a dear old place—and I wish you were
both here to enjoy it with us. It is nice to say *"us"* and not me.
I am going to live this summer out to the fullest extent. Keep
well and happy. Love to Miss Beall and our pets and ever so
much for your dear selves. I kiss you with all my heart.

Your loving child,
Anna M. Lester

Anna had underlined the Hôtel St. Paul in her Baedeker guidebook. Using the coordinates on the foldout map, I found Fettenhennen Street. Baedeker categorized hotels by amenities such as telegraph office, luggage dispatch, or lift. Some hotels were "less pretentious." The thrifty Lester ladies chose one near the bottom of the list, noted as "still less pretentious."

Begun in 1248, the Cologne cathedral was completed in 1880, eighteen years before Anna and Edith visited. The twin spires have openwork circles of geometric crosses and mandalas, held by iron clamps. The sides of the pointed towers are pimpled with rows of studs, giving a rickrack edge to the towers. Cologne cathedral was the tallest structure in the world until the Washington Monument outreached it in 1884.

Edith and Anna probably read about the city's coat of arms. Three crowns represent the Three Wise Men. According to legend, the cathedral houses their bones in a golden sarcophagus. Eleven black teardrops are either the tears of St. Ursula and the 11,000 maidens martyred by Atilla the Hun, or they represent the black ermine tails of the royal cape.

Anna marked in purple pencil some of the paintings she saw in the Cologne museum. One showed Queen Elizabeth signing the death warrant of Mary Queen of Scots. In another, St. Francis receives the stigmata. When she saw a picture of Moses being borne to heaven by angels, she probably thought of Moses, her beloved cat at home.

Baedeker says that Eau de Cologne may have been invented by J.M. Farina of Domodossola in 1709. Visitors to Cologne could buy a case of six "ordinary medium size" bottles for seven and a half marks. In later years, if my ladies dabbed Eau de Cologne *(Kölnisch Wasser)* on their wrists, they may have thought of the city where they began their summer adventure.

June 26, 1998 Rome, Georgia, my sixty-first birthday
*Dream: I'm crossing Broad Street. A big parade pours down our main street, but I get across. I'm walking under some power lines.*

On my birthday morning, I woke up thinking about street names as psychological clues. The year I turned forty, I had multiple dreams about Second Avenue and its bridges. In that decade, I crossed over into a second way of doing things: I left tradition and moved into art. As I approached age sixty, I had dreamed often of Broad Street. The dreams amused me because much of my artwork had focused on the female body and women's issues.

I liked the idea of a wide, broad street, but also the connotation of a street for women. Rome's fine ladies always shopped in the Broad Street stores. At the opposite end of Rome's social continuum, at least one woman could be characterized as a "Broad on Broad."

---

Peggy Stone Snead, Rome's premiere madam, ran an illicit house from the late 1940s until the early 1970s. Peggy had an international reputation. Some say she was the richest woman in Rome. Without doubt, Peggy Snead had power. Policemen came by at Christmas for their bottles of whiskey; the house only closed during the yearly Coosa Valley Fair.

Peggy's cash income re-circulated through Rome's economy. Snead's taxi service had designated pickup locations for Peggy's customers. She and her employees shopped in Broad Street stores for jewelry and wigs. The "girls" were guaranteed healthy by routine checks at my Uncle William's medical office. At Christmas, Peggy brought gifts to Dr. William's staff: gift-wrapped bottles of *Ma Griffe* perfume from Esserman's.

When Peggy cruised Broad Street for a parking place, people on the sidewalk tittered. Peggy's pink hair matched her pink outfits, and a curly pink French poodle rode on the leather seat of the pink Cadillac convertible.

Sherrie Bacon told me that she and her mother were shopping on Broad Street one day when they saw a pink convertible parked in front of Esserman's.

"Don't stare," Sherrie's mother whispered, but she was too late. Sherrie had seen and recognized the poodle in the convertible.

Despite its dyed pink fur, the dog was familiar. He had been a troublemaker in Sherrie's neighborhood before being banished for bad behavior.

"Poodle Doodle!" Sherrie yelled.

Hearing his former name, Peggy's dog leapt from the convertible and ran to Sherrie's arms. Her mortified mother may have fainted on Esserman's green marble doorstep.

The encounter reflected two facets of Broad Street shoppers. Dignified Old Rome women bought hats with veils. Rich edge-of-town women needed lingerie for undercover activities.

———◆———

Because it was my birthday, I drove to my mother's nursing home to thank her for birthing me. Several years before, when she was entering the tangled woods of dementia, my mother had forgotten, for the first time, that it was my birthday. Snip, snip, the umbilical cord snapped. I was in free fall, a leaf severed from the mother tree.

The nursing home hallway was a breath-sucking gauntlet. One woman's pink sweatshirt said: London, Paris, Rome, Georgia. Her curled hand reminded me of a carved bamboo backscratcher. A burn victim kept his turtleneck pulled over his head. I became Ichabod Crane chased by this headless horseman in his mobile cocoon. Behind me I heard his muffled moan, "Hep! Hep! Hep!"

Another Sleepy Hollow skeleton clutched my arm: "Honey, will you take me to the cemetery to see my husband's grave? It won't take long. Honey! Honey! Please, honey!"

I unpeeled her fingers, gagged on the Lysol of custodial care, and walked down the hall. I concentrated on the names on each door to see who the current inmates were. I looked twice to verify one name. A blue "No Code" sticker rested next to the nameplate of a Miss May Day. The first line of a new poem simmered in my head: "May Day was a No Code." Her name echoed every resident's silent distress signal. All the shriveled hands waved semaphores that pleaded "S.O.S."

My mother's generic room was the antithesis of her former homes. Aluminum chair legs replaced Queen Anne mahogany. The cracked tangerine vinyl upholstery lacked the panache of embroidered linen. When I tilted the plastic blinds, Mamie winced in the light. Even if she had been able to focus outside the window, she could not have seen the birdfeeder from her low hospital bed. On the bed-side table I kept a tape player set to loop cassettes of Chopin waltzes, but the cleaning staff switched the tapes to country music radio. When I pushed open the door, Johnny Cash had greeted me with, "I'll walk the line."

I scraped the metal chair across the beige floor tiles to sit by my mother's bed. Swaying like a metronome, I sang "Swing Low, Sweet Chariot." That chariot was taking its own sweet time coming for to carry Mamie home. I massaged the scrawny fingers that once wore diamonds, and I noticed the age spots on my own blue-veined hands. I remembered our many shopping trips in Atlanta.

When Broad Street stores were insufficient, crisp air sent us to the city for fall clothes. Our mutual love of fabrics could have come from Bannester Lester and his daughters. We touched every dress, determining the cloth's weight, drape, and degree of sleaze. In a plush fitting room, a woman with pins in her mouth hemmed our skirts, while my young sister Edith swung her legs and begged for an ice cream sundae at lunch. Rich's department store mailed the packages to us if we didn't want to carry them on the train or in the car. The rustle of tissue paper disgorging a satin dress was ear ambrosia for Rome women.

My mother aged. The system changed. No soignéed Atlanta matron pre-selected dresses and hung them in a celadon green dressing room. Revolving racks stuffed with dresses and coats made Mamie dizzy. I steadied her on the Lenox Square Mall escalators. She sighed, "If I could just find my department."

My mother's "department" was now the rack of hospital gowns at Kessler's Broad Street store. I chose blue, pink, or lavender flower prints. I could not buy teddy bear or candy cane gowns for my once elegant mother. The only fabrics Mamie touched were the thin sheet and cotton blanket on her plastic-covered bed. The camaraderie of our lady days had ended.

---

For my birthday lunch, I joined Mary Ann Mew and Marsha Black. In the late 1970s, Mary Ann and I had belonged to a support group. After the women's movement filtered to Rome, we decided we could do more than organize bake sales and carpools. We called ourselves the NINGS, which was short for No Guts No Glory. I had just snagged a solo show in Washington, and the other women were starting or reviving careers.

After we women of NING ate our sack lunches, we wrote our résumés on the empty brown paper bags. Following NING meetings at Virginia Bellew's house in the Lindale mill village, we went to the West Point Peppcrell Mill Store. We tamped down our nascent feminism with Vera Therapy: flowered linen dishtowels, potholders, and psychedelic pillowcases.

Marsha Black's house had provided refuge during the worst years of caring for my mother and father in Fieldwood. We compared stories of elder care. Marsha had found wads of S&H green stamps, licked and glued in folders, in her mother's dresser drawers. I countered with the WWII ration books and the Eastern Airlines stock certificates I'd found in Mamie's attic. We wondered what we were saving that our children would find worthless. Eight-millimeter cameras? Betamax tapes? Three dozen sterling demitasse spoons?

---

June 27, 1898 Bonn, Germany. AML journal.
Left Köln at 8.30 A.M. for Bonn, reached here at 10.30. Went to Beethoven's house, saw the room in which he was born. Then went to Schumann's grave—had dinner then sat out on the terrace all the afternoon. Now Edith is making a sketch from the window.

*Bonn, Germany.* Edith Lester 1898

June 27, 1998 Rome, Georgia

According to Baedeker, the Beethoven museum contained the composer's piano, quartette instruments, ear trumpet, musical scores, and letters. The garret in the back building where the composer was born had been preserved unaltered. Visiting these music shrines must have pleased my grandmother. I found ivy leaves from Beethoven's house pressed in Edith's linen-covered sketchbook.

While the ladies prepared to cruise the Rhine, I went to my air-conditioned studio in the Carnegie Building. The metal door swooshed behind me as I walked into my cool cavern. The cement block walls were pale industrial green, not artist-studio white. Gray commercial carpet covered the cement floor. The thick walls insulated me from traffic noise. Eastern light from the single high window fell on my worktables. Baskets and boxes held wood block scraps from a cabinet shop, metal tools from a foundry floor, and stacks of textured handmade paper.

If I closed my studio, I would need to (literally) dismantle *The Gynecologist*, one of the assemblages I made for a show in Washington, D.C. in 1982. For *Capital Profiles,* I constructed furniture portraits of powerful American men. *The Admiral's Bathtub* had his phallic submarine and a Neptune trident. *The Cardinal's Closet* contained postcards of naked Greek Gods. *The General's Desk* was littered with bullets and missiles.

For *The Gynecologist*, I chose the mantelpiece as a female symbol. Fire tools and pokers surrounded my "fire" place; beefy logs rested on the iron grate. A fire screen provided modesty, while a white porcelain glove mold held a speculum inside the chimney birth canal. Around the hearth, I assembled macabre tools that a Victorian doctor might have used to manipulate a woman's womb—or her personality. I balanced white eggs on the mantel, a tribute to the ovaries removed by Dr. Battey and to Rome's spring equinox egg stand.

I fastened an antique meat grinder on one end of mantelshelf. The meat grinder had amused me when I found it at a flea market. The manufacturer was the Climax Company.

*The Gynecologist*

Repressed Victorian women probably enjoyed grinding sausage in their Climax meat grinders.

Propped against one wall of my studio was a twenty-foot wooden ladder, which I had pulled from a dumpster behind our local mall. I had leaned the ladder against George Washington's throne in my *Monumental Erections* exhibit in 1985. I later learned that the Greek word for ladder is *klimax.*

I shocked and amused gallery patrons when I discussed the vaginal chimneypiece, male dominated medical practices, and the meat grinder named Climax. I was the saucy child on the curb pointing at the ruler's retinue. To my unscaled eye, the Emperor was naked as a jaywalker.

———⊷———

Less scandalous than my exhibited sculpture, my paper products sold well and paid my studio rent. In 1996, I designed a set of postcards using Lester family memorabilia. I copied Edith Lester's Berlin concert programs, Anna's Paris books, and menus from their transatlantic ships. For my Dream Boxes, I designed paper from music scraps, postmarked envelopes, and ticket stubs.

One small piece of cardboard I had used said *Eintritts-Karte. Beethoven's Geburtshaus.* In June 1998, I knew that my grandmother entered Beethoven's birthplace on June 27, 1898.

———⊷———

Writerblocks were the newest product for my studio line. I collaged wooden blocks with Japanese and Nepalese paper and slathered them with white glue. I added an exaggerated list of avoidance ruses. Not as altruistic as my grandmother's Sunday School rules, my "should" list came from my inner taskmaster. I turned my verbal procrastinations into small three-dimensional artworks, but I didn't know if art was blocking my writing or vice versa.

# WRITERBLOCKS

sharpen pencils • call your mother • stare into space • drink some coffee • go buy legal pads • visit the sick • bake brownies • climb Mt. Fuji • take a walk • peruse the dictionary • send for writers guidelines • watch tv • change typewriter ribbon • boil pasta • deadhead petunias • check the mail • balance the checkbook • water the plants • clean out the refrigerator • apply for a grant • stare at the blank page • take a hike • buy stamps for SASE • line up pencils on desk • have a beer • read newspaper • take clothes to Good Will • change screensaver • procrastinate • check mail again • talk on the phone • change fonts • count cars in the street • file nails • clip coupons • blow nose • read high school annual • hang indents • clean oven • alphabetize the spices • Clorox the grout • wash the car • refold maps • practice tai chi • fly a kite • repaginate • deflea the dog • repot the cilantro • swim English Channel • iron dust rags • watch soaps • surf the net • spellcheck • clean out rolodex • file a flight plan • kill a hog • go to Kinko's • read obits • table the contents • curl butter • sit in sweat lodge • clip nose hairs • twiddle thumbs • unwind phone cord • read fan mail • rake leaves • make love • declaw cat • play squash • take sauna • shave toes • beat drums • stain the deck • flip channels • eat a watermelon • do research • foot the notes • clear gutters • jet wash driveway • write Aunt Rachel • polish chandelier • rearrange furniture • defrost freezer • refinish table • call the weather • read cruise brochures • climb Long's Peak • separate eggs • pumice heels • pickle peaches • grind pepper • pit cherries • string celery • sort paper clips • run amok

*Susan Harvey 1998*

I took a load of sticky collaged blocks out to the parking lot to dry on the hot asphalt. I had raided my kitchen cabinets for whop-sided jellyroll pans, bent spatulas, and rusty wire cooling racks. In my studio, I baked blocks, not cookies.

My female forebears wore white cotton gloves in hot weather. My trashcan held dozens of stiff latex gloves, tacky in more ways than one.

———— ❦ ————

> June 28, 1898—up the Rhine. AML journal
> Got up in time for the 10.45 boat and just did have
> breakfast over when it came. The day was lovely—a perfect
> one for the Rhine—clear and cool—so cool that all our
> winter clothes were necessary. Reached Mainz at 9 P.M.,
> went to the Central Hotel.

Having seen Robert Schumann's grave the day before, perhaps my grandmother hummed the rollicking theme from his Third (*Rheinische*) Symphony as she stepped on board the Rhine steamer.

From the Anna's Baedeker guide, I learned that "upwards of 100 steamboats" navigated the Rhine, and the average number of steamboat passengers exceeded one million annually. The fares were "very moderate, those for voyages up stream being one-sixth less than for those in the reverse direction."

Passengers could get a *table d'hôte* (fixed-price) meal at one o'clock. Baedeker warned that the "waiters occasionally offer worthless books, maps, and panoramas for sale at exorbitant prices."

The Baedeker Rhine River map unfolds to about twenty inches by six inches. The pale blue river snakes between the brown hills. Helpful arrows show the direction of the river's flow from south to north.

On June 28, 1898, Anna underlined "Lurlei." The water nymph named Lore lived at Ley, a jutting rock above St. Goarshausen. Baedeker says the rocks are 430 feet high, and the river is at its narrowest and deepest at this point. The famous echo is not audible

from a steamer, but may be "wakened from a small boat in the quiet
of early morning or late evening."

I saw Anna's sense of humor and her love of cats. She underlined
the castle of *Neu-Katzenelbogen*. The "Cat's Elbow" was nicknamed
the Cat(*Katz*). The guide says a nearby rival stronghold was derisively
called the Mouse(*Maus*).

My grandmother's *Legends of the Rhine* book told me more about
the "water-witches, nymphs and gnomes" associated with the mighty
river. The frontispiece engraving of *Die Lorelei* shows a beautiful
young woman perched on a rocky outcropping. Her golden tresses
fly in the wind back toward a full moon. Stars pierce the sky between
the clouds. With her left hand, the Lorelei holds her harp. With the
right hand she makes a come-hither gesture down to the water where
a boat crashes in the dark waves. From her lair, Lorelei lured shipmen
to their watery graves. The book says that "the listening shipmen hear
the echoing clang of a wonderfully charming voice."

Heinrich Heine's poem, "Die Lorelei," was so popular in
Germany that the Nazis could not suppress it. They marked its
author as an "unknown writer" rather than acknowledge Heine as a
talented Jew.

I had confused the singular Lorelei with the plural Sirens, the
mythical Greek bird-women who lured ships onto the rocks. Perhaps
all cultures have legends of seductive women who entice hapless
sailors. These fables spring, I suppose, out of fear of magnetic female
power. Beware the rocks of misogyny and anti-Semitism.

June 28, 1998 Rome, Georgia

Schroeder's New Deli courtyard on Broad Street had been the
setting for Poetry Night for eleven years. When Sherrie Bacon and
Jon Hershey of the Rome Area Council for the Arts organized the
first Poetry Night in 1987, the isolated writers of Rome coalesced
into a literary community. Rain did not dampen our spirits or our
courtyard oratory.

Following that first heady night of verse, writer Al Braselton
started a writing support group called Postscript. We met at Marlin's

Restaurant on lower East Third Avenue. Rome's founding spring
bubbled underground next door. An adjacent parking lot had been
the site of the Third Avenue Hotel, once home to writer Calder
Willingham. From a booth at Marlin's, I could see Bannester Lester's
grocery store building across the street. I did not know that a decade
later, I would write the Lester family stories.

Postscript moved from Marlin's to my Third Avenue back
porch. When the writing group disbanded, five of us decided to
meet sporadically, "on a whim." We finagled an empty room at
the Days Inn where we could hide from hungry husbands and
home-working children. The hotel was on Lumpkin Hill, the
former site of the Rome Female College and the Albert Sidney
Burney home.

WHIM became an acronym for Women Hiding in Motels.
Mildred Greear is our senior Whimmer. A gifted teacher and poet,
Mildred mined her Mississippi and North Georgia roots in earth
celebration. Rena Patton taught creative writing at Darlington
School and researched Cherokee Indian history. Artist Bambi Berry
assembled exquisite handmade books and assemblages from Japanese
paper. She wrote poetry with equal grace. Nancy Griffin made public
television documentaries in Boston before she returned to Rome. She
and I shared Cuttino blood from France.

---

In addition to my WHIM friends, the June Poetry Night crowd
included Rome writers, college students, and one eighty-year-old
Harvey groupie. Athlene Forsyth was a petite music teacher who wore
pastel tweed suits and came to all my art shows and lectures. After the
readings, Athlene grabbed my tomato sandwich essay.

"I must have this!" she said, as she scurried from Schroeder's
courtyard.

June 29, 1898—Mainz to Frankfurt. AML journal
Went to the Cathedral then sat on the terrace by the Rhine
until time for dinner. Missed the 2.20 train, but got off on

the 4.50 for Frankfurt. Two funny women were in the car with us. One forgot to give her friend the house key until after we had started off. There was such a time as she had and threw it out the window.

June 29, 1998 Rome, Georgia

While Anna and Edith traveled to Frankfurt, Barbara Knott spent the morning in Rome, doing her book research. My mouth puckered from my tour guide patter. I heard my mother's voice touting the beauty of Rome's dogwoods in spring and fall. Barbara made specific, helpful comments about *The Pissed Princess*. She invited me to attend Zona Rosa, Rosemary Daniell's writing group, on July ninth in Atlanta.

I wanted my writing to pop out of the toaster, perfect the first time. I was learning that re-writing is like making pancakes. You have to throw the first one away, in order to get to better versions on the seasoned griddle. Like other novices, I dreamed of a rescue person, an agent, a publisher, and *The New York Times* bestseller list. During the summer I learned that these fantasies are premature without crafted, polished work. How could I tell when my writing was done? If *The Pissed Princess* had been a Bundt cake, an inserted broom straw would have come out sticky with raw batter.

Barbara brought me perfect peaches from an Atlanta farmers market. From my grandmother's secretary, I took out the china bowl Sister Anna had painted for her father to use when the Georgia peaches were ripe.

Anna had taught china painting at Mary Baldwin College. The decorative art was popular with ladies, but the physical loading of the kiln may have contributed to Anna's ill health.

I held the delicate bowl with two hands. Eggshell pink bathes the inside, and a small honeybee hovers near peach blossoms painted on the robin's-egg-blue exterior. Bannester Lester poured cream onto his peaches, as I did. The taste exploded into homemade peach ice cream, churned on my grandmother's back porch.

June 30, 1898 AML journal
Enjoyed Frankfurt—the light was good in the Cathedral—
then went over the old bridge and along the Main to the
Museum of Pictures—stayed there until one o'clock then
went for dinner—afterwards took a [street]car ride—back to
the Hotel for a nap. Left at 5.22.

Baedeker uses the old spelling of Frankfort (ford of the Franks).
In 794, Emperor Charlemagne held a convocation of bishops there.
When my ladies walked over the Old Bridge, they may have seen the
medieval iron cross near Charlemagne's statue. A cock perched atop
the cross, in reference to the architect's promise. He said he would
sacrifice to the devil the first living being who crossed his new bridge.
The rooster ran afoul of the architect's vow.

According to the guide, the Central Railway station was one
of the finest and most convenient on the continent. Allegorical
sculptures pictured the Geniuses of Steam, Electricity, and
Agriculture. I unfolded Anna and Edith's picture book of the city. The
red leather cover was bright, as was the gold lettering in a fancy font.
Photographs showed three iron spans of the railroad station interior,
where trains puffed smoke on their designated tracks. Outside the
station, women wore long skirts and big feathered hats. Men and
soldiers milled about. Bicycle riders pedaled next to horse-pulled
carriages. A porter may have pushed the sisters' luggage on a two-
wheeled cart to the Deutscher Kaiser Hotel near the Bahnhof.

The Eschenheimer Turm, erected from 1400 to 1428, has a
crenellated walkway with small turrets around a large central one.
Rapunzel might have leaned out a window. Edith and Anna could
be on the open streetcar running on tracks in the paved street. These
pictures showed civilized life in Germany: the railroad cars, horse
and buggies, fountains, the four-sided clock in the crossroads of
Kaiserstrasse, the fountain of Justice, and the monument of Emperor
William I.

Men in spiffy hats and women with parasols circle the
monument that honors Gutenberg. My ladies also saw the monument

erected in 1844 to Johann Wolfgang von Goethe, twelve years after the poet's death.

Anna, the art teacher and student, took her Baedeker to the Städel Art-Institute. Her purple pencil marked paintings of John Huss at the Battle of Constance, The Wise and Foolish Virgins, and Ezzelino in prison, refusing spiritual consolation and resolving to die of hunger.

The ladies refreshed themselves at the *Palmen-Garten*. Their accordion picture book shows a steel enclosure with tall oasis palms reaching for the grey glass. Smaller palms surround a tumbling waterfall. An insert shows a lawn tennis game played in the *Neugarten*.

If time travel were possible, I would have joined Anna and Edith for dinner and music in the elegant *Palmen-Garten*. I wondered what happened to the glass building and to the art museum during the wars that followed. When our Hollins Abroad group visited Frankfurt in 1957, the damage done by allied bombing was evident. I was thankful to have the detailed photographs of the city my ladies saw.

After Frankfurt, Anna and Edith will visit Heidelberg, one of their favorite cities. I needed to rest my eyes before diving back into the fine print and topographical maps of Baedeker.

—⇥ ⊕ ⇤—

June 30, 1998 Rome, Georgia
*Dreams: I'm in Switzerland with David and the kids going up and down mountains. We are looking at the clouds covering the Matterhorn, waiting for the clouds to lift and clear. Later, I'm in a vacation house. A note on the back door says to plant the sage.*

My morning dreams told me to seek patience and wisdom (*sagesse*). I hoped to find them by following my traveling ladies.

# The Summer of 1898

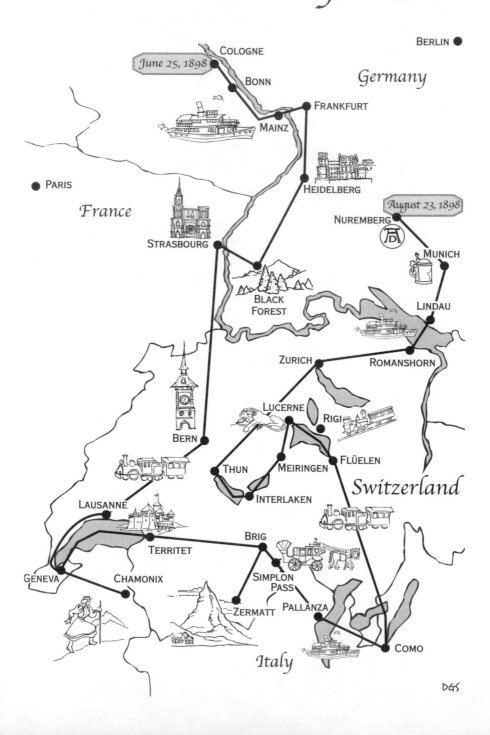

BERLIN

COLOGNE

June 25, 1898

BONN

Germany

FRANKFURT

MAINZ

PARIS

HEIDELBERG

France

NUREMBERG

August 23, 1898

STRASBOURG

MUNICH

BLACK FOREST

LINDAU

ZURICH

ROMANSHORN

LUCERNE

RIGI

BERN

FLÜELEN

THUN

MEIRINGEN

Switzerland

LAUSANNE

INTERLAKEN

BRIG

TERRITET

GENEVA

CHAMONIX

SIMPLON PASS

GENEVA

ZERMATT

PALLANZA

COMO

Italy

DGS

# The Julys of '98

*People travel to wonder at the height of mountains, at the huge waves of the sea, at the long courses of rivers, at the vast compass of the ocean, at the circular motion of the stars, and they pass themselves by without wondering.*

Saint Augustine

July 1st, 1898 Heidelberg, Germany
Pension Internationale, Mrs. Hoffmann, Anlage 10
My dear Papa and Mama,

Monday morning we went by boat to Bonn, and it was so cold and windy I could not enjoy it much. Anyway, the "beauties of the Rhine do not begin to present themselves" à la Baedeker, until one leaves Bonn. After having dinner at a garden we passed, we went and sat for a long time on a terrace facing the Rhine and the Seven Mountains in the distance. After supper we took a long walk on the bank of the Rhine.

The next morning I prepared for the water by putting on my winter flannels and woolen [shirt]waist. We were on the boat from 10:45 to 9 o'clock, when we reached Mainz. I was very agreeably disappointed in the Rhine trip, for I had heard several people say it wasn't worth taking. The weather was beautiful. Indeed it was all lovely. The legends connected with the old ruins make them very interesting, outside of the scenery being so pretty. It looks like a bay, and continues wide up to Mainz. It was hard to realize that I was seeing the "vine clad banks," because the vines are not cultivated as I supposed. They look like bean vines, tied to sticks not three feet high.

Mainz was very nice but only the Cathedral was of much interest to me. We stayed overnight and left the next afternoon for Frankfurt. As soon as I changed my waist we went to the Palm Garden and stayed until nearly 9.30. We got our supper there and listened to the music. The Palm houses and ferns were beautiful. In fact, the whole place was charming.

Yesterday evening just in time for supper we got here [Heidelberg]. If it stops raining after dinner we will walk out to the old Castle. It is said to be one of the grandest ruins in Germany.

Of course we will walk out to see the famous dueling place. I believe a duel is to be fought today, from what I overheard at the breakfast table. This is a large pension. We have decided that Mrs. Hoffmann is English and married a German, for some things here are decidedly not German and some are. For instance, there is plenty of drinking water on the table at meals, and the beds are made so that one's eyes are *not* to the window. Then again she has regular German pillows and feather coverings. There is at least one American fellow here. I knew he was by his looks, then I heard him say "you all" which settled matters. The people at our table are English and they didn't know until this morning that whiskey is made in America, thought it was purely a Scotch and Irish production. They asked the American fellow about it and he was naturally very much surprised that they didn't know that.

Coming from Mainz, a woman on the car asked me if Sister could understand German, and when I said "no" wanted to know if I was German! What do you think of that? The people down in these parts speak such curious German and so indistinctly that I can scarcely understand them. I don't know if they all have false teeth that don't fit or what the matter is. Please excuse pencil, there is no ink in here, and I didn't want to go downstairs to write. The rain is still coming right straight down, so I don't know if we will get any thing at all done today.

I am sure I don't know from where my next letter will be written. It all depends on how long we stay here. Let Joy [Harper] read this for on Sunday I only had time to write her a postal. Sister is well and joins me in much love to you two dear ones.

Devotedly,
Edith Lester

July 1, 1998 Rome, Georgia
*Dream: I'm in the middle of an intersection, like Rome's Five Points. I'm on a gynecological table getting a pelvic exam by an aide or a P.A. The traffic and people don't seem to matter.*

I decided to work through (again) Julia Cameron's *The Artist's Way*. I dribbled my stream-of-consciousness morning thoughts onto paper as she recommends. I had been skirting depression, whip-stitching the hem using bias tape. Was I about to have my period? Why not my comma, or my ellipsis? Sorry, can't swim today, I have my ellipsis: a heavy repetitive period. Drip, drip, drip...

Anna and Edith have left the Rhine for the Neckar River and the lovely city of Heidelberg. In the Baedeker guide, I found Anna's purple pencil mark beside Mrs. Hoffmann's pension at *Anlage 10*. I learned that *Anlagen* are public grounds, perhaps a grassed area like a parkway median.

The oldest human remains in Europe, a lower jawbone, were found near Heidelberg. The castle construction began in 1300 and ended with high Renaissance architecture. The elaborate Heidelberg castle gardens *(Hortus Palatinus)* of Emperor Friedrich V were once called the eighth wonder of the world. Designed by his wife's drawing teacher, the parterres had hydraulic fountains and musical devices in grottoes. Later the botanical gardens were a favorite place of the poet Goethe when he stayed in Heidelberg. I wonder if Anna and Edith saw his bench or knew about the gingko tree that inspired his poem, "Ginkgo biloba." In 1815, he attached two leaves to the poem and sent the page to a former lover. His theme of unity and duality appealed to me as I followed my female duo in Germany and looked for unification in my fractured life.

The Baedeker map showed the layout of the major sites on either side of the river. Anna and Edith could visit the red sandstone castle that dominated the city or cross the bridge to the Heiligenberg (Holy Mountain) on the north side of the Neckar.

---

In her book, Julia Cameron predicts that the Universe will respond if I stake claim to my creativity. On my calendar I marked in red the dates of July 18-31, in case a miracle allowed me to pop over to Switzerland. While I envisioned a book with pockets for postcards and letters, the Universe worked the phone lines.

From the *Rome News-Tribune*, editor Pierre Noth called. Athlene Forsyth had taken my tomato sandwich essay from Poetry Night into his office. "This should be published!" she said. He agreed. I never predicted that my first literary agent would be eighty-year-old Athlene. I checked the spelling of Durkee, Henckels, and Hellmann. Pierre said he'd run the article on a Sunday. When I told Pierre that I was time-traveling with my grandmother and great-aunt, he asked how I could do this without being there myself. Was I a reporter or a seer?

At David's office, I became a mediator as we discussed his career malaise. His secretary and I saw his lethargy; he needed to retire or get new energy for another decade. He was the Paralyzed Prince to my Pissed Princess. Perhaps my next character would be "Merlinette." We needed a female magician to transform our unstable Camelot.

Outside in the parking lot, a crow cawed, a signal that my father's spirit was wafting overhead. I questioned the King-Father of my fairy tale: Why hadn't he left enough gold in the coffers to send me to Europe? Couldn't he cut some celestial cords to set our Queen-Mother free?

> July 2, 1898 Heidelberg, Germany AML journal
> This morning we went over the town—across the old
> bridge—had a fine view of the Castle. Sat by the river Neckar
> and came back here to rest so we could take a long walk this
> P.M. but it began to rain while we were having dinner and
> has not stopped. So I will write some on my letter.

When our Hollins Abroad tour group visited Heidelberg in July 1957, we lunched in a student restaurant with vaulted ceilings. We saw no Sigmund Romberg princes. I stopped an American lady from entering the *Herren*. She thought it meant "hers," and that *Damen* was "da men." After lunch, we took the funicular up to the Schloss. In my diary I noted the lovely red stone façades of the castle and the nice view, but I did not know my kinswomen had been there.

I pulled down the glass and pewter stein I had bought in Heidelberg. I washed off the dust of forty-one years. When I flipped open the stein cover with one thumb, lusty young men sang the drinking song from *The Student Prince* operetta: Drink! Drink! Drink!

Sunlight from my kitchen window turned the glass top into a prism. The rainbow colors enhanced my ginger ale toast to Anna and Edith.

July 2, 1998 Rome, Georgia
*Dream: I've forgotten my hair appointment. I go by my studio, which is in a basement, and Sprints the dog is down there. I've forgotten to feed him. David has been feeding him, or he'd be dead.*

David came home from work full of ideas. Perhaps Merlinette had snapped his inertia suspenders.

"Let's rearrange the den, move the sofa, put the TV against the window, and add a door into the hall. I could play my stereo as loud as I want."

"It's a stopgap move," I said. "I'd still be able to hear the squeaking basketball shoes and the referee whistles when I'm up in the White Room. I may move my office down the hall to young David's old room. We'd need five coats of primer to cover those dark blue walls."

"What if we made a garage under the house after you finish clearing the boxes from Mamie's? At least my car would be off the street."

"The basement playroom is almost soundproof. You and your TV could hibernate down there. I could pitch your food down the steps. You'd need a new ceiling and floor and total rewiring for your electronics. Could you part with your traffic light and parking meter? Don't even ask what happened to your Lionel train set. You can look in the coal cellar, if you dare."

Every time we tried on a new house scenario, something required remodeling or rewiring. We bumped our elbows and banged our heads on the floor plan of a 1920s house.

"Nothing feels right. Let's get a hamburger and ride around." David got his keys.

We ate baby Whoppers and onion rings, and then drove to Five Points, once a crossroads of African-American businesses like the Spider Webb Café. When the area was urbanely renewed, East First Street became Spider Webb Drive. Martin Luther King, Jr. Boulevard became a wide parkway that led to Maplewood and Fieldwood.

Across the road from the Coosa Valley Fairgrounds, a circular church has a roof that uplifts like a waterspout. In a bizarre real estate twist, the Christ Temple Rapture Preparation Holiness Cathedral occupies the former site of Peggy Snead's infamous brothel.

"I met some American boys in Vienna in 1957 who knew that Peggy's was in Rome, Georgia." I said.

"You know," said David, "I probably got into my fraternity at Georgia Tech because of Peggy's."

"What?"

"Yeah, when they heard I was from Rome, they thought I could take the guys on road trips to Peggy's."

"Wow. I never knew that was your fraternity credential. I thought it was your brains and good looks. Let's drive through Maplewood and then by Troy's for old times' sake."

———— ⟡ ————

In the 1950s, David and I often went to an elevated empty lot in the Maplewood subdivision. Lone Pine Hill was a trysting site for high school sweethearts. On the night that Ludie Harvey married Fred White, I had changed from my buttercup yellow tulle bridesmaid dress, David had hung up his tuxedo, and we went to Lone Pine Hill. David kept a moth-eaten Army blanket in the trunk of his 1956 Chevrolet. We spread it on the ground and collapsed onto the scratchy olive drab wool. Blades of damp grass stuck through the blanket holes and mingled with the scent of pine straw. We breathed these earthy bouquets and watched the stars through Lone Pine's branches.

After midnight, I loosened the yellow satin ribbon from my ponytail and tied it on a pine tree limb. My act was instinctive. I did not yet know the Celtic ritual of tying cloths to sacred trees.

Sometime after 1956, our scrawny pine tree met a chainsaw. Lone Pine Hill was leveled and populated. We drove to Troy's Barbeque on North Broad Street. While dating, David and I often stopped here for barbeque and lemonade. We'd park at the covered drive-in area where a carhop attached a tray over the rolled-down window. One summer evening, David pulled me across the vinyl front seat. With one hand, I drank my lemonade. With the other, I repelled his octopus arms: "If you don't stop, I'll pour my lemonade in your lap." During his next foray toward my blouse buttons, I tilted my paper cup. Lemonade hit the crotch of his Levi's.

David scrambled to wipe off the sticky upholstery. I had shocked him, but he saw the steely side of his future wife.

———— ⟡ ————

We drove through more suburbs. I rejected the houses with mal-proportioned dormers, skinny plastic columns, fake Palladian windows, and pseudo-Tudor stucco façades. The sun had set when we parked in front of our Third Avenue home.

"Hey!" I joked. "This is a nice house, why don't we live here?"

"Maybe if we...."

"Enough!"

David went to his den and arranged his CD's in alphabetical order by composer. I went upstairs to be with my ladies.

Heidelberg, July 3, 1898

My dear Mother and Father,

After dinner we started in the rain for the Castle garden but by the time we got up there the sun came out and we concluded we would go through the ruins there. I must say I enjoy the view *from* an old place more from the outside. If they would leave some of the furniture and things inside for me to see it would suit better.

We then sat out on the old balcony and enjoyed the breeze and view from there. Afterwards walked round the terrace and had a lovely view of the castle and country around. The wind blew me until I was too sleepy to hold my eyes open. And the ground was too damp for me to take a nap. We started down again. Saturday A.M. we went round the town—saw in a few old churches, the outside of the university and the Students Prison—will go inside on Wednesday—when it is *free* as we expect to stay here that long. Then we got some cherries for Edith and 20 pfg's [pfennigs] worth of Huckelberries for me—and came back to dinner. We got these refreshments thinking we would make a trip to the Königstuhl in the afternoon—and knew we would get hungry—But bless you it began to rain at dinner and did not stop until after 6 P.M. By that time nearly all the cherries were gone—and I had found out that my berries needed sugar to make them go down. So after tea, we got a tiny bit of sugar.

Sunday A.M. we started to walk at 9.30 and went way to the top of that place Königstuhl—it was a walk and no

mistake. We took our berries and two rolls—when nearly to
the top sat down on a rock to eat them. Lots of people were
going our way, so when one party passed—one said "*Guten
Morgen*" and "*Guten Appetite*." Edith returned the Morgen
and said thank you. We were sorry afterwards we had not
said, "We have the appetite but no spoons." It was rather
inconvenient to bite up those berries covered with sugar, for
our noses would dip in too—and there was no water near.
We then went a little way and came to the top. Then up a
tower 93 feet—and saw the view. It was then 12 and our
dinner is at one—so down we came at double quick—and
actually got here on the stroke. My knees were so tired I
could hardly get down to dinner.

Anna M. Lester

July 3, 1998 Rome, Georgia
*Dream: I'm at a beach with the kids. I'm fascinated because I can see the
stars in the daytime. Lots of them—the constellations are very clear, like a
fluorescent star map drawn on the sky. I see a dolphin outline next to the
Dolphin constellation. Starbursts like fireworks. I'm showing people how
neat the sky is.*

The heat broke a bit—only 90 degrees instead of 105—but it
was too hot to attack the basement boxes. David decided to take
the day off to play golf. I, the workaholic, also took a break. Julia
Cameron prescribes a weekly "artist's date" to foster creativity. On an
impulse, I took my Self on an excursion to Kingston, a small town
about fifteen miles from Rome.

As I drove along the winding Kingston Road, I passed Edgefield,
an imposing rock house on a hill above the highway. My Cuttino
cousin, Martha Glover Griffin, had lived at Edgefield. When I was
about ten, Martha gave me my first art lessons. Martha was one of
many strong women who taught at Shorter College. In the 1950s,
Franziska Boas taught modern dance disguised as movement or
physical education. On occasion, she danced the evening Vesper
service in the rose garden.

Franziska, the daughter of noted anthropologist Franz Boas, came to Shorter after an outstanding New York career as a dancer, ethnologist, and dance therapist. She and Martha Griffin lived on the secluded Griffin farm. They hosted archaeological digs on the river-bottom land, where Native-American arrowheads sprouted after a rain. Margaret Mead (a student of Franz Boaz) once came to Edgefield for dinner. Franziska bought goats from Carl Sandburg's wife's herd and raised them on the hillside.

Martha and Franziska were members of the Rome Council on Human Relations in the 1960s. For security, the council often had covert meetings at night at the Edgefield house. Along with other council members, Martha and Franziska received threatening phone calls and harassment from anti-integrationists.

In 1982, I dedicated my *Leitmotifs* exhibition to Martha Griffin and Virginia Dudley, my seminal art teachers. The last time I saw Martha Griffin was in the Shorter College gallery at the opening of that show. Virginia Dudley had died the year before.

I saluted these visionary Shorter College women. The ballet music from *Swan Lake* lifted me along the Kingston highway.

In Heidelberg, Edith and Anna walked up to Königstuhl, a 1700-foot peak called the King's Throne. Kingston, Georgia, was as close to Königstuhl as I would get; the word root meanings may be the same. I drove into the historic district—a row of buildings on Railroad Street. Kingston had spruced up its main street with painted storefronts, trees, and lampposts. Self and I peeked in store windows and ate the fried chicken plate at Morell's Café. No huckleberries on a hillside.

Inside an antique shop, piles of furniture hid under damp newspapers. Collapsed ceiling fragments were brown with water stains. Through the dirty windows I spied a wooden horse and some archifrags. My mother-in-law bought me some gold champagne glasses here years ago. I'd used them twice. The stench of mold, mildew, and death seeped from the doorway. My shoes bumped into a man slumped on the doorsill. He was a grey-skinned phantom, the shell of an antiquarian.

"Is this still a shop?"

"Yes, but we're closed today," he whispered.

This haunting vignette chilled the July day, as if a dream sequence had invaded my waking life. The town of Kingston was lethargic, as was the antique mall in a deserted school building. In the woods near the flea market, a sign announced: Ugly truck contest. Call Jim.

When David came home from golf, he helped me move furniture. He knew that when I couldn't change my life, I rearranged the living room. We hung one of Sister Anna's oil paintings over our Hong Kong chest. The canvas had been black when I found it under the rafters of Mamie's attic, but professional cleaning revealed scarlet drapery and a classical plaster bust. The initials, A.M.L., rose from a dark corner in gold Old English script.

Under the dining room window sat a long wooden counter. According to the neighbor who had put it in his gutter, the counter came from a Broad Street store—enough reason for me to haul it home. I placed a brass wire hat stand from The Fahy Store on top of the wooden counter. If objects have emotional memory, the hat stand and the store counter may have known each other in their former commercial lives.

In Vienna in 1958, my final New Year's Day resolution had been to "Be a *LADY*." Forty years later, I hadn't attained that status, but I had artifacts from the Argo-starched life: an Army-Navy tablecloth from China, Madeira linen biscuit holders, and hem-stitched cocktail napkins embroidered with roosters. One hunt board drawer held two dozen Irish linen napkins monogrammed with an Old English "B" for Burney.

One project dominoed into another. Dust balls and dead flies behind the wooden counter required a trip downstairs for the vacuum cleaner. In the basement I noticed that water drooled from the dehumidifier. Upstairs for the mop. Downstairs to swab the floor. Back up to the laundry room.

I opened cabinets over the washing machine where I had stuffed clean rags for polishing silver. Our silver was locked in a hall closet in plastic bags. What was the rag quotient for a good housewife? How many silver tea services made a southern belle? The gospel according to Alline Harvey had been: A lady can never have too much sterling silver or too many diamonds. Susan Harvey's gospel mandated Russell Wright American Modern china from the 1940s. I pitched some rags and stacked my collection of granite gray plates, lug bowls, and dimpled saltshakers.

On the top shelf sat a pressure cooker and large serving dishes. I hadn't pressure cooked since I sterilized baby bottles on Okinawa. Stacks of videos sat on top of our broken VCR. David didn't drink, but he had a monogrammed sterling jigger. We had a wine rack but no wine. I had three steam irons, but I never ironed unless hard pressed.

From our parents we had inherited the requisite beverage equipment: sterling goblets, wine glasses with spun glass stems, martini shakers, swizzle sticks, and seltzer bottles. We had designated glasses: highball, old fashioned, and cordial. When I opened the cabinet that held my dad's leftover liquor, the essence of my parents' Fieldwood dinner parties floated from their ice bucket and wine cooler.

---

My mother, radiant in a flowered print dress, greeted guests at the glass-paneled front door. Ice clattered in the ice bucket, amber liquid gurgled into glasses. After country ham, squash casserole, graham biscuits, and Charlotte Russe, Mary Gilbert led her guests down two steps to the living room. The piano lamp shone on her silver hair as she accompanied her friends in Stephen Foster songs. They started with "Way down upon the Swanee River" and ended with "My Old Kentucky Home, good night." Uncle William's deep bass voice covered the sound of James Smith clearing the bar. A closed kitchen door muffled the clank of hollowware as Sallie Reid washed the silver.

The heavy brass box lock of the front door clicked shut as laughing guests departed down the flagstone walk. The house smelled of gardenias, Jack Daniel's, Maxwell House, and cigarette ash.

---

I took the memory with me to my own living room where white
woodwork framed saddle brown walls. In the early seventies, my wall
color choice had been a rebellion against pastel parlor tints. I craved
drama. One of Rome's best painters mixed the color as I watched.
David was uneasy about what he called "baby shit brown."

For twenty years, the brown suede color had pleased me, but
as I looked around the room, I realized I lived with furniture not of
my choosing. Other than the Hong Kong chest, the shoji screen,
and the Japanese hibachi coffee table, other people's things filled our
house. I might have picked an Eames, Barcelona, or Wassily chair
instead of Alline's green velvet Louis Sixteenth fauteuil. We ate at
the poplar table from the Burney home. In the 1960s, I could have
chosen Danish modern teak or rosewood from Hong Kong. On state
occasions, we might eat from Georg Jensen sterling instead of my
mother-in-law's Francis the First.

The riptide of possessions towed me under. I was the
overwhelmed man in the Kingston doorway whose antiques collapsed
around him.

July 4, 1898 Heidelberg AML journal
Started up the Philosophenweg—but the sun was so warm
we took a shady road towards Heiligenberg—to the Tower.
Got pretty flowers on our way back—and just did get here
in time for dinner.

July 4, 1998 Rome, Georgia
In the university town of Heidelberg, philosophers and teachers
walked and talked on the path across the river from the old town.
Anna and Edith may have walked across the *Alte Brücke* to reach
the *Philosophenweg*, the Philosopher's Way. They could have walked
up the serpentine *Schlangenweg* (snake path). They probably
got warm because the temperature is higher on the north side
of the river. The southern exposure and gentle winds make a
Tuscan climate, perfect for Japanese cherries, cypresses, lemons,
pomegranates, yucca, and gingko trees. Gardens provided places to

sit, rest, and philosophize while enjoying the view back toward the old city and castle.

One of my Vienna resolutions had been to develop a working and living philosophy. So far, the closest I had come was when I wrote down Harvey's Laws in 1980. Harvey's First Law: Just because something is a good idea and someone ought to do it, does not mean that I, Susan Harvey, have to do it.

I may have been violating my own first law by following my ladies on a trip I could not make. I trudged on. The ancestor police nipped my heels.

＊

To celebrate the Fourth of July, Pete and Suzy Gilbert marched their grandchildren from East Fourth Avenue to our house on Third Avenue. My brother looks like Jason Robards. A urologist by profession, Pete's avocations include fishing in his country lake and playing his guitar on the cabin porch.

For our nation's birthday, Pete had slung a CD player around his neck. He marched in a military mince step to "Hooray for the Red, White, and Blue." Gilbert kids waved flags, Thomas beat a drum, and wide-eyed Reid rode in a stroller. From my basement I resurrected the rhythm band instruments that came from Edith Lester Harbin's music studio. Granny's great-great-grandchildren banged her cymbals and clanged her triangles as we paraded down the East Fourth Street sidewalk. I used a small mallet to mark time on a hollow mahogany woodblock.

We passed the corner where Edith Lester studied at the Southern Conservatory of Music. In later years, she often walked her dog, Dickens, along these walled sidewalks after hours of teaching piano. Her Rome Music Lovers' Club had sponsored concerts in Rome, including the band of John Philip Sousa. My grandmother entertained Sousa with a reception at the Harbin home. The spirits of Edith Harbin and John Philip Sousa may have marched along the sidewalk with the Harbin descendants. Or, Edith may have preferred to be in Heidelberg with Sister Anna.

At the Gilberts' house on East Fourth Avenue, we ate pork ̣
ribs, coleslaw, and grilled vegetables. Aunt Elizabeth Warner Harbin
(Boofie) joined us. Boofie was a petite no-nonsense woman. She
trimmed her own grey hair and wore cotton dresses, catalog sweaters,
and ballerina slippers. At age eighty-nine, she was a free woman.
After Uncle William died, she no longer had to deliver his lunchtime
martini to the Sun Mountain nursing home.

We spoke of long-gone summers when men wore straw hats.
Boofie had saved one of Uncle William's white linen suits—the
uniform of southern gents. We discussed the meaning of seersucker.
Could it be a seer who was suckered? Boofie described the white lawn
dress with rolled and whipped lace that she wore to watch Ellen Lou
Axson Wilson's funeral cortège pass down Broad Street in 1914. With
her nurse, five-year-old Elizabeth stood near The Fahy Store while her
parents attended the First Lady's funeral. Charles Jacques Warner's
quartet sang, "Art Thou Weary, Art Thou Languid?"

Our aunt's vibrant memory made our mother's dissolved brain
cells more poignant. We blessed our food with Boofie's favorite prayer
from *The Book of Common Prayer*.

> *Oh Lord, support us all the day long, until the shadows
> lengthen, and the evening comes, and the busy world is hushed,
> and the fever of life is over, and our work is done. Then in your
> mercy, grant us safe lodging, and a holy rest, and peace at the
> last. Amen.*

We exhaled and repeated the final phrase. "Peace at the last" was
what we wanted for Mamie. And for ourselves.

---

After lunch, I sat on the Gilberts' front porch and ruminated
about East Fourth Avenue, the widest street in the Between the Rivers
neighborhood. Nineteenth-century artifacts punctuate the 300 block.
Across the street, a rider could tie his horse to the iron hitching posts.
Buggy passengers could step onto curbside granite blocks. If you were
invited into the garden next door to the Gilberts' home, you would

enter through the wrought iron gate that once led to the Rome Female College and the Albert Sidney Burney home on Lumpkin Hill.

Pete inherited our mother's love of history. He brought out to the porch a photograph of Fourth Avenue's major event. During the occupation of Rome in 1864, General William Tecumseh Sherman and his staff posed by a spool-leg table placed in a yard across the street from the Gilberts' house.

The photograph reminded me of the Dutch militiamen in *The Night Watch* by Rembrandt. Both groups of men strike cocky poses, although the Yankee soldiers lacked plumed hats.

From Fourth Avenue in Rome, General Sherman telegraphed President Lincoln in Washington about his proposed March to the Sea. The resulting flames from Yankee torches destroyed the house where Sherman stayed, along with Rome's foundries, hospitals, railroads, and bridges.

Ghosts inhabit (at least) two houses in the 300 block. In the old Charles Bass house across the street, a mother ghost mourns her dead children. On the corner of Fourth and Fourth, the large white house once belonged to the Printup family. When they sold the house, the sales agreement stipulated that the Printup daughters would have lifetime tenancy. The current owner thinks the ladies are still in residence. Sometimes lights turn on in their former room.

The Printup sisters could have been watching me from a second floor window as I turned their corner onto East Fourth Street. Miss Ava might be creating her elaborate feathered fans. Wearing high-buttoned shoes in July, Miss Alida could be practicing her violin.

On the sidewalk across the street, Lola Legg might be walking her paraplegic cat by holding its tail in the air like a wheelbarrow handle. At any moment, Madeleine Kuttner could roar over the hill. Her horn blasts would alert neighborhood children to come unload groceries from her car.

---

In the middle of the East Fourth Street block, a narrow lane gives rear access to Fourth Avenue homes and swimming pools. "The

Alley" once bordered the brick towers of the original Shorter College. The young women students were forbidden to lean out of the arched Gothic windows to talk to boys who clustered in The Alley. Irate teachers chased the interlopers with brooms. The boys became known as B.A.T.s or Back Alley Trotters.

The white-shingled house at the end of The Alley had been home to the Lester and Harbin families. I remembered Fourth of July afternoons on my grandmother's porch. I heard the crunch of rock salt and ice as James Smith cranked the wooden ice cream churn near the back door. Rusty springs of the porch glider squeaked with the weight of Granny Harbin and her friends. Rocking chairs harrumphed over warped boards on the wooden floor.

After lemon sherbet and teacakes, we children bounced on the "joggling board" in the back yard, a remnant of our Low Country heritage. In my mind, I crushed a crimson fleuret from the sweet shrub on the lower terrace. The spicy smell took me to Easter afternoons when the competitive voices of seventeen Harbin grandchildren reverberated in the tiered yard.

"I found the golden egg!"

"I saw it first!"

"Did not!"

"Did, too!"

In July 1898, vines had shaded the porch at 309 East Third Street. Bannester and Eliza Mary Lester sat and read the letters that I was reading in July 1998. Perhaps Dickens, Danny, and Moses caught the scent of their far-away mistresses from the crinkly envelopes with German stamps and postmarks.

Heidelberg, Monday, July 4!!

Dear Mother and Father,

This morning we went to the Tower over on the opposite mountain. Started down at 20 minutes of twelve, stopped and got some lovely flowers—then got back here at

dinnertime. Now we are waiting for it to clear up so we can
go to the Castle again. Edith says she will be back in Berlin
on the 22nd of August and would like a Draft sent her some
time so it will reach her between 22nd August and Sept 1st—
same address—in care of Frau Welle. I think I better have
mine a little earlier as I have to buy my ticket back from Köln
to Paris. So get Brown Bros. to send you a Draft for $100 on
some good bank in *Münich*, Germany. Then you can send it
to me at the Geneva address—in care of Cook. You may as
well do this as soon as you get this letter then it will get here
in time for me to have the letter forwarded.

Now do not worry over this. I only want to be sure I
have a plenty. I find the trip will cost a little more than I had
planned so I want mine in Münich. I am in it now and would
rather spend a trifle more and see it comfortably than not at
all. I may never be here again. This is a charming place. You
ought to see the American flags that are out—quite a number.

If I did not have so much else to see I would like to stay
here two weeks. Have been to the Castle again this afternoon
and the view is simply *charming*. But my how stiff I am. I
have said a number of times that *you* would not like to climb
these hills. I must stop now for we want to mail this tonight
so it will catch the Wednesday boat. With much love and
plenty of kisses—your loving child.

Anna M. Lester

I shared Anna's travel philosophy: Spend a trifle more and see
it comfortably. I have never regretted staying an extra day or two in
Switzerland or France. Anna had budgeted her savings for Edith's
study and for her own; the summer of travel was a treat for both. At
her death, Anna had funds remaining in her savings account. She
could have gone to Italy to paint in the winter instead of coming
home to die. Her prediction was correct. She never returned to
Heidelberg. I knew I'd probably die with money in the bank that
could have gotten me to Heidelberg. *Carpe diem, manqué.*

July 5, 1898, Heidelberg AML journal
Went to the Castle this morning—then after dinner we
took that long walk to the Wolfsbrunnen. Then down to
Ziegelhausen, then back to Heidelberg—just about six
miles! I was so tired I could scarcely move—Went right to
bed immediately.

July 5, 1998 Rome, Georgia
After I traced the sisters' route on the Baedeker map, I was
exhausted. Wolfsbrunnen (wolf fountain) was a favorite resort of
Frederick V and his wife Elizabeth (daughter of James I of England).
A legend claims that, at this spot, wolves tore to death an enchantress
named Jetta. Edith and Anna climbed 590 feet to Wolfsbrunnen.
They then descended to the river Neckar and crossed to Ziegelhausen.
There, according to Baedeker, "boats are always ready to take walkers
back to Heidelberg by the river."

In Georgia, El Niño stole the rain, and La Niña brought heat.
My dreams hid in wildfire smoke like Interstate 95 in Florida, which
was partially closed by flames that no one could put out. The nightly
news held metaphoric horrors. Drivers blinded by smoke crashed
into other cars. Women mourned their cats who perished in the fiery
woods. Brush fires devoured houses and melted cars.

My brainstorming mind returned after vacationing in the
desert of hormonal deprivation. I looked up seersucker: striped
Indian cotton, from the Persian for "milk and sugar." I drank some
seersucker *café au lait* while women in hats drove by my house. The
indelible Bible Belt tapes whirred: Good people should be in church.
After eleven, when the church traffic died down, I stepped onto the
front porch in my jeans to water my pots of sultana.

As a Good Christian Act, I took Psalm 23 to the nursing home
to read to my mother, although the Manor was not an idyllic green
pasture. Before she entered the valley of death shadows, Mamie loved
gardens and mountain streams. She filled crystal vases with peonies,
quince, and Tropicana roses. Her body was too stiff to fold into a
wheelchair to roll out and see the hanging baskets of geraniums along
the Manor walkways.

David, Good Christian Man, came home from church. While I made sandwiches, he removed the phone receiver from its hook and dangled it in the air. As it swiveled, all the twisted knots unfurled. I was thankful that he untied my knots, but I observed his unconscious behavior. I never saw the cord congestion.

July 6, 1998 Rome, Georgia
*Dream: the building shakes in an earthquake. Out the window I see the City Clock lean over and crash. I drive down a road I've never been on past an estate being restored next to a stream.*

If the City Clock represented my timing mechanism, my body and I were at risk. I had to trust that the new road was good. The restored estate—our house or our finances—sounded positive. The newspaper reported that the Moscow markets got pummeled. Financial analysts appropriated verbs from the sports pages: thrash, pound, hammer, tumble, and rout.

From the Internet I learned that the Heidelberg Castle Museum had reopened. The city scheduled castle illuminations and fireworks during the summer. The Castle Festival would feature the traditional Heidelberg romance, *The Student Prince*. I would not be there.

> July 7, 1898 Heidelberg AML journal
> We went to the castle for the *last* time. I wrote a little in my journal and tried to take in the beauties of nature and castle in between times. Edith writes Joy. A nice day—I hate to leave Heidelberg so much.

July 7, 1998 Rome, Georgia
*Dream: I'm in a place that we're moving out of. A few toys are still on the floor. Let them go. Someone puts an envelope at my place. The beautiful paper has inscribed words in old ink. Wooden blocks covered with paper are similar to my Writerblocks but with different colors and fewer words. I'm upset that someone has copied my idea. I walk out to the dumpster where I left my old green Samsonite suitcase. It's gone! The trash has been picked up. I visualize a new bathroom with travertine tiles and cabinets with spiral labyrinth knobs. I dream of a new bedroom.*

The Black Forest was the next destination for my ladies. To prepare, I pulled out my maps of Germany from 1985, when David and I spent one night in the southern part of the *Schwarzwald*. At that time, I didn't know Edith and Anna's 1898 route, but the romantic name screamed "fairy tale land." A Zurich tourist official had recommended the town of Hinterzarten. We took three trains to get there.

At the Hotel Schwarzwaldhof, our *Doppelzimmer* had a window box of red and white petunias. In the twilight, we strolled up the hill and into Hansel and Gretel woods. Little Red Riding Hood could have been on her way to her grandma's house. Dried needles from the fir trees cushioned a fragrant path, and the flowers were spectacular. One two-foot wide blossom looked like Queen Anne's Lace on Vitamin B12. Before bed, I sat by the hotel window to gulp the good air and watch the moon rise.

Hinterzarten had a rich resort atmosphere, but healthy and woodsy—like Gatlinburg before it became tourist flypaper. When we went to Gatlinburg with my grandmother in the 1940s, she must have been nostalgic for the river rocks and noble fir trees of the Black Forest.

---

July 8, 1898 Rastatt, Germany AML journal
Reached Rastatt last night then after seeing the town went to Weisenbach on the train. Then walked to Forbach, that is we started to walk but rode on a wagon all the way, much to my delight for I am tired. The view down the Valley was beautiful. A most beautiful day.

July 8, 1998 Rome, Georgia, to Atlanta, Georgia
*Dream: I'm in a house and we're cleaning up. I'm at Berry College on the back campus. I realize I've left my purse in the Art Building (!) and have to go back. I've done a lecture on Neolithic art and say, "I've got the Stone Age down cold." I go down to the Art Department to look for my purse.*

After the clarity of Baedeker's city maps, I didn't know if I would locate the small villages on the sisters' trek, but I found one index entry for Rastatt. I turned to page 334. Sister Anna had left her mark. In the margin next to Rastatt, her purple pencil had noted: July 7, 1898. Baedeker gave a distance scale for kilometers and English miles, but I couldn't calculate how far they rode in a wagon along the curving Murg River to Forbach. Baedeker describes the "wild and beautiful" valley of granite rocks, brown streams, and green meadows. "The slopes are richly wooded with pines, firs, and a few beeches. The valley is seen to best advantage when descending."

I flipped through more pages, past the towns of Baden and Freiberg. A section on the Duchy of Baden boasts: "Of all the wooded districts of Germany, none presents so beautiful and varied landscapes as the Black Forest." Industries were clock-making and the manufacture of straw hats, brushes, and wooden wares. Baedeker adds: "In this prosperous district, beggars are unknown."

A blank page followed the description. Some small blue dots made a pattern on the creamy paper, like a star map of the Little Dipper constellation. I turned the page to a detailed map. Rastatt sat at the top, squeezed into the map margin. The pale blue River Murg meandered from north to south. Anna and Edith had taken a "pokey" train from Rastatt to Weisenbach, where the railroad ended. Even with a magnifying glass, it was difficult to read the town names in the brown mountain ranges.

Small ink circles dotted the map. They corresponded to the dots I'd seen on the blank side. Of course. My meticulous great-aunt had abandoned her purple pencil to mark their route in dots of blue. The dark ink had penetrated the paper. I could easily have passed over this map. Now all I had to do was follow the breadcrumbs from Sister Anna.

Like my great-aunt, I like to document. In Switzerland and England with Sister Edith, I marked and dated our routes. Perhaps, in a century, a great-niece will find my yellow highlighter markings as useful as Anna's inked dots.

I hated to leave the ladies, but after spending two nights in Atlanta, I would be in the cool mountain forests of North Carolina.

I couldn't find two watches and a clock. I'd misplaced Boofie's birthday check, which I had put in a safe place. I was losing time and money in real life and my suitcase and purse in dreams. When I read Anna and Edith's letters, I was in a warped state while a black hole slurped time through a straw. Swoosh. Hours were gone.

Like Waffle House hash browns, I was smothered, covered, scattered, and fried. The hormone medication helped, but hot flashes exploded when I panicked or got anxious. The compounding pharmacy was supposed to send my estriol cream, but it hadn't arrived. I loved swimming, but the chlorine left me tired. I had moisture on the brain and stagnant water in my basement. The creative juices surged, but the flow was jerky and compulsive. I didn't feel good, but I couldn't stop. My City Clock might crash.

⸻ ❦ ⸻

I drove to Atlanta with German language cassettes playing in the tape deck. Sister Edith had finished her graduate courses, and we would celebrate her certification as the only low vision therapist in Kentucky. After my hectic morning, Saint Anthony, the patron saint of lost items, found one of my watches, and my prescription arrived from Colorado. As I was leaving, Waldenbooks called. They had received Rosemary Daniell's book, *The Woman Who Spilled Words All Over Herself.* I could read part of it before meeting Rosemary at her Zona Rosa group the next night. I thought of the saying: "God is never late, but he is rarely early." Perhaps he would be Just In Time with a ticket to Switzerland.

When I entered the lobby of the Hyatt Regency Hotel, I could have been in any country, on any continent, as excited to meet my sister as Anna had been in Cologne. Edith and I are kids in a hotel. We analyze the personalities behind the front desk and give them nicknames. We check the amenities, the view from the window, the foot elevation prospects. Will we use a chair cushion, the tote bag, or the ironing board?

As we talked and laughed, we heard music rising from a piano in the atrium lobby. Granny Harbin would have approved; she wanted

music everywhere. When we left our room, we discovered that a
player piano was running a programmed concert, with not even a
piano stool for the ghost musician. We walked around the atrium
balcony, and the player piano serenaded us. Instead of Mozart in
Heidelberg, we heard, "Oh! I wish I were an Oscar Meyer Wiener."
We laughed. At least Oscar, Meyer, and Wiener were German words.
Wiener is the adjective for Vienna (Wien). "*Wiener Blut*" (Viennese
blood or spirit) by Strauss would have pleased Granny Harbin more
than the hot dog jingle.

We pretended we were in Europe going out to dinner. We were,
as usual, the first diners of the evening in the Polaris restaurant on top
of John Portman's seminal building. All the world's atrium hotels are
toadstools sprung from this prototype root. The rooftops of Atlanta
were not European, but as we rotated around the skyline view, we
enjoyed lobster bisque, crab cakes, and prime rib.

While Edith chatted with colleagues at her vision conference, I
walked through product displays for the visually impaired. Here was
equipment my dowager character would need: walking canes, huge
calculators, talking computers, and infrared night vision glasses. The
vision aids would have helped at the hotel; the bedside table lamp
bulb was twenty-five watts. I leaned under it to study the Baedeker
Black Forest map. I read Edith some of the Lester sisters' letters.

We looked through Granny Harbin's souvenir postcard book.
We'd been to many of the European cities, but we felt a centennial
tug as we turned the cardboard pages of the leather-bound album.
An Antwerp postal showed a dogcart full of milk cans. Colorful cards
depicted the towers of Heidelberg castle. Winged monks flew in the
sky above Munich.

I sat up on the bed. "Oh, my goodness, the year 2000 will be the
one-hundredth anniversary of Anna's death."

"We must have a wake for Sister Anna." Edith waved her hands.
"I could wear Granny's black picture hat, you could wear Eliza Mary's
mourning jewelry. Could we find some horse-drawn carriages?"

"Stop! Remember Harvey's First Law: we don't have to *do*
everything we can *dream up*."

Edith thought that Anna was channeling herself through me, that I'd grabbed the baton in a reincarnation relay race. Along with her possessions, I had inherited some of Anna's unfulfilled ambition. I knew that I would go to Myrtle Hill Cemetery on October 17, 2000 to say farewell to Anna. I hoped we'd both rest in peace.

July 9, 1898 Zwickgabel AML journal
Walked about seven or eight miles. I should not have gone so far but did not know it until I was past one place where we could have stopped. Then had to go on or turn back. Got to the Inn at 3 P.M. and went to bed immediately. How my head and back did ache! Could not sit up any more that day.

July 9, 1998 Atlanta, Georgia
After paying for an exorbitant breakfast and outrageous parking, I drove out into the ninety-nine degree heat. At the Readers' Loft, I showed Mary Morris my studio products: Writerblocks, travel journals, postcards, and dream boxes. In an antique shop, I saw Bakelight radios, Monopoly games, toasters, Mixmasters, and comic books. I searched for a Russell Wright water pitcher. I heard the term "mid-century modern." If items from my childhood were vintage, so was I.

Fighting heat exhaustion, I gulped water at Eclipse di Luna, where chairs hung from the ceiling. Grilled salmon salad with hearts of palm fortified me enough to get to son Dave and Jaynee's house in Peachtree Park. After a nap, I read Rosemary's book. Her stories were encouraging, and many of her techniques were things I already did. On the way to the Zona Rosa meeting, I stopped to get my water level checked. My car and I were overheating.

Rosemary was welcoming and very supportive of her protégées. We talked about my Pissed Princess project. I signed up for her two-day workshop on July eighteenth, my fantasy date for Switzerland. Rosemary quoted Stéphane Mallarmé: "Everything in the world exists in order to end up as a book."

Maybe Anna and Edith Lester tromped through the Black Forest just to be in a book I might write. We do things for our own adventure, but our journals and photos leave clues for inquisitive granddaughters.

I left the meeting early because the floral "Joy" of the woman beside me gave me a headache. Also, the setting sun triggered my homing instinct. I made it around the perimeter highway to the Dunwoody home of daughter Katherine and Tim Kenum.

> July 10, 1898 Zwickgabel, Germany AML journal
> Laid up for repairs. Wrote home, read our little book then went to bed again. Thought best not to go on until the morning. Such a place. Chickens in all parts of the house. Hay stored away upstairs—and every thing dirty except the beds—and our food. The woman tired herself in giving us a good dinner.

July 10, 1998 Atlanta, Georgia, to Linville, North Carolina

Katherine, her son Harrison, and I drove to North Carolina to visit daughter Mary and the Beaver family at Grandfather Mountain. Harrison and I played car games while Katherine drove. Her van handled the mountain roads better than a diligence, but the motor smelled hot when we arrived at Mary and Walt's stunning wood and shingle mountain home. The house sat just below the National Forest in woods of mountain laurel and rhododendron. Germanic architecture showed in the eyebrow windows and cedar shake roof. The excavated hillside was a tiered rock garden of rudbeckia, cone flowers, and lantana. One columbine plant recalled Colorado. Inside, Mary had placed bent twig tables next to her grandmother Harvey's Victorian loveseat; she had replaced Alline's aqua velvet upholstery with a red toile print.

Rattan chairs from my parents' home faced a valley view from an upstairs bedroom window. Mamie and Doc would be pleased that their love of mountains trickled through their descendants. Mary and her four boys often hiked down into the boulder field and rocky streambed next to the house. Katherine had memories of college study in Switzerland and hikes in the Rocky Mountains. In honor of his Colorado grandfather, son Dave had proposed to Jaynee on Trail Ridge Road. Long's Peak in Colorado and the Matterhorn in Switzerland were family pilgrimage sites. Mountain air was our aphrodisiac, our oil from Aladdin's lamp, and our mingled corpuscles from Lester and Gilbert bloodstreams.

On a living room table, Mary displayed a book she had chosen from Mamie's library: *A Wreath from the Woods of Carolina*. When I opened the wildflower book, the flyleaf inscription startled me. An eleven-year-old hand had written: Minnie Lester 1868. "Sister Minnie" read this book thirty years before Anna and Edith tramped in the Black Forest. Minnie Lester Brower's death in 1878 may have fed Bannester Lester's anxiety for the safety of his surviving daughters. Perhaps the women felt compelled to complete their sister's truncated life.

July 10, 1898 Zwickgabel, Germany
Dear Mother and Father,
Here we are down in the Black Forest spending Sunday. It is so cool that even Edith is content to have all the windows closed and wears her Jacket. We sent you a Postal the afternoon we left Heidelberg—then went to the train and rode as far as Rastatt—reached there about 9 P.M. and went right to bed—thinking if it stopped raining by morning we would start on at 9 A.M. but when we looked out at 6 A.M. it was still pouring so we decided to sleep more and go at 1 o'clock if it cleared.

After breakfast it took us just 40 minutes to see the town, all the places of interest—then we came back and got our things fixed for our tramp. Had dinner and started on the pokiest little train you ever saw—went as far as it could to the end of the line at Weisenbach then got off and started to walk. It was 5 and 1/4 miles to the place where we intended spending the night. At first my satchel seemed light, but before we had turned the first corner I had to sit down, open it and get out my rubbers. The road there was muddy. Then I went on getting hot, hotter, hottest, pretty fast. That satchel got like lead and the sun was on me. I changed hands every two minutes—and all the wagons we met were going the wrong way—finally after about a half a mile we saw one coming our way.

[The wagon had] only a pole through the center, but I determined to ride if Edith would do the asking. Just as I thought we were going to let it pass she did ask if he would take our GePack. The man said *"Ja"* and got down and then asked if we did not want to ride. I said yes in a hurry so he spread out his two horse blankets between the back wheels and made a good place for us—by that time two wagons behind were waiting on us. The road was too narrow to pass so he called a man to move the pole a little so we would be more comfortable. I hopped on as one would on horseback using the chain for a stirrup. Then I laughed and could enjoy the view, which had been and was lovely. Only I could not see or think of it while the satchel grew so heavy. We tramped all the way, by sitting on that wagon! It was fine and the view was beautiful. Everybody we met laughed and said *"Guten Tag."* Got to Forbach at 4 P.M. instead of 7 as we expected.

We intended starting the next day at 8 but it was after nine—was cold, too. Same result about that satchel. The first wagon going our way we put our things in and walked behind for several miles. Then the driver was nodding—I said I was going to sit on the pole behind and he opened his eyes just as I was about to try. So had the politeness to ask us to ride, which we did as far as he went. Of course we pay for the rides. Then as soon as we left him, the Diligence came by our road so we sent our things on ahead to the next town.

After we stopped for our baggage we walked 3 miles and carried those things. It was the longest 3 miles I ever saw. I thought we never would get to this Inn. And if you could see the Inn you would laugh. The beds however are fine. I immediately took one and rested until 6 P.M., then we had tea and I got in bed in a hurry to keep warm. I was so cold my teeth were chattering—9th July—and all my flannels on too!

———————

For dinner at the mountain house, Mary prepared a friend's tomato recipe. The tomatoes were ripe from a mountain garden. She peeled and chopped them into a bowl with crushed garlic and chunks of ripe Brie cheese. She stirred extra-virgin olive oil and chopped basil leaves into the mix. A few hours later, the oil and tomato juice had softened the Brie. We spooned the mixture over hot pasta and dipped slices of French bread in the remaining garlic sauce. A sprinkle of sea salt from Ile de Ré connected us to France. Delicious.

I told my daughters that the Rome newspaper might print my article about Ladye's tomato sandwich. We agreed that the new Brie recipe would become a summer classic.

———————

July 10, 1898 Zwickgabel, continued:

You would laugh if you had seen our supper. The old woman said she would have omelet, salad, milk, bread and butter. Well, the omelet was nothing but great pancakes— like they make here and I do not eat. She put rancid oil in the salad and that was spoiled. Such nice salad. I was awfully sorry—because I was tempted to eat it anyway. The milk, butter and bread were good. This A.M. we had coffee, bread and an egg, all very good indeed. So we told her not to trouble to put oil on the salad for dinner, we preferred it without. We are upstairs. Just across the hall is the hayloft and a nice black and white cat's in there—but will not come out to see me.

This forest is beautiful. I hope we can finish seeing the parts we have planned by Tuesday, then go back to Rastatt for our things left there—and continue our route by the ticket. I sent you my list—of course we do not expect to stop at all those places but we could if we had time and money enough—will finish this later.

July 11—The old lady seemed anxious Saturday to wait until her daughter returned to give us supper. Edith says I had no business to tell you our oil on the salad was rancid, but I do not see why if I wanted to. It was the truth. Dinner yesterday was fine! They really tired themselves. Beef, eggs, milk—salad (no oil) rolls, wild strawberries, whipped cream, and real live waffles!!! Think of that—I was struck dumb.

We decided not to go on as it would be only a short way we could make by night but must start early this A.M. First thing this morning rain was just coming down so as the daughter says it has set in for 4 or 5 days—we are going to retrace our steps (in a buggy) at 3 P.M. in time to catch the Diligence and go by train back to Rastatt tonight. Then on to Strassburg in the morning. So our Black Forest trip is ended for a while, at least. Mighty sorry. We could have seen more but it could not be helped. I am out of news now so good bye.

Anna M. Lester

July 11, 1998 Grandfather Mountain, North Carolina
*Dream: I drive my car out Kingston Road, near Fieldwood, where trees have been trimmed. Lots of construction and traffic. I hit a roadblock, have trouble turning around. Lots of people at Fieldwood Road. I walk out into the pasture. Strange airplanes fly overhead, gliders with jets, wings, red, white, and blue. I ask Paul O'Mara if there is an air show going on.*

If I couldn't have the Black Forest, nothing could be finer than to wake up in the mountains of Carolina. I smelled coffee. Perhaps Mary would make waffles. But first, I steeped in my dreams. The air show dream pulled me back to a crazy day in the Fieldwood pasture in 1992.

———

In its inscrutable wisdom, The Georgia Department of Transportation had decided to widen the Kingston highway and build a new access road through the Gilbert pasture. As a humorous protest against the D.O.T., I invented a mythical flock of "Dotty Birds." Using the letterhead of BTR (Beware The Ruse) Labs, I wrote a press release announcing the impending arrival of the rare Dotty Birds.

A theater friend had given me three sets of white wings with black spots. I played the matriarchal role of "Dotty Matrix." For my bird spouse, I recruited my son's visiting friend, Hall Ott. He gamely donned black cycling pants and six-foot wings to be "Polka Dotty." Nancy Griffin was our offspring, "Little Dotty Swiss."

On my phone recording, Miss Wren Tin Tin gave aviary "updots" as the migratory birds left the Gilbert Islands in the Pacific and headed for Georgia. After receiving my phony press release, a Tallahassee weatherman called to check out these strange happenings. With a straight face and crossed fingers, I answered the phone in an old maid's voice:

"BTR Labs, Miss Marsha Henna speaking."

"May I speak to, uh, Dr. Arnie Thologist?"

"Oh, I'm so sorry, Dr. Thologist is out standing in his field. He's tracking the Dotty Birds by Dottler radar. May I take a message?"

He hung up. I loved the spoof.

Early on the morning of the spring equinox, I went to the Fieldwood pasture and marked a landing strip. My wooden stakes had polka-dotted fabric strips. I hammered them between the red and

*The Dotty Birds 1992*

yellow utility company stakes. At ten o'clock, lab-coated attendants
from BTR Labs assembled. Wearing white gloves, members of the
Rome "Autobahn" Society raised their field glasses to watch the Dotty
Birds emerge from the cedar trees. Chirping "Dot-dot-dot-dot" and
flapping their wings, Polka Dotty and Dotty Matrix performed a
mating dance for the assembled crowd. Dave's friend, Van Willis,
played Pastor Land of the Flock of the Truly Diverted. He presided
over a reaffirmation of the feathered couple's marital vows, to the
delight of little Dotty Swiss.

After Dotty Matrix unveiled some spotted eggs in the barn, the
trio flapped off to Clocktower Hill for the annual Standing Ovation
Egg Balance. Paul O'Mara photographed the Dotty Birds, and Dave
(Dr. Arnie Thologist) made a jumpy video between laughing fits.

Faded strips of polka-dotted fabric hung in the maple trees until
the bulldozers arrived. Humor assuaged my grief: the Dotty Birds
video is more valuable to me than the lost pastureland.

⸺ ⬦ ⸺

At breakfast with my family, I read Edith Lester's addition to
Anna's letter, one hundred years after it was written:

July 11, 1898 Zwickgabel (continued)
Dear Papa and Mama,

Sister wants me to finish her letter but I don't know
how I am to do it when she has told all there is to tell. This
is the most charming rainy day I have ever had the pleasure
of seeing. The clouds cover the mountaintops and first it
rains east, then west, then south, then north, then straight
down in the middle. If I had an interesting book I would be
as happy as a "big sunflower nodding in the sun" but alas!
there is absolutely nothing to read, not even a guide book,
for I didn't bring my Baedeker of Switzerland along, and
the Black Forest finishes this one. I thought I would amuse
myself by making a sketch of one of these "mourning pines"
by this little creek but, bless your heart, the picture makes

*Mourning Pine.* Edith Lester 1898

the pine look as if it was nearly dying *laughing* instead of weeping so I had to give that amusement up. After all, I don't believe I have missed my calling by not being an artist.

Edith Lester

I had brought Edith's small linen-covered sketchbook with me to the mountain. I showed the kids the page that said, "Edith's Sketch, July 11, 1898, Mourning Pine." Because of her letter, we could imagine

*Rain Bound.* Anna Lester 1898

my bored grandmother, pencil in hand, drawing what she saw in the
Black Forest. She correctly assessed her limited drawing ability. The pine
branches droop, and the chimney smoke spirals like a child's drawing.

At the other end of the sketchbook, Anna sketched the same
pine trees and a stream with rocks. She wrote, "Zwickgabel July 11,
1898." Thanks to the letter, I could decipher her faint, penciled
words: "Rain bound."

I showed Mary and Katherine where our Lester ladies were in the
Black Forest. Zwickgabel was difficult to find on the Baedeker map.
The word is printed in a minuscule font across brown mountains and
small streams. I wondered why Anna had not marked it with a blue
dot. She did mark towns higher into the mountains. These must have
been the ones they missed due to bad weather. My rain-stymied ladies
bundled down the Murg River valley in a diligence to Weisenbach
where the rail line began

⊣━⊗━⊢

I opened my grandmother's postcard book on Mary's long trestle
table and showed my grandsons the colored cards. One postal had
been written on June 28th, Christopher's birthday. Drew wanted a
copy of a December 6, 1898 drawing, one day from his birthday.
Clay copied the drawing of the horse and the women who were "Out
for the afternoon" in Paris. My mother had found the drawing in
Sister Anna's possessions, but months would pass before I discovered
the identity of the artist.

> July 12, 1898 Strassburg AML journal
> Came to Strassburg today but I felt tolerably used up, and by
> night was too ill to stay out of bed. Went to the Cathedral
> and saw all we could except the clock strike 12. Went to St.
> Thomas church to see the monument then back to the hotel
> and such a dinner—I could not eat it.

July 12, 1998 Grandfather Mountain
*Dream: I'm at the spring at Granny's farm. Then, I'm in a house with*
*David. He's opened windows and doors to air it out, both windows in the*

*kitchen. I bring in sprigs and branches of quince and white peach to put
on the piano, just as my mother did each spring.*

*Dream: I'm at Hollins, where all the freshmen are moving into dorms. I
walk across the front quadrangle grass, then realize there's a rule: "Hollins
women don't walk on grass," so I get back on the brick path. I go into the
dorm and start giving some vitamins to the girls.*

I heard my family drinking coffee downstairs while I lingered to
get my dreams on paper. After breakfast (and vitamins), I took my art
supplies to the porch. The boys and I folded and glued paper boxes at
the wooden table. Cool breezes spun up from the valley on their way
to the forest behind us. I wanted to encapsulate that time: clicking
scissors, burping glue bottles, shuffling paper, and the companionship
of creativity. The whole clan then climbed up the backside of the
mountain to the field where the Scottish Games take place. As I
puffed up the hill, I wondered how I could have considered the Alps.
I did not have the stamina of my ladies in the Black Forest.

That night we picnicked in a hillside pavilion overlooking craggy
Grandfather Mountain. The Celtic setting recalled stone circles I had
seen in England. From the fire pit ashes, I pulled some sooty coat hangers
left from a marshmallow roast. We bent the hangers into dowsing rods,
and I taught the kids to dowse for underground energy lines.

July 13, 1898 Strassburg AML journal
At 12 o'clock I managed to drag myself down to the cathedral,
got there early, so sat down in a corner to wait. By the time
it was 12 by the old clock the space in front was crowded, so
we were glad to have such good places and watched all the
performance. Had lunch and started for Berne.

July 13, 1998 Grandfather Mountain
*Dream: I'm dyeing my hair, moving furniture, and getting in touch
with David.*

After breakfast, I took Anna's Baededer and Edith's Rhine book
with me to the rope hammock next to the forest. Anna sounded

weary and sick after the damp Black Forest, but her determination
forced her to see the sights. Any visit to Strassburg (Strasbourg)
included the cathedral clock's noon performance. The Rhine legends
book told a gory tale. In addition to building his fine cathedral,
the Magistrate wanted an "artistic clock." An old man made an
exceptional timepiece with a large "World-ball," rising and setting
sun, and eclipses of the Moon and Sun. Mercury pointed his staff at
all "changements" when each constellation stepped forward.

Because the proud Magistrate wanted sole possession of the
unique clock, he ordered the clockmaker's eyes put out so that he
could never replicate his work. The clockmaker begged to complete
the final part of his masterwork in the steeple. Later, after they
blinded him, the authorities realized he had sabotaged the clock. The
wheels were frozen.

Despite the legend, the Strassburg clock drew crowds to see
the cherubs turn an hourglass and hit a gong. The twelve apostles
paraded in front of Christ; a cock crowed and flapped its wings. The
personification of Death advanced each quarter hour to seize the
clock hammer. The Redeemer stepped forward to send back Death—
except on the full hour.

I wanted the Redeemer to push back Anna Lester's death.
She may have been too exhausted to make notes in her Baedeker
about Strassburg. No purple pencil marks indicated their hotel
or underlined the sights they saw. My heavy magnifying glass had
opened wide the stiff guidebook pages. I was the first person in a
century to unfold the crisp maps. I left the bookmark where Anna
last placed it. The woven green tape had left a stain between the
Strassburg Cathedral Tower and the Statue of Gutenberg.

———

From the swaying hammock, I heard the underbrush shuffle of
the forest. Behind me, a path led down to the boulder field and the
streambed. One year at our Easter gathering, the forest floor wore a
blanket of trout lilies. The spotted leaves and delicate yellow blossoms
mingled with the Triple Goddess leaves of trillium. Some people, like

wildflowers, are early bloomers bursting into the filtered sunlight of
early spring. Others require the more sedate summer shade to mature.
I was too late to be a trillium, a violet, or a bloodroot blossom. I was
an autumn weed or fruit: cattail, red sumac, buckeye, or a hickory nut.

My reverie ended when the kids spilled me from the hammock.
We drove to the summit of Grandfather Mountain to see the caged
black bears. The air was thin and the Mile High swinging bridge
was earthquake shaky. The park headquarters resembled the stark
Victorian hotels perched on the Swiss mountains my ladies would
soon visit. How did the altitudes of Gornergrat and Rigi compare
with Grandfather Mountain's 5964 feet?

> July 14, 1898 Berne, Switzerland AML journal
> Got to Berne last night in a pouring rain. Went to Villa
> Frey and had tea then took a hot bath and tumbled in bed.
> It cleared more today, we went to the Cathedral and the
> snow mountains came in view a few minutes later. Bought
> cherries, tomatoes, saw the old clock then came back to rest.

July 14, 1998 Rome, Georgia

Having left the Rhine Valley and the Black Forest of Germany,
Anna and Edith were now in Berne, the first stop on their
counterclockwise circuit through Swiss lakes and mountains. The
founders of Bern (Berne in French) named the city after the first
animal killed in 1109. Bears (Bären) gave the Swiss capital its
name. The city's first seal, flag, and coat of arms have images of the
famous bears.

Berne sits on a peninsula in a curve of the Aare river, a tributary of
the Rhine. The old town has covered arcades, lofty bridges, and fountains.
Berne was known for its views of the Alps and the phenomenon known as
"Alpine glow." After dusk hit the valley, the snow-covered peaks held the
sun's pink glow for a few spectacular minutes.

Five years after the sisters were in Berne, Albert Einstein moved
to the city and developed his theory of relativity. In *Einstein's Dreams*,

author Alan Lightman makes a statement appropriate for
the mechanical clocks of Berne and Strassburg, and for my
summer's journey:

*And each person knows that at some time he must confront the
loose intervals of his life, must pay homage to the Great Clock.*

———※———

The muggy air of Rome strangled me after the clear mountain
atmosphere, but even in that pristine environment, I had heavy
dreams every night. Our house was falling apart, I was falling apart,
and I needed insulation from the Dow Jones barometer on television.
While I was gone, Russian stocks and bonds had soared. In France,
people celebrated Bastille Day.

David wanted to begin house repairs, but I needed time to
come back into the Rome world. I had promised to revise *The Pissed
Princess* and priority-mail the manuscript to Rosemary Daniell before
her workshop on the eighteenth.

But first, I had to "confront the loose intervals" of my mother.

———※———

I parked outside Mamie's nursing home and put on mental armor
against the Lysol smell and pitiful residents. As I wove through wheelchairs
in the hall, a haggard woman grabbed my hand, "Hep! Hep! Hep!"

I wanted to yell back: "Hep! Hep! Hep! HEPA filter!"

My siblings and I played the nursing home charade. Family
photos, greeting cards, and daffodils said to the staff: Look at all the
people who love this feeble woman. Each December we decorated a
small Christmas tree on Mamie's bedside table. On her hall door we
hung the corn shuck wreath that once decorated the Fieldwood house
front entrance.

"Surely, this will be the last time we hang the corn shuck
wreath," I told Sister Edith every Christmas.

"Surely, Lord have mercy upon us," she supplied the canticle refrain.

On New Year's Day, with an expletive, I would frisbee the wreath
onto the top closet shelf and start another 365-day countdown.

As I sat by my mother's bed, I envisioned my own final room. I wanted the white or taupe walls of an art gallery, black pedestals for Anna's statue of Venus and my metal sculpture, and black and white photographs by Owen Riley, Jr. on the walls. I wanted my women's power altar of rocks, spiral fossils, and the summer solstice photo of sunrise on the Etowah Indian Mounds.

I left the nursing home by a side door to avoid the main hall. Monotone moans and sighs came from behind doors. The staff had added an aviary to amuse the patients, but it was hard to tell who was chirping at whom.

— ⊨ ⊜ ⊧ —

After sorting the mail, I plowed through the accumulated newspapers. While I was gone, the *Rome News-Tribune* had printed my tomato sandwich essay. I was published—thanks to the bravado of Athlene Forsyth. One funny fly in the mayonnaise was a bizarre typo. When I wrote of my mother-in-law's summer luncheon table set with china, crystal coasters, and sterling iced tea spoons, I described her starched, crocheted place mats. My computer had highlighted "place" and "mat" and suggested that I use one word: placemats. With the rapidity of click and choose, it offered alternative spellings. I had clicked on a single word choice and, instead of placemats, I ended up with "starched, crocheted *placentas.*"

Sigmund Freud and Buckminster Fuller might have appreciated my keyboard slip. I had read Fuller's theory of precession. He observed that real meaning takes place on the periphery, at right angles to our conscious path or intent. We do one thing in a straight decisive line, but in our unconscious, slightly out of focus on the periphery, we're doing another, more intuitive thing. The honeybee thinks he's drinking nectar but—at ninety degrees—his wings are pollinating the flowers.

Like Fuller's honeybee, I had typed a straight, non-controversial essay and unconsciously encoded a reproductive symbol. Because many of my sculptures and performance pieces had been sexually explicit (wombs, yonis, phalli), a few friends thought I had done this on purpose. Weird. When life gives you surplus placentas, crochet them into placemats.

I called Sister Edith to tell her about the placenta blooper. She had just heard that our dad's oldest sister, Rachel Gilbert Brown, had died in Cincinnati.

July 15, 1898 Berne, Switzerland AML journal
Such a beautiful view this morning. I was just charmed, all the whole range of mountains came in full view. We went to see the Bears. Had lunch then in the afternoon went to Gurten and such a magnificent view came to us there. Got too cold to stay until after sunset.

July 15, 1998 Rome, Georgia
While Edith and Anna hiked to Gurten, a mountain near Berne, I unloaded my car from the mountain trip. I carried in tote bags of books, my journals, and hiking boots. How easy it had been to tour Switzerland in 1985 and 1987 with only one small bag. At that trip's end, my tee shirts and turtlenecks were stiff with travel sweat, but many were refugees from the Good Will sack. I had given them one more adventure before I threw them in a Swiss trashcan.

I took my oldest hiking boots to England in 1997 for tramping through Cornwall bracken and stone circles in Dartmoor. I intended to abandon the shoes to lighten the return load, but I could not let go of the shoestrings. Those boots had taken me around the Glastonbury Tor labyrinth, up Mont Saint Michel and Saint Michael's Mount, into the chambers of West Kennett long barrow, and up the steep steps to King Arthur's Tintagel. How could I abandon those foot-friendly boots with sacred soil embedded in their treads? The boots came home.

Sister Edith joked that my boots were now family relics, like Sister Anna's Alpine walking stick. I doubted that my disintegrating vinyl travel bag would acquire the mystique of Anna's steamer trunk. I considered pitching the hiking boots to save my descendants the dilemma. Instead, I listed on the box the places the boots had been and stashed them on my top closet shelf.

———⊶⊕⊢———

The phone rang. I recognized the western twang and hearty voice of a realtor in Colorado. He made his annual inquiry about buying the Elkhorn lode, my gold mine claim in Left Hand Canyon near Boulder. I gave him my standard response. I kept the property for sentimental reasons; my ancestors were pioneers in Gold Hill.

Julia Cameron says the Universe answers if we take action on our dreams. Depending on the size of the mess of pottage, the sale of my gold mine might have bought a plane ticket to Switzerland. I wanted to get to Europe, but I was not ready to abandon my Gilbert birthright to follow my Lester ladies.

> July 16, 1898 Lausanne, Switzerland AML journal
> Had our breakfast then came to Lausanne. Found a place
> then after having tea went to Dr. Dufour to see about my
> glasses. Bought a few pictures and an umbrella as mine had
> given out then had supper. The man said it would take six
> days to make my glasses.

July 16, 1998 Rome, Georgia

Rain hinted of cooler weather to come. The postman delivered a postcard of black bears. The Lester sisters bought a postcard of the Berne bears in their pit. After I saw the caged black bears on Grandfather Mountain with my grandsons, I had mailed a postcard to my sister and one to my home address.

———⊶⊕⊢———

Afternoon brought a sad journey. My dear friend, Mildred Greear, was moving from Rome. Mildred was one-fifth of the WHIM constellation. Rena Patton had moved to Savannah. Bambi Berry, Nancy Griffin, and I were the last WHIMs standing in our domino row.

Mildred and Dr. Philip Greear lived on the western side of Mount Alto, Rome's highest mountain at 1496 feet. With a ball of

ice in my gullet, and my trunk full of sacked newspapers, I drove
the hairpin curves up to the Greears' house. For years, Mildred had
built retaining walls using newspaper bricks. I was delivering my final
contribution to the Great Wall of Greear.

A truck and two cars stood in the driveway. A small tree sat in
a child's red wagon; burlap covered the near-naked roots. Mildred
would leave behind no portable vegetation. She would transplant
the sapling to her new yard in Helen. The northeast Georgia tourist
town mixes Bavarian and Swiss clichés. Mildred would live among
lederhosen and mock Alpine chalets.

I deposited my newspapers in the lower back yard. The brown
paper sacks joined thousands of pages of cruise brochures, old letters,
and offers of free credit. Mildred's newspaper walls supported her
chicken house, asparagus beds, and orchard. A future archaeologist
may unearth geologic strata of my mail: pizza coupons, Victoria's
Secret catalogs, grant application rejections, and excess art show
announcements. My L.L. Bean catalogs had supported rows of
Mildred's Kentucky Wonder beans.

Mildred in white overalls was a caretaker angel bent over
her vegetables. She was Gaia with dirty fingernails, a generous
handmaiden to the earth goddess. She shared ruffled leaf lettuce,
brown eggs from the coop for mayonnaise, and bunches of fragrant
mint. No one left Mildred's garden empty handed. I would miss her
affirming welcome and fierce loyalty.

The cast iron stove in the Greear kitchen was cold. No more
cornbread in its wood-fired oven. Philip, a noted scientist and
environmentalist, sat in his rocker; Mildred perched on a stool. Their
daughter, Carol Britt, stood up. I had the only straight chair at this
wake. Mildred reached over and grabbed my hands.

"Susan! If you're ever going to move, start packing *now*. This is
the hardest thing I ever did that wasn't important."

"This is entirely voluntary. We are *choosing* to move." Philip
decreed.

"I think the Prince has spoken." Mildred muttered.

"I recognize the voice of the King." I whispered.

As I stood to leave, Mildred said, "Susan! I've discovered a kudzu room on our property at Helen."

Carol Britt said, "Brother Delbert has warned the kudzu that Mother and her machete are coming." We knew that Mildred would tame a creek-side wilderness into an Eden of corn, tomatoes, sugar snap peas, and peonies.

On the way to my car, I stooped to pick a leaf from Mildred's bloodroot plant. In 1991 I had reproduced the plant's leaf for the invitation to my exhibit, *Blood Root*. Red juice dripped from the stem to stain my fingers with Native-American war paint. At home I pressed the leaf between waxed paper sheets. The McNulty family Bible held the four-leaf clovers I'd picked from my grandmother's yard. What book was sacred enough to preserve blood and root from Mildred's earth? I chose her own chapbook, "A Species of Ruin." I stacked three dictionaries on top of the slim booklet. Mildred would appreciate the weight of words.

> July 17, 1898 Lausanne, Switzerland
> My dear Mother and Father,
>      We are way down here on Lake Geneva now. It was cloudy [when we left Strassburg], and before we reached Berne at 9 P.M. it was pouring—I wondered how we could see any monuments. They fixed our room and brought in *hot* water—the first we have had—I was so glad—took a bath and went to bed. The next morning we peeked out and found the sun was trying to shine—also trying to rain but the sun whipped out at noon—and we had already been out to see the lay of the land. So just after lunch started again— and sure enough in a short while the snow caps looked out of the clouds a little. We visited the Cathedral then went up in the tower—half way up we saw the [snow] caps for the first time.
>      We then ran around a corner to see an old clock at the strike of 4—at each hour Bears come out and walk round

then a cock crows. Got there just a second too late for the whole performance—saw a few Bears and [heard] a cock crow once. I was tired then and went back to the house and took a nap.

When we opened our window next morning I saw a flag on top of a hill—so said to Edith that is to tell us the mountains are in full view—so we hurried breakfast and went to a lookout terrace and such a sight! The whole row of beautiful white mountains back of the blue ones. I had to wear my dark glasses—stayed a *long* time seeing them. The Jung Frau [Jungfrau] was in full view. This is pronounced "Uungfrau" and means young wife.

We then went to the garden to see the live Bears—back to lunch then started for that mountain where the flag was flying to see the view from there. It was awfully hot going up—but cool on top—and if you could only have seen that lovely mass of snow. You know, Berne, when clear out, has the most extensive range of Alps in view from any one place. We had intended staying until after sunset—to see the "after glow" or Alpine Glow—but I got so cold even wrapped up that it was impossible. I was awfully sorry—for I wanted that beautiful tour. We came down as quickly as we could, but it was so steep—could not *run* any. I was warm when we reached the bottom. Then we saw the mountains all pink in the distance. You see we would have had to stay until 8:30 to get that from the top.

Had tea then went to bed—and left next day at 10:50 for Lausanne. Got here at 2 P.M. went to the oculist at 5.30 and now I hope to have good eyes in a week. My glasses were not right and that has been the trouble he says for a while. Yesterday we visited the Cathedral then in the afternoon the view terrace—saw the sun set and watched the Lake until 8:30. The water is the most beautiful Blue.

Anna M. Lester

July 18, 1898 Lausanne to Geneva AML journal
Went for a box and after putting in everything we could
possibly do without, sent [mailed] them back [to Paris and
Berlin] and, after fixing our things, went on to Geneva. It
was so hot! Went right to Cooks and got our mail. Such a
charming letter if I only could have one every day!! The lake
was beautiful and we sat out until the sun was quite down to
see the glow on Mont Blanc. It was so beautiful!

July 18, 1998 Rome, Georgia to Atlanta, Georgia
From the north side of Lake Geneva, Edith and Anna could
see Mont Blanc in the distant French Alps. Soon they would be at
the foot of the mountain in the town of Chamonix. This day had
been my target date for Switzerland, but even though the DOW had
peaked at 9337, no financial *deus ex machina* had swooped down to
spirit me to Geneva. I activated Plan B: Rosemary Daniell's two-day
workshop in Atlanta. I did not know that Destiny had a Plan C for
me in November.

Rosemary discussed the importance of journals. For my daily
notebooks, I reversed the concept of Righty Tighty and Lefty
Loosey. My Left Brain Notebook was rigid with appointments and
deadlines. When I completed a page I folded it in half, leaving
access to the notes on the back: Cousin Janie's phone numbers,
directions to Anne Webster's house, the hours of Sports Authority,
and the price of their water barbells. Before I left town, I called on
my character, "Antoinette Check-it-Off." Using her sharp pencil, she
and I attempted to complete the tasks on my Left Brain lists. What
remained went onto an "On Return" page. In this way I didn't carry
the mundane future in my head while I traveled.

My Right Brain Journal was fluid with dreams, thoughts,
rants and raves—a slippery reflux from the stewpot brain. In the
back pages I germinated seedlings in cold frames, a foster home for
nascent ideas. In a workshop with Carolyn Forché, I'd learned to
save excised phrases and titles. These snippets might be too clever for
a current work, but if I added water, they might sponge up into new

sculpture, poetry, or performance. Current contenders were "Crow Magnon," "A Haggle of Witches," "Herbaceous Borders," and "Strobelights to Heaven."

Rosemary added a third notebook to track the writing life with an evaluating, weighing voice. I was to develop criteria of what I wanted my work to be. What books did I like to read? What was my natural style and voice? Where did I fit into the literary world? If I fit at all.

---

July 19, 1898 Chamonix—Glacier des Bossons AML journal
Early we started for Chamonix. In the Diligence a party of English people were going too. Got to Chamonix in time for lunch then all went for a walk to Glacier des Bossons.

From Geneva, Edith and Anna detoured from their Swiss route to visit the town of Chamonix in the French Alps. Edith had packed her blue satin bloomers for hiking, and Anna brought black pantaloons from the Bon Marché store in Paris. They had shortened their long skirts to make hiking easier. I don't know where they purchased their Alpenstocks. These long hiking staffs with metal points were necessary for the rocky terrain and icy glaciers they visited.

The Glacier des Bossons was in the Chamonix valley, close to the famous Aiguille du Midi (Needle of Midday). In the sixteenth century, during rapid glacier expansion, the local clergy exorcised the glacier demon before it gobbled up houses, barns, livestock, and citizens of Chamonix.

July 19, 1998 Atlanta, Georgia
*Dream: I'm going up a path in woods. Trees have fallen over the path and we're going around or through them, stepping over the branches. We meet a black man on horseback coming down the path, so we know we can get through. There's a stream with rocks at an intersection with light.*

Rosemary Daniell had given us a homework assignment for the second day of her workshop. She asked, "What fatal flaw are you prone to?" To what fatal flaw was I prone, inclined? I needed to flip my flaws from prone to supine—face up. My answer was: I am fatally prone to the passive voice.

This flaw was evident in my Tomato Sandwich essay, and I knew I had to switch *The Pissed Princess* from passive to active voice. My grammar pop-up suggested that the active voice makes a livelier and more persuasive sentence. Right. Sounded like tough-love literary psychotherapy for a bona fide southern belle who still owned a hoop skirt. Southern women embody the passive voice; we avoid any activity involving sweat or confrontation. The Princess needed major surgery.

I could cull the passive voice from *The Pissed Princess* manuscript, but how could I claim my own active voice in the tense present? My brain's Army sergeant turned imperative: Take charge. Stop whining. Quit wishing. Get diligent. Dig yourself out of the Black Forest muddy ruts. Keep walking.

Rosemary's workshop lasted three hours longer than scheduled. I had an hour to get home before dark, when my eyes revert to blind potatoes. A bolt of lightning warned of a brewing storm in the northeast. In Acworth, I pulled under a Rodeway Inn canopy until the storm passed and the sunset blazed in the west. Unlike Anna and Edith, I saw no bell-ringing Alpine goats in my shelter.

July 20, 1998 Rome, Georgia
*Dream: I'm riding in a car with part of my French group. Who is driving? I have a little child in my arms. I'm reading a book to everybody, a charming children's book with sweet illustrations. We all sing the "Marseillaise" in honor of Bastille Day. We ride by the City Clock, which is either decorated or something is going on.*

July 21, 1898 Mer de Glace AML journal
I took a mule to the top and the rest walked. We then crossed Mer de Glace and came down on the other side. I did not like Mauvais Pas. It took us all day. In the evening we looked through the telescope at Mont Blanc, saw all very plainly. The sunset was beautiful.

I could translate *mauvais pas* as "bad step," but I had never heard the mountaineering term. A color photograph mounted on cardboard gave me a visual explanation. On a sheer rocky hillside, men descend the mountain on rock steps. They wear suits and derby hats and grasp iron railings clamped to the rocks. A misstep would send a hiker tumbling down the cliff. The title on the photo says: Mont Blanc, Mauvais Pas. On the back, Edith Lester signed her name and the date, July 1898.

July 21, 1998 Rome, Georgia
*Dream: I am some place like an Alternate ROOTS meeting. A woman is doing a performance up on a mountain. A stage platform is built out from the mountain, supported by rocks and stones. The performance moves through a train. I get off the train temporarily, and then we're going downhill. The brakeman has taken off the brakes, and we're going fast like a roller coaster. The braking mechanism consists of wooden sticks in the tracks. I may be facing backwards as in a previous dream.*

Alternate ROOTS is an organization of dancers, actors, musicians, and performance artists. My participation had included some solo performances at the Annual Meeting in Black Mountain, North Carolina. The annual meeting was in August, but I was off that train for the summer. Like the woman in my dream, I was facing backwards on my summer roller coaster.

———◈———

I called Sister Edith in Kentucky with a Lester Ladies Alert: Granny and Sister Anna were crossing the Mer de Glace. Edith has their surviving hiking stick. She said that son Grant would chop some ice cubes with the Alpenstock. That steel point had not touched ice in one hundred years.

Our grandmother's souvenirs included a photograph from the Mer de Glace. The yellowing image shows a nineteenth-century hiking party crossing the glacier. The women have on feathered hats and long skirts. They carry Alpenstocks. The men wear slouchy hats and hold furled umbrellas. With a magnifying glass I studied each figure. One woman is about to step over a crevasse. Could that be adventurous Edith? The last lady in line lags behind the group. Perhaps she is the reluctant Anna. We'll never know if this photo depicts their glacier crossing. It could be another group of tourists making the popular excursion.

*Mer de Glace*

My Hollins Abroad journal reminded me of the July day in 1957 when our group went from Geneva to Stresa, Italy. We drove through the French Alps to Chamonix, where we had an hour's wait near the train station. I had forgotten that some of us raced to take the funicular up to the Mer de Glace. We had time for a quick dash to the glacier and back down to our waiting bus. At twenty, I was the same age as my grandmother when she visited Chamonix with Anna.

—————◇—————

July 22, 1898—Geneva AML journal
Started early to go back to Geneva. Went to Cooks, to see the waterfalls—then sat on the edge of the Lake—Took our boat at 5.15—the Doctor appeared again to say good bye—Reached Territet at 9 P.M.

July 22, 1998 Rome, Georgia
*Dream: I'm in Paris, and I can see all the sights. Something about*
*changing clothes. I'm showing grandson Harrison the Eiffel Tower.*

Our steamy weather made reading old letters outside impossible.
I wanted to join my ladies at the prow of a lake steamer chugging
eastward across the lake from Geneva to Territet. As we approached
Montreux, I would watch for the Castle of Chillon, a small fortress
on the border of the lake.

When George Gordon, Lord Byron, passed through Switzerland
in 1816 with Percy Shelley, they visited the famous Castle. They heard
the history of François Bonivard, a monk who had been imprisoned
from 1532 to 1536 for his political views. Byron's response to the
touching story was a long poem, "The Prisoner of Chillon." Byron
wrote of the tragic figure whose pacing wore tracks in the stone floor.
When released, Bonivard was nostalgic for his prison where he had
coexisted with spiders and mice. From his window, he had seen, "A
lovely bird, with azure wings, And song that said a thousand things."

> July 23, 1898 Territet—Chillon castle AML journal
> Today we went to the Prison of Chillon, a very pretty place
> and a lovely view of the lake. It began to rain and we came
> back here in the [street]car—got pictures, now it is raining
> and I am so sleepy. Am hungry too.

July 23, 1998 Rome, Georgia
Despite my urgent desire to join Edith and Anna, I knew I
would have had trouble reading their letters and maps, taking notes
of the sights, and dealing with train timetables. I would have needed
three 1998 days to match each day in 1898.

In search of allergy relief, I bought an Alpine Air system for our
musty basement. The purification system cost almost as much as a
ticket to Geneva. I could have been in Territet, Switzerland, on my
way to Zermatt with the sisters. That scenario was impossible, so I
breathed ersatz Alpine air, stared at my Matterhorn poster, sipped
sugar-free Swiss Miss hot chocolate, and yodeled a bit.

A thunderstorm boomed in the west, moving in from
Alabama. We needed the cooling rain, but it interfered with my
swim and with using the computer. I gave myself permission to
lie in bed, listen to the rain, and read at three in the afternoon.
Water dripped from the leaves of the peach tree outside my
window. The car wheels on the wet street sounded like bandages
being ripped from flesh.

Rosemary Daniell's book says that the writer can read what she
likes instead of what she *ought* to read. This advice was affirming
to someone with a literary inferiority complex. In a museum, I can
make quick visual assessments: that painting's geometry derives from
Mondrian, those voluptuous females are Rubenesque, or that lighting
mimics Caravaggio or James Turrell. Literary symbols and style must
be dug word by word from stacks of pages and then be processed by
the brain. I lagged so far behind, I'd never catch up.

My public school education had flaws, but my grammar school
teachers gave us a lasting gift. Our weekly Memory Gems were
topaz stones engraved in our brains. We had learned poetry "by
heart." I could recite, "Abou Ben Adhem, (may his tribe increase!),
awoke one night from a deep dream of peace." In the spring, my
heart warms as well as my brain cells at Wordsworth's words: "I
wandered lonely as a cloud." I looked out the window at the rain
and remembered the plaintive Verlaine poem: *Il pleure dans mon
coeur, comme il pleut sur la ville.*

The storm passed. The house was quiet. Too quiet. Lightning
had zapped the air-conditioner compressor. Great. The compressor in
my car was also at risk, and one door handle was broken. I looked for
metaphors. Compression? Decompression? Get a handle? Get a grip?

July 24, 1898
Territet, in sight of the Castle of Chillon
Dear Mother and Father,

    The Castle of Chillon really is a charming place and
much more interesting than I had expected. But I would not
have liked to be chained to that stone pillar with only a yard

of room. The view of the lake is beautiful from every front.
It is blue and green too and pink according to the light on
it from the sky and sun. I am hoping the man in Lausanne
will send my glasses on in the early mail. I do hope now my
eyes will be a good as new for this is a fine Oculist. I went to
the best in Europe. Dr. Dufour. I hope Father got my letter
telling him to send me $100 more in care of Cooks. For I
will need it soon.

[On July 19] we had a delightful drive of about 15 miles
up the mountain road in the Diligence. Then we reached
Chamonix! What a charming place that is. I wanted to stay
even longer. The snow mountains were out but not Mont
Blanc. Walked to the foot of Mer de Glace. Just as we left
there—3 miles from the Hotel—I saw the whole valley had
gotten very dark and a tremendous storm was coming. So
we ran until we got to a farmhouse. No one was in the house
but the old man who was minding the cows. We stepped
inside the stable, only a foot off from their front door but he
came up and in French told us to go in the best room and sit
down, that everything was at our service.

Edith and I went in and the puppy and kittens came
running in to be petted and the little monkeys got a good
share. I almost squeezed the kitten to death, for Moses' sake.
We heard the goats coming home. In the morning a boy
takes all the goats of the village out for the day. They wear
cowbells and the cows wear church bells! Great big things
the size of a gallon can, but the tone is not harsh. Well, here
the goats came, ringing their bells, the woman went to the
door and called out her names and the goats left the flock
and rushed into the house way up to the door of the best
room, were met by father, mother, and children!

It hailed and poured and when we found it did not
intend stopping we set out for 2 1/2 miles, just took what
came and went on. The next morning everything was as
clear as a bell. Mont Blanc out in full view. I could see the

observatory on top 15,000 feet up in the air! I did not want
to go inside at all even to eat breakfast, but of course had to,
for we were going to the Mer de Glace. I took a mule up for
I do get so awfully hot and it was 1200 feet up. The mule
and I carried the wraps for our party, also the lunch. Only
the two sisters, Edith, and I went—the cousin was afraid she
would slip on the ice crossing. They would not send a mule
without a guide and a boy so it made it cost a little more.
We had not intended having a guide except for crossing the
ice, but this one went all the way. The mule only took me to
the top then the boy brought him back. The guide met us
and carried our wraps. We ate the lunch on top of the hill
then descended into that sea of ice. We put on our winter
cloaks and woolen socks over our shoes, then proceeded to
cross. I must say I did not enjoy it much but Edith did.

We stopped several times to eat ice then we went down
the other side back to Chamonix, reached there minutes of
six. Had started at quarter after ten A.M. I really enjoyed
going on that mule. I could see every thing and did not get
warm but my, oh how stiff it made my right leg. I have not
ridden in so long.

The view all day was perfectly lovely and the sunset
beautiful. I left dinner and went out in the street to see
Mont Blanc. Then crossed over and took a peep at him
through the large telescope. Could see the path where we
had gone up that day, the house on top, and both the half
way stations, where they rest on the way up. At the first one
I even saw the clothes hanging on the line and all just as
plain as if I had been there near at hand. I had to tell him
good night though after a while and leave him with the
stars—while I packed my straps [suitcases] and went to bed.
Early on Friday we started [for Geneva] and the drive in the
Diligence was so delightful.

I think of you all a great deal and will be glad when my
face is turned towards home again. I have found it impossible

to make any sketches. Only staying a day or so in each place is not conducive to work. I am tired and it takes all my time seeing things and fixing my straps and things up ready for a move forward. I shall rest a week after I return to Paris before beginning work. To paint I would have to stay at least ten days in one place for I do not feel settled enough for work you see. It is a great disappointment to me for I have my colors and papers with me but no time or energy. Absolutely all we do is to go and see and send one letter home each week, once in two to Mlle Ballu, Edith sends a card or letter once in two weeks to Joy. That is all we can find time to do. If you all could be here with us how much fun we would have.

Anna M. Lester

---

I heard how Anna missed her painting during the summer. Artists need time to inhale a place. Anna's workaholic voice crept into her plans for the fall. She wanted to justify her time and expense. Was she proving her worth to herself or to her parents? I did not know how much of her obsession, her jitters, and insomnia came from her "time of life." Perhaps tuberculosis had its own psychological symptoms.

By contrast, Edith Lester's letter to her best friend, Joy Harper, has youthful enthusiasm. She uses their childhood nicknames of "Jack" and "Jill." I wished I could send my grandmother 300 francs to climb Mont Blanc while she was young.

July 24, 1898
Territet, Switzerland
Dear Old Jill,

I haven't had a letter from you in a month of Sundays, so it seems to me. The last week I have enjoyed most I believe of my trip. On Monday we went to Geneva, and gee whiz! wasn't it blazing hot! We got our ticket for Chamonix and decided to leave on the early train Tuesday morning. A party of English people went on the same train and we rode

all the way in the same coach with the three ladies. We left
the train at Le Fayet and took the diligence to Chamonix. It
was hot and dusty or the trip would have been delightful.

After lunch, although it was cloudy we went for a walk
to the Glacier des Bossons. There were seven men and five
ladies in all, and during the whole time I found out the
names of none of them. There was a grey haired lady, who
hopped instead of walking, and a cousin to the two sisters.
The older sister we took to be married, for she had that
married look, and the younger sister had curly yellow hair,
and was really very funny. Our names for the men were
the baldheaded man, the sunburned man, the pug nosed
man and the man with the grey beard, the man with the
light moustache, the fat man and the little man. Isn't that
an array? The pug nosed man wasn't really *pug* nosed, but
it was an awfully funny nose. He turned out to be a doctor,
so now we call him "the Dr." which fits him much better.
Well, they were all very nice except the fat man and the little
man. They may have been nice too, but they didn't have
much to do with anyone except themselves. The sunburned
man looked as if he was going to die laughing, every time
he began to talk, so of course everyone else did laugh. The
baldheaded man always began a sentence very seriously
and gave the last few words a curious unexpected twist that
was ridiculous, and generally sent us off in a giggle. Light
mustache was the other one in the party besides myself who
carried a Baedeker, while the Dr. was one of these people
who make all glad when he comes into a room, and likes to
please other people.

Long before we reached the Glacier it began to rain
some but we didn't stop for that. We got a little wet, but
having on short skirts it wasn't so bad. The sunburned man,
the doctor, the grey haired lady and I amused ourselves by
going out of our way and climbing up to the very foot of the
Glacier. We stood on it and ate some of the ice, and wanted

to carry some to the others, but it would melt. There was an icy wind from under the water where the water ran out, and a hot breath came from across the top every few minutes. We overtook the others and continued our way up. The distances are so deceiving, one thinks the little red chalet where the ice grotto is is only a step, but we women never got there at all. The bald headed man went by another road, came down and said the grotto was really not worth going in, as it is only an artificial hole cut in the ice. We looked at a watch and found it only an hour and a half until dinner so we knew we must hurry back.

The next morning we awoke to find it perfectly clear and Mont Blanc standing forth splendidly. That was our first near view of it. We could easily see that speck on the top, which was said to be the observatory. I looked through a telescope and then saw it distinctly. We decided to take an all day excursion. Sister hired a mule, so as not to get over heated and we let it carry our wraps, lunches, etc. so we had only ourselves and our Alpenstocks to look after. We ascended Montanvert in two hours and a half. At the half way station we had some milk. On top we had lunch and milk and rested nearly an hour before crossing the Mer de Glace. I gathered some beautiful alpine roses going up, but they were too stiff to press. They smell just like our honeysuckle.

We put on woolen socks over our shoes to cross and it was high fun, not one-tenth part as hard as those men made it out. I enjoyed chopping up ice with my stock and was sorry when we reached the other side. The moraines were harder to cross than the ice, because in climbing over stones and boulders one never knows if one will slip.

The "Mauvais Pas" afforded me much amusement, because I never get dizzy. The Mauvais Pas is where the path goes straight down the side of the cliff with tiny little steps cut in the rock. That sounds terrible, but it has an iron rail

on one side, which makes it easy as falling off a log. The
view from that place was beautiful. Sister didn't like that
much, because her head swims so the guide stayed close
to her all the time. We had to cross a beautiful waterfall,
where the water went roaring and dashing over the cliff, on
a narrow footbridge *without rail*. That was nice too, only
everything was so much easier than we expected that we
hardly realized that we had accomplished the long talked of
feat! I wanted something exciting and if anyone would have
furnished the three hundred francs to ascend Mont Blanc I
would have gone up, only now it is made so easy with guides
and porters and I would not have found even there what one
reads about.

Well, we got back at six o'clock, eight hours out, when
Baedeker says it takes five, but we took our time and rested
lots of times to enjoy the view. You should have seen us
kneeling down to drink out of those ice cold streams. My! It
tasted nice.

It was two years yesterday since I sailed from New
York. Do you realize that it has been so long as that? The
next year will go only too quickly for me as for what I must
learn is concerned. But not quick enough to see you and
the home folk.

Sister is in bed and I must say good-night. Two weeks
from to-day there is no telling where I will be, but if I can I
will write you a letter.

I have an awfully big appetite and I am afraid I will go
back very fat and brown. The last I don't mind, but I can't
wear gloves while it is hot.
With lots of love from your devoted Sweetheart,

Jack—E. Lester

Sister has just waked up and asked, "Where are we?"
She thought she was putting her head out of the diligence at
some station.

July 24, 1998 Rome, Georgia to Louisville, Kentucky

I called my air conditioner repairmen, put a few things in a suitcase, photocopied Anna's postcards, got cash at the bank, and then headed for the Birmingham airport for a flight to Louisville. With my sister and her family, I would attend Aunt Rachel Gilbert Brown's funeral in Cincinnati.

In the Ethridges' brick Victorian house in the historic Cherokee Triangle, I saw where Edith had placed Mamie's furniture from the Fieldwood house. I sat in one of Mamie's wingback chairs next to Granny Harbin's curio cabinet. Edith took out the miniature chalet that Granny had bought in Grindelwald and her own souvenir chalet from Zermatt. The Ethridge children, Elizabeth (Biz) and Grant, joined us at the dinner table decorated with prints and photos of the Matterhorn and mountain chalets. We fondled the Alpenstock while I told them our ladies would soon be in our family's favorite Swiss town.

Granny Harbin's stories and memories had started our obsession with Zermatt. Sister Edith spent time there on her 1973 sabbatical in Europe. In 1974, she took our parents to Zermatt where a laughing Mamie fell into a snow bank in May. Mary and Katherine Harvey visited Zermatt during their study abroad. Son Dave skied near the Matterhorn during his college trip.

> July 25, 1898 Territet AML journal
> Had to stay in Territet one more day, because the woman
> did not bring our wash and my glasses did not come until
> 12. In the afternoon we took a trip on the Lake to Meillerie,
> France. That was pleasant, then after dinner we took a walk
> up the Gorge. Got back at 9 P.M. Felt however that a day
> had been wasted for Zermatt.

July 25, 1998 Louisville, Kentucky to Cincinnati, Ohio

The four Ethridges and I drove to Cincinnati for Aunt Rachel's memorial service. Her grandson, Scotty MacLeod, played his bagpipes as we entered. An oboe trio from the Cincinnati Conservatory of Music performed, and friends and family shared stories. I read my dad's favorite Walt Whitman passage about tramping a perpetual journey. We ate dinner with the Brown-MacLeod clan at a German restaurant. The rough outdoor tables under grapevines were as close to a Biergarten as Sister Edith and I got that summer.

> July 26, 1898 Zermatt AML journal
> Reached Zermatt at 3 P.M. and took a walk, then came back
> to dinner so we could take a good nights rest for the next
> day. Stopped at Hotel Terminus.

The train from Brig to Zermatt opened the town to many tourists in 1891. Anna and Edith reached Zermatt thirty-three years after the first successful ascent of the Matterhorn. Perhaps they knew the book *Scrambles amongst the Alps* by Edward Whymper, a British artist and engraver. On July 14, 1865, as the Civil War ended in America, Whymper and his party raced an Italian team to be the first to master the east face of the Matterhorn. They achieved their goal, but not without a toll paid to the mountain gods. On their descent, a rope snapped, and four of the group fell to their deaths. Although Whymper was in shock, he sketched an eerie formation in the sky. He saw three crosses and a great circular arch, perhaps formed by an unusual alignment of ice crystals or a sun reflection in fog. Whymper said he was haunted nightly by the memory of his companions sliding away down the mountainside.

July 26, 1998 Louisville, Kentucky, to Rome, Georgia
*Dreams: I'm at a speaker's meeting. I'm changing clothes in a big barn or studio. I go riding with David, then with the women. We're going to a reading or writing conference. We go down a river in a boat. Someone has restored some buildings and a marvelous bridge over the river: a house bridge enclosed with a roof.*

The heat and humidity in Rome were intense after cooler weather in Kentucky. David reported that nothing happened while I was in Louisville. No one had died. We'd had no rain. No news from the kids. I threw a load of his underwear in the washing machine and joined the ladies in Zermatt.

July 27, 1898 Zermatt AML journal
Got up early, had breakfast and started to the Riffelberg at
7:30. At ten we had reached the Riffel Alp. It rained and
we stopped in the church—waited a half hour. We then
went about halfway up Riffelberg and it began to pour. No
umbrellas, so after meeting a number of people who said the
view was bad, we came back. Got soaking wet!

July 28, 1898 Zermatt, Switzerland
My very dear Mama and Papa,

We are up in the mountains again and
now have a splendid view of the Matterhorn
from our window. Yesterday we had a great
experience. We were going to make an all
day excursion to the Riffelberg and Gorner Grat so made
an early start at 7.30 A.M. It was beautifully clear so we
took no umbrellas with us. They are rather in the way when
climbing. The Alpenstock takes up at least one hand and
in steep places, two. Then I had my jacket and lunch and
Baedeker and Sister had her cape and part of the way my
jacket. She decided to walk as we could take our time. It
was very enjoyable walking to me especially and I didn't
even get warm. About nine thirty I noticed some clouds
and presently heard a guide say to a German lady on a mule
behind us that we would have rain. We were just in sight of
the hotel on the Riffelalp, when it began to sprinkle and we
had to hurry into a little English church that is being built
up there. We stayed until it stopped raining and then started
for the Riffelberg, an hour's distance, straight up the side of
the mountain. We had no view however because everything
was covered with clouds.

Just then it began to come down like everything and as
we could reach a house sooner descending than ascending
we did the former and waited in a little hut until the worst
was over. We decided there was no use to continue our way,
as we were already damp and there would be no view on top.

It was very provoking as we were so nearly up. We hurried up and had just reached the little refreshment house when the third hard rain began. There we waited an hour, got some milk and ate our lunch.

The rain showed no signs of stopping and we were getting chilly from sitting still, so we started down. It took us an hour and a half to reach the hotel and all the way it poured. We were not the only ones caught for we met a lot of people. We had not been here a half hour before it cleared off beautifully. Wasn't that horrid? The Matterhorn never was free from clouds, though the sky was blue, so I don't know what the other high mountains did.

We gave our shoes, skirts and my jacket to the maid for they were dripping. But, curious to say, the rain did not reach our shirtwaists. I took the ribbon off of my hat and washed it, and put it in the sun to dry, and we put our hats to press. Then we bathed our feet in hot water and got in bed for a nap. I put my hat in the sun and it got dry enough to trim before dinner. It really looks better for the washing for some dust had stuck to it and it got sprinkled in Chamonix, so now it is as clean and good as new. Nothing got hurt except the mull [muslin] on Sister's hat. We ourselves are none the worse for wear, but awfully sorry we were detained in Territet until Tuesday.

We have met one or two very pleasant people but none as nice as the English crowd at Chamonix, and none to make excursions with, though everybody makes the same ones. Sister was rather disappointed in the Matterhorn because it was not covered with snow as Mont Blanc was. Mont Blanc is more rounded and the snow sticks, whereas the Matterhorn is very rugged and so steep that the snow does not stay on long. Today however it is white with fresh snow from yesterday's storm so Sister is much better pleased. I think too it is prettier to be white than brown. We see a plenty of brown mountains that are not high enough for snow.

This town and Chamonix consist of one street, a
depot, post office, some stores with pictures, wooden
animals, Alpenstocks, etc. and the rest of the place
hotels. Of course, the chalets are dotted all over the
mountainsides. We got a few very pretty pictures. That is
about all we do buy because they are easier to carry. When
we returned [from town] we dressed for a five-hour walk
after lunch and then went down to the table, this time
carrying *umbrellas*, Alpenstocks and jackets. As soon as
lunch was over, we went outside and it was *raining* and
it has been coming down ever since. It really is too bad,
because there is no use to leave here until it does clear,
because our next trip will be over the Simplon Pass down
into Italy. We must cross in a stage[coach], a nine-hour
ride, I believe, and as the view is the principal thing, there
would be no pleasure in going in the rain.

It is cool enough here for my flannels to be very
comfortable. We were very glad to get back to a hotel
because we found Miss Farnell's fare at Territet very plain
and not enough for my enormous appetite. No place is
it like home eating, but when a number of courses are
served, I manage to get most enough to satisfy me at the
time, but a half hour later I am hungry again. I really
believe I could eat all day. I miss the cherries terribly.
During June and July they are splendid over here, but now
they are not so good and it doesn't pay to buy them. The
other fruit is too high.

Don't worry about the Simplon Pass, we will not walk
it but will cross in a stage [diligence] probably with a lot of
other people. I must say good night now. Hope it will be
clear tomorrow. Sister joins me in love to Miss Beall, the
pets, and oceans of it for you two dear ones.

Devotedly,
E. Lester

July 28, 1898 Zermatt AML journal
Another day of rain. Such luck! I want to see these beautiful
things and leave before my purse is empty. I wish the Good
Lord would send us a bright day or two *now*.

July 28, 1998 Rome, Georgia

David and I went to Zermatt with Edith and Larry Ethridge in
July 1985. From Geneva, we took a train around the northern shore
of Lac Léman (Lake Geneva). We munched cookies and nectarines
and pressed our noses to the window. The lake steamers we saw were
descendants of the boat Anna and Edith took across the lake eighty-
seven years before. Like they did, we marveled at snow-capped Mont
Blanc in the distance. We passed Lausanne, Montreux, and Territet,
but we did not know that the ladies had seen the Castle of Chillon.
When we passed Aigle, we did know that daughter Katherine had
taken the train from there to Leysin for summer school in 1983. She
and her friends nicknamed the Montreux-Oberland-Bernois (MOB)
train, the "Move Our Booties."

At Brig we got the BVZ (Brig-Visp-Zermatt) train up to
Zermatt. Kiko had not been in Zermatt in ten years and the
rampant commercialization depressed her. The Orion Hotel faced
a new building, and a crane blocked our view of the Matterhorn. A
striking clock woke us at dawn. Hammers banged, and earth-moving
equipment growled in the dirt outside our windows.

We dropped our bags at the quieter Jagerhof Hotel and
jumped on a train up to the Gornergrat summit at 10,170 feet.
The Gornergrat-Monte-Rosa-Bahnen opened on August 20, 1898,
just a month after Anna and Edith hiked the mountain on foot. At
the end of the rail line, the view was spectacular: Monte Rosa, the
Matterhorn, Kleine Matterhorn, and Castor and Pollux. Bronzed
women had on halters, walking shorts, and hiking boots. The serious
hikers carried alpine sticks, big-lensed cameras, and hefty backpacks.

We climbed over to a rocky ridge and ate our sandwiches,
fruit, and cookies. Edith and I remembered how our dad always
took chocolate on mountain hikes. We toasted Doc with Toblerone

*Gornergrat 1985*

chocolate triangles; their shape matches the Matterhorn. The founders of Toblerone hid the image of a bear in the Toblerone logo, to honor their home city of Bern.

We took the train down as far as Rifflealp, where the fir tree line began. From there, we walked. Maybe we saw the church where Granny and Sister Anna took refuge from the rain, but we didn't yet know their letters. Maybe they had stopped at the refreshment hut where we drank lemonade. We sat on one of the red viewing benches. Wild azaleas, clover, Queen Anne's lace, daisies, blue bells, and hemlock needles made an Alpine potpourri.

Our descent took two and a half hours with stops to absorb views from other convenient red benches. For weeks before the trip, David and I had hiked up Clocktower Hill in Rome, chanting "Gorner Grat, Gorner Grat." Our training helped, but the path was steep. David cut through the woods on some curves of the path. I felt young and healthy—the best I ever felt in my life.

───◈───

Like Anna, David and I felt taut purse strings on our Zermatt trip, but we made a twentieth-century splurge: a helicopter ride around the Matterhorn. We pushed a button in a hillside, and a James Bond elevator lifted us to the landing pad. When the helicopter zoomed in, we climbed aboard. From the whirlybird we saw tiny climbers ascending the Matterhorn. Some stood victorious on the mammoth peak. The helicopter excursion cost fifty dollars, but we knew we might never pass that way again.

While David shopped for an Alpenstock with a Zermatt crest, I visited the Zermatt Museum. Next to stuffed goats and marmottes, one display case had guest registries from old hotels. The one from the Mt. Cervin Hotel covered 1896 to 1899. I knew that Granny and Sister Anna had visited Zermatt, but I didn't know their hotel name or exact dates. I located the museum director, who worked at the Post Office. He tried thirty keys before one fit the lock on the case. I went through the July hotel register page by page, looking for Edith and Anna Lester from Rome, Georgia. According to the director, the other hotels of the era had been Monte Rosa, Terminus, Zermatterhof, Angleterre, and Victoria. I was disappointed not to find Anna and Edith, but tracking the Lester sisters proved to be addictive.

I visited the charming English church, unaware that Edith and Anna had worshipped there. The cemetery had graves of people who had perished in the mountains; their climbing axes were attached to their gravestones. People were buried in rows in the order in which they died, instead of in family plots. Women and children tended the flowers on graves. I saw my first edelweiss—growing on a grave.

The tombstone inscriptions were capsule stories. Ellen Emma Sampson was killed by falling stones on the Thriftjock in 1895. Edith Carr died in a crevasse on the Weisshorn Pass, age 25. F.C.B. perished on the Matterhorn during a terrible snowstorm in 1886, age 48. W.E. Gabbet—fell from the Dent Blanche. "In the midst of life we are in death."

I adopted the motto of Donald S. Williams, who died on Breithorn in 1975. Below his axe on the tombstone are the words: "I chose to climb." This intentional creed for risk taking is the antidote to fear, regret, and mothers' tears: I *chose* to climb.

———————

Edith and I chose to celebrate our forty-fifty birthdays with a return trip to Switzerland in 1987. We began our three-week trip on

Rigi—where Anna and Edith will be on August sixth. With *Swiss Rail Pass* freedom, we searched for sunshine. May was off-season: no flowers, hotels closed, slushy weather. A dreary Zermatt smashed our memories of colorful window boxes in the summer of 1985. The town was cold, rainy, and gray. The fir trees were brown. We vowed never to go back to Zermatt before the geraniums come up from the valley.

We clutched our memories from 1985 and stepped onto the train to go down to Brig. On a strong impulse, I pulled Edith off the train. I had to try once more to locate Edith and Anna in a hotel register. By then, I had seen their Zermatt postcard from the Hotel Terminus. At the post office, the museum director said they didn't have the hotel's register, so that door closed.

As we waited for the next train, the clouds cleared enough for us to see the majestic Matterhorn. After two years, I had forgotten how the mountain dominates the town. Since then, a shrouded Matterhorn has haunted my dreams.

---

When Katherine and Tim Kenum got engaged in 1990, they considered a wedding in Zermatt. We calculated that we could fly the principal people to Switzerland for the same cost as paving our back yard. Katherine and Tim went to Switzerland and talked to Zermatt church officials, but there were legal complications. They decided to be married in Rome, so that older relatives could attend. I was disappointed. In the style of Miss Isabel Gammon, I had composed a fantasy write-up for the *Rome News-Tribune*.

"The winsome willowy blonde bride carried a bouquet of multi-colored Alpine wildflowers. The statuesque mother-of-the-bride wore a dirndl skirt in becoming pastel shades; her hiking boots were laced with festive ribbons. Guests enjoyed cheese fondue while yodelers provided jaunty music. Cowbells were rung as the happy pair departed."

July 29, 1898 Zermatt AML journal
Today we have been all the way up to that Gorner Grat!
I walked and got awfully tired but kept on. The view was

superb! I could have stayed a week but of course had to leave after lunch. Snow began.

## July 30, 1998 Rome, Georgia

Sutton Bacon, my friend Sherrie's son, came to advise me about replacing my old computer. My stalled adult brain needed a teenaged tutor with jumper cables. We spent two hours discussing the flashy new iMac from Apple. We decided on the G3 233mHz. I didn't know what an internal zip drive did, or if I could use the fax modem I had. Sutton said I must have a domain name. Sounded regal until we discovered that there were multiple Susan Harveys. One of the imposters owned my castle address.

Several years later, on my birthday, Sutton the Diligent called with great news: my desired domain was available. I registered for www.susanharvey.com.

### July 31, 1898—Zermatt AML journal

We are going to church this morning then after lunch we leave so as to cross the Simplon Pass tomorrow. Today is perfect! Not a cloud in the sky.

## July 31, 1998 Rome, Georgia

*Dream: I'm having a dinner party. I'm in the kitchen of the old Fieldwood house. The guests are already there. I'm fixing a plate of lettuce. Do I have enough? There's a chicken dish but it needs a sauce. I go get more plates but need help. I have pretty Lenox plates but they are dirty. Just not ready for this meal.*

My dream of not being prepared may be universal, even though I had ample china resources. Was I chicken? What part of my chicken needed saucing up? My life? My work? My marriage? Or option D: All of the above?

I searched all afternoon for a small book I had bought in 1985 on Rigi, a mountain that overlooks Lake Lucerne. In an excerpt from *A Tramp Abroad*, Mark Twain describes his climb up the mountain. I wanted to reread it before Anna and Edith reached Rigi on August sixth. Saint Anthony, the overworked saint of lost things, was vacation, or else he had rejected me as a client: "Of course she can't find anything in that mess!"

———⚬———

For my artist's date I went to the Red Lobster for lunch. I negotiated with the waiter. With my grilled trout I wanted no potato, no rice, no bread, no salad, just vegetable medley, zucchini sticks, and water. Continuing my solo date, I roamed Office Depot in search of expandable file folders. I bought a large tub of paper clips. My mother's metal clips had rusted on her papers, so I chose plastic-coated ones. From the multicolored assortment, I would segregate the black clips to use with my manuscript chapters.

Black was my favorite color, a commentary on my mood and my desire for simplicity. Most of my sculpture was black because color distracted from the linear shadows against a white gallery wall. No true southern lady would lust for a black and white room, nor would she pick an office supply store as her artistic treat for the week.

Since I could not find my book on Mark Twain's Rigi ascent, I stopped at the library for *A Tramp Abroad*. I found over 170 listings for Twain and Samuel Clemens. *A Tramp Abroad* was in nearby Cedartown and could not be put on request.

The weather cooled a bit. Son Dave came up from Atlanta to play golf with his dad. In a mechanical miracle, they got David's red 1980 Vespa running. Just in time for Italy.

# The Augusts of '98

*…Winds thwarting winds bewildered and forlorn,*
*the torrents shooting from the clear blue sky,*
*the rocks that muttered close upon our ears,*
*black drizzling crags that spake by the wayside…*
"The Simplon Pass"
William Wordsworth

On August 1, 1898, Anna and Edith Lester reached the halfway point of their journey. After a night in Brig, Switzerland, they boarded a diligence to cross the famed Simplon Pass into Italy. Since the mid-thirteenth century, this passage has connected the Lepontine Alps and the Pennine Alps.

Augustinian monks started a hospice at the pass in 1235. William Wordsworth wrote a poem about his Simplon walking tour in the summer of 1790. In 1805 Napoleon engineered a military road to invade Italy. Anna and Edith's stagecoach followed a winding route through the pass at 6590 feet. Today's travelers barrel underground through the Simplon Tunnel, the longest rail tunnel in the world. The Italian city of Domodossola is at the end of this mountain passage.

August 1, 1898 Hotel de la Poste, Simplon
My dear Mother and Father,

You can see where we are—about half way across this pass. We started at 6 A.M. today and have remarked that at home we could not be dressed in flannels and have capes on and then ride in the sun at twelve o'clock and not be too warm. The man told us we would wait 2 hours—so we have had lunch and now have some time on our hands. You amused me when you said this is the only place you were afraid of. It would be safe for one woman to walk the whole way alone. This country is inhabited all over I think. At least I do not think I have been out of sight of houses since I came to Switzerland. You may be sure we never do anything where there is *any* risk. I am too careful of our dear little selves for that. In fact I have *no* desire to go places where I might slip off.

By five o'clock we will be in Italy, then for a few days we'll be enjoying the Lakes there. I am so glad you are keeping up with us, it is almost more than I can do to keep up with myself. We jump from France to Switzerland and Italy and back so soon it would take a racehorse to follow.

Get Mark Twain's A Tramp Abroad from the Library and read it if you want to know what we are doing. Don't believe *all* he says for one must know when he is making fun to enjoy all he goes through.

I got beautifully sunburnt going up to that Gorner Grat. Now all the dead skin is coming off. I never thought of that in such a cold place. We walked on the dry snow there in the mule track between banks of snow 7 feet high. Such fun and all in July! It snowed on us for an hour then we got to the flower line and stopped to pick beautiful forget-me-nots, violets, and all sorts of pretty flowers. Did not get back to Zermatt until five so you see were walking just about ten hours. That was not bad for me when I had to climb over four thousand feet, do you think so? I'll be all right in my new face soon—had on my dark glasses and did not realize the sun was so bright.

I wish from the bottom of my heart you were all over here with us this summer and could see and hear all we do. I am getting a Photo from each place so I can show you as near as possible when I come home. The time will go fast I hope now and soon we will be together. I guess I must stop now and will add a few lines on this paper when we stop tonight. Chamonix and Zermatt are gems—I want to go back and stay a month at each place. This pass is *beautiful! Good bye.*

Anna M. Lester

August 1, 1998 Rome, Georgia

Celtic people celebrated Lammas, a harvest festival, in early August. The cross-quarter day bisects the sun wheel, halfway between the summer solstice and the autumnal equinox. As the sun slipped another notch toward winter, light came through my dining room windows from a different angle. I felt the portent of Emily Dickinson's slanted winter light. The fall pollens invaded my nasal cavities. Lammas season demanded new pens, spiral notebooks, file folders—and antihistamines.

August 2, 1898 Pallanza, Italy
Dear Mother and Father,

It was so late after we reached here—Pallanza—last evening that by the time we had supper I was ready for a hot bath and bed. We were coming just 14 hours. And let me tell you—after we got to Domodossola we were in "north Georgia." Corn fields, beans, and all sorts of things—crossed the Silver Creek—went up Billy Jones road and in fact they might have called out Rome, Ga! instead of Domodossola. Coming from Gravellona to Pallanza smelt like the woods too. There we saw mimosa trees in bloom and magnolias, plenty of roses. The lake is very pretty and we are going on that today so hope not to feel the heat. The reason we think it warm is because we have been in such a cool place. You would have laughed had you been with us—just before we reached the town a hand organ was playing in front of an Italian house and lots of the people sitting around—and two young men with their arms clasped around each other were dancing. The whole thing—colors and all was quite a picture—and funny too.

The rest of our drive yesterday was through a wild gorge—one of the best in Switzerland. As we came to the first Italian village we had to stop for customs. The man wanted to know if we had chocolate or cigarettes—I said no. So he looked under the carriage seat and all round but not in our straps—then let us pass. We asked if he wanted to see our passports and he said no—these customs are all in a house anyway. I am writing this while we wait to have our breakfast brought so do excuse the looks—We want to be off as early as possible and I thought I would mail this before going so you would know we were safe and well—and across the Simplon Pass. Edith joins me always in love.
Your own little daughter,
Anna M. Lester

August 2, 1998 Rome, Georgia
David and Dave played golf while I worked. I tried to slow down but got manic about my computer decision. Dave said: Mom, you're not *supposed* to work on Saturdays. I guess he can turn his work off. Since my work is in my head, it's hard to find an escape hatch for fun.

At Kroger I bought zucchini, eggplant, and peppers to grill. I got first-press, extra-virgin Italian olive oil and some fresh mozzarella cheese from Denmark, Wisconsin. I chopped basil leaves from my garden, and the two Davids and I dined alfresco—as Italian as we could get on East Third Avenue.

We celebrated my computer miracle: the G3 233 desktop had gone down $300 overnight. I ordered the CPU, extra RAM, an external Zip drive, and upgrades for my software. I designed a FOR SALE sign for my old Macintosh: Classic model never driven more than 50 mhz on the Infobahn by a bifocaled lady in tennis shoes.

August 3, 1898 AML journal
It took us all of today to reach Como. Very tiresome indeed.
It poured rain and came in the car so we put up umbrellas!
So much for 3rd class in Italy.

August 3, 1898 Como, Italy
My dear Mama,

We reached here this afternoon. Had a pleasant stay at
Pallanza and a most delightful trip on Lake Maggiore. Saw
a beautiful sunset and the fine full moon. It took us from
eight until three-thirty to get here today because we had to
stay over three hours and a half in Varese. It was awfully hot
so we got tired and took a nap as soon as we got here. After
supper went for a walk by the lake. Everything looks exactly
like Georgia as far as nature goes. It looks so natural too, to
see everybody with fans, as at home. I never see one in Berlin
except at operas. Tomorrow we will take a trip on the lake.
This [postcard] is a picture of you when a girl. We hope you
will have a pleasant birthday and many many happy returns.

With love,
E. Lester

Because of our May 1987 trip with Edith and Larry Ethridge, I
could picture Anna and Edith in the Italian lakes. Our foursome had
gone from Chamonix to Locarno by way of Vallorcinc and Martigny.
No one checked our visas. After Brig and Domodossola, we changed
to a creeping train that hauled milk and firewood over the mountains
to Locarno. We never left Switzerland, but the canton of Ticino was a
strange mixture of Swiss and Italian. We didn't know that Edith and
Anna had traveled just south of here in 1898. Our balcony at Hotel
Zurigo overlooked the sparkling Lake Maggiore. Waves from passing
lake steamers lapped the peaceful shore.

The sunshine felt wonderful after rain and snow and cold. I shed
my red and black hiking boots for the first time in ten days. David

bought a black executive Swiss Army knife engraved with his name, then we had supper at a small trattoria, up a side street in the old quarter: melon with prosciutto, creamy pasta with smoked salmon, and a light cake with a cinnamon rum sauce.

At five o'clock the next morning, the sky was a clear sapphire with a hind-quarter moon reflected in the lake. About six, the birds went wild in the chestnut trees below our window, and waiters put bright yellow cloths on tables for a breakfast buffet. We joined Kiko and Larry under the tree canopy for their May twenty-first anniversary breakfast: coffee and good brown French bread and cheese. We couldn't keep our rooms, so we elected to fulfill Larry's major wish: a trip on the Glacier Express.

A fast train took us from Locarno through the Gotthard Pass into rain, then blinding snow. We got off at Goeschenen, huddled in the waiting room, and decided to take the next train south and save the Glacier Express for the following day. From the train station we called Doc and Mamie because it was also their anniversary. Kiko talked to Biz and Grant. When we talked to Mary and Walt we heard big news. A second baby Beaver was due in December. We took the first fast train south, this time to Lugano on Lake Lugano. We watched the snow turn back to rain. In Lugano, our room at the Hotel Walter had a view of the lake and mountains. During our supper at Café Mary, we toasted the new Beaver baby.

August 3, 1998 Rome, Georgia
*Dream: a new book has been published, printed in Bulgaria. I'm looking at the type settings: bizarre varieties of fonts.*

Katherine and I were going to visit Ludie and Fred White in Chapel Hill by way of Grandfather Mountain. I woke up in trip-prep mood. Heritage Motors thought their machine would be fixed soon so they could repair my air conditioner. Antoinette Check-It-Off, my taskmistress, worked my list: arrange a party for Thomas Mew at St. Simons, talk to the upholsterer about welting for Katherine's Victorian chair, meet with gift shops at Rome History Museum and Berry College about selling my products.

I called MacConnection about a monitor cord for my new computer. They serenaded me while I waited on hold.

"Love is a many splendored thing...."

The musical interlude swept me to a hilltop in Hong Kong, where William Holden embraced Jennifer Jones. How sizzling hot they were in 1955, and how slinky I had felt in the silk brocade *cheongsam* David bought me in Hong Kong.

I held the telephone receiver with one hand and unloaded the dishwasher with the other. The music stopped.

"This is Van, may I help you?"

"Don't hang up!" I screamed, but Van only dealt with software. I needed the technical enhancement hot line.

"All of our representatives are busy helping other valued customers."

I started cleaning out the junk drawer next to the refrigerator: twist ties, garbage disposal wrench, mystery keys, rusty screws from the bentwood chairs, refrigerator magnets, dozens of dead pens, expired warranties. I tugged on a gold elastic cord. From under a stack of coupons, out popped the bottle opener I called Ariadne's Church Key. Like Daedalus, I needed a thread to guide me through the junk drawer labyrinth and the computer world.

Jill at MacConnection told me my monitor would work if I had a 15-pin plug. I ran upstairs and stood on my head, but I couldn't pull the plug out to count the pinholes. Airborne Express had my G3 on a truck. My teen guru, Sutton Bacon, would soon leave for Emory University. I needed to clear the office before we spread out the new equipment.

In the afternoon, I floated with my neighbor, Libby York, in the Gilberts' pool. We noticed the Lammas change of light. At five the sun moved past the magnolia tree and sent oblique rays through the claret leaves of the Japanese maple. A few dry hackberry leaves rustled across the cement walkway, early refugees escaping through the border fence. I knew that the underlying leaf hues are red, yellow, and orange. Summer green is camouflage, a mask to wear to the country club for lunch. In autumn, midlife leaf ladies show their true colors in one last jingle and jazz before being raked to the nursing home.

They sashay in ethnic duds: African safari cloth, Jakartan batik, and tie-dyed sunbursts of riotous living. I wanted to be an autumn leaf woman and show my true colors.

> August 4, 1898 Como, Italy AML journal
> Took a trip on the Lake of Como. The Villas were lovely, especially near Tremezzo and Cadenabbia. I had addresses for those places but we could not stop on this trip.

August 4, 1998 Rome, Georgia

Anna's journal entry has a wistful tone. Her address book had notes of hotels recommended by friends. She knew which pensions served eggs for breakfast or included wine with dinner. She thought she would have another trip to Italy. In 1987, we had tracked near Anna and Edith's path. Perhaps they were watching when David and I made a lightning run to the Villa Favorita in Lugano to see an exhibit of Fabergé eggs. We dashed back to the hotel for our bags, up the funicular to the Staztione to meet Kiko and Larry for our 11:30 train back to Goeschenen. By that day, the snow was heavy on the ground but not falling. We took a small red train to Andermatt to catch the Glacier Express.

*Glacier Express 1987*

After they added a dining car, we dropped the cheese and apples we were eating and followed the conductor to the *Speisewagen*: a veneered-wood jewel box trimmed with brass. The tables had small lamps and fold-down brass rings to hold wine bottles. The angled bowls of the wine glasses kept the liquid level as we went up steep hills. Outside, the world was solid white as we ate veal au citron, carrots, green salad, ice cream, and cookies. The fresh snow made a wonderland. The table lamps gave us light in the tunnels. We had been smart to detour to Lugano and come back the next day.

⸺◈⸺

The doorbell rang. Airborne Express delivered my computer. After Sutton Bacon arrived, he and David stretched an extension cord up the stairwell to my office from a grounded downstairs outlet. We inserted plugs and—miracle—my monitor and printer worked with the new unit. While David tucked the excess wires under the baseboard, Sutton installed a screensaver view of snow-capped mountains with trees and a lake. I craved that Swiss landscape, but I had no time to play with my new toy. I pitched tote bags in the car and drove in the twilight to the Kenums' house in Atlanta.

⸺◈⸺

From Como, Anna and Edith took a train north to the Lake of the Four Forested Cantons. The *Vierwaldstättersee* is the fourth largest lake in Switzerland. One of the connected fingerling lakes dangles like an appendix down to the city of Flüelen, where the ladies boarded their lake steamer. On their way to Lucerne at the western end of the lake, they would have passed the bald Mount Rigi and the peak of Mount Pilatus.

> August 5, 1898 Lucerne AML journal
> Came to Lucerne. The day was very warm and it was a comfort to get off the train at Flüelen and take the boat across the lake.

August 5, 1998 Dunwoody, Georgia
*Dream: I'm in a medieval room with four-poster bed. A spider sits on the*
*windowsill. Someone says there may be spiders in the covers. I check the bed.*

When my summer dream of Switzerland died on July 18, I
marked the last two weeks in October for a possible trip to Paris,
but Princess Harvey saw calendar constriction. After this trip to
North Carolina, I would go to a wedding on Saint Simon's Island. In
October I would stay with Harrison while Katherine and Tim went
to Colorado. Mary and Dave had fall reunions at Darlington School
in Rome. David and I planned to celebrate his fortieth reunion
at Georgia Tech. After we attended a retirement prep seminar in
Milwaukee, we would fly to our nephew's wedding in South Carolina.

With a financial windfall, I might walk Sister Anna's
neighborhood in Paris in late fall, but my travel window closed to one
inch above the windowsill. I flagged a few days at the end of October
and in early November. Cheaper airfare, fewer tourists, but I could
predict a cold fog on the Seine.

> August 6, 1898 Lucerne AML journal
> Went up the Rigi, was rather disappointed. Edith says I
> am spoiled. But really one ought to see this *before* going
> to Chamonix. On our return went to the P.O. and got
> our letters!

August 6, 1998 Grandfather Mountain, North Carolina
Katherine, Harrison, and I drove from Atlanta to the Beavers'
mountain house. We were glad to escape Georgia humidity, just as
Anna and Edith were relieved to leave Italian heat. With the Beaver
family, we went down to the lake for end-of-summer frivolities
and trout and tacos. A radiant moon rose over the prominence of
Grandfather Mountain. I walked along the lake and thought of Anna
and Edith on the shore of Lake Lucerne. Their mail had brought
unexpected news from their brother.

At age thirty-nine, Fleetwood (Bubber) Lester was engaged to a
young woman about Edith Lester's age. Fleetwood's restlessness had

taken him to California and then to Texas, where he met Miss Lillie Belle Price.

I had only snippets of information about my great-uncle. Edith Lester mentions her brother's "problem," but is never more specific. In a Rome history book, I had seen Fleetwood listed as a resident of "Poverty Hall." These apartments for single men were located above the Lester Store on East Third Avenue. The "Poverty Hall Boys" probably wanted to escape their parents' strict morality.

> August 7, 1898 Lucerne, Switzerland
> Letter (in pencil) from Edith
> My dear Mama,
>
> It's awfully inconvenient to have only one ink bottle, for Sister and I are nearly having a squabble as to who is to use it first in writing to Bubber's "lady love" as he calls her. We don't know what to say so both want to get the letter off of our hands. Bubber's letter was sent to me from Berlin and came in the same mail that our other mail came in yesterday. It was rather a surprise to us, I assure you, but I am very glad for him if he continues to be as happy as he seems to be now.
>
> Yesterday we went up on the Rigi, but not on foot. It is too warm for climbing here, so we ascended and descended on the train. If you read Mark Twain's A Tramp Abroad you will see what he says about the bridge where he repented of his sins before going over and then found that it was no use because he got over safely. He does say some perfectly ridiculous things in that book. You and Miss Beall must read it and enjoy and laugh over it as I did.
>
> The view from the top of the Rigi was beautiful and very extensive. About a hundred and twenty miles of snowcaps could be seen on one side, and lakes and pastures and towns on the other. But the snow seemed so far off after the Gorner Grat, where we walked through it and were snowed on. I expect we should have seen the Rigi first to thoroughly enjoy it.

I have just finished washing my hair and now it is pouring down rain, just like a summer rain at home. You know in Berlin it very seldom comes down hard as it does in Rome. Yesterday afternoon a little while before time to dress for dinner a big storm came up. First it blew and slammed window shutters, turned over flowerpots, etc, at a great rate. Then it hailed and rained down cats and dogs. At this place we are not in the same house where we eat, so the storm kept us from going to dinner. We did not starve, however, for we happened to have some things left from lunch. For a change we have been having our lunch in our room. Pickles, tomatoes, rolls, cake and fruit, all of which were nice and did not cost much. We went to church in the morning and heard the same minister preach that we heard last Sunday in Zermatt. Wasn't that funny? I imagine that this is his church and he was only in Zermatt on a visit. There are a powerful lot of Americans here and you should see them hang around the jewelry stores. Everything here is expensive, even to the pictures, so we only look in the windows.

This morning after an early breakfast we walked out to see the "Lion of Lucerne." It is a large lion carved out of the rock he is in, lying with his head  on his paws and a broken spear in his side. He is dying but is still trying to protect the Bourbon coat of arms. It was made in honor of the Swiss [Guards] who fell on August 10, 1792. [Hundreds of mercenary Swiss Guards died defending the Tuileries Palace of Louis XVI.] It is fine! But the copies in wood and ivory never have the right expression.

Sister and I both wrote to Miss Price yesterday, and I also wrote to Bubber. I hope they will be very happy, but if he fails to tell her the *whole* of the past I would not take many chances on their happiness. If he tells her himself all now it will probably be all right, but if she finds it out after

they are married she is sure to feel very much hurt because
he never told her. She would have a right to I think. There is
no use to think she will never find out, because that doesn't
work. I am sure if she really loves him, she would trust him
all the more, but I don't know what will become of the trust
if she finds it out afterwards.

Two weeks from today I will be back in Berlin. Love to
all and a double share for your birthday. Kiss Papa for me.

Devotedly,
E. Lester

My dear Mother and Father,

Edith is writing and I am sure I do not know how
much or what she has told you but I am to write some too,
she says. In the first place, we were quite taken off our feet
Saturday afternoon by the contents of Bubber's letter. I am
very glad he is so happy. The letter Bubber sent me must be
in Paris, but I am going to let it stay until I return. Direct
my first letter to Paris, care of Cook and Son, 1, Place de
L'Opéra, until I tell you my address. I may have a new one,
as Madame Grégoire has answered and says I can have a nice
sunny room for 30 francs—that you see is much cheaper—I
have written her again however, so cannot tell you yet just
what I shall do.

I was so glad to get the [bank] draft yesterday—now
I need not worry. You see we jumped the track and went
to Chamonix and Zermatt, which was not booked in our
ticket, but they are the gems of our trip and I would not give
them for all the rest put together.

Won't it be fun to be at home again? I can scarcely
wait for the time to come. By the way, we only got cheated
once in Italy. Someone gave us a bad franc—one older than
1860. I did not know they would not pass as we would not
have been taken in then—even that little bit. And we came
back to Switzerland with *no* Italian money on our hands. I

calculated pretty close on that. Now we must do the same in going from Switzerland to Germany.

We would enjoy 3 nice peaches, too. And any quantity of *cider*. I am starved for that so lay in a good supply ready for me, please.

Keep well and happy—for we are coming soon—have made all our plans. Love to Miss Beall and the pets—and a heart full for both your dear selves—your own little daughter.

Anna M. Lester

———※———

My grandmother had often spoken of Zermatt and Chamonix, but I first saw the word "Rigi" in the spring of 1985. A single line in a Switzerland guidebook said that Victorian travelers on the Grand Tour of Europe—including Mark Twain—went to Rigi to watch the sun rise. I was in my sundial art period, so while in Lucerne with David and the Ethridges, I persuaded the group to gamble on a Rigi sunrise.

"Susan, do we know any one who has actually *been* to Rigi?" my weary sister asked me, as our steamer chugged across Lake Lucerne.

"Only Mark Twain," I said.

The Japanese man next to us laughed.

I later learned that herdsmen had pastured cattle on the mountainside of Rigi for centuries. J.M.W. Turner painted three impressionistic watercolors of the Rigi in the 1840s. His *Blue Rigi*, *Dark Rigi*, and *Red Rigi* show the mountain at different times of day. In 1868, while my Lester family was moving to Georgia after the Civil War, Queen Victoria toured the Alps. Bearers carried the queen up the Rigi in a sedan chair. Mass tourism increased after the opening of the Vitznau-Rigi railroad in 1871.

When our foursome got off the lake steamer at Vitznau, the red train was about to leave for the Rigi summit. We grabbed our satchels, stepped aboard the Vitznau-Rigi-Bahn, and went up the mountain—with no reservations. On the steep ascent, the angled

seats allowed us to watch the spectacular view below. At the end of
the line was the Rigi-Kulm Hotel. At 5900 feet, the altitude slurped
our breath. The view encompassed the Alps, lakes, cities, and green
rolling hills with trees.

Getting rooms was not difficult because most tourists deserted
the patio tables at sunset and descended on the last train. Very few of
us remained at the spooky hotel, a prime site for a murder mystery
or clandestine spy operations. We imagined that the mountain was a
chunk of Swiss cheese burrowed with tunnels. The antennae poking
from the ground might connect to Swiss Army underground bunkers.

That night, in our third floor rooms, we flung open the creaky
casement windows. The sweet breeze countered the mustiness of the
feather beds. I could see the moon and the twinkling lights around
the lake below. The sound of cowbells invaded our bedroom all night,
but we slept in Alpine peace. The next morning I got up at 5:45 to
see the sunrise, the prescribed activity on Rigi. From my window I
saw people walking up to the *sommet*. Downstairs, the front door
was locked, but I found my way through a dark bowling alley to a
side door. My chest heaved as I minced to the summit where a small
group gathered to watch the sun come through the haze. The red ball
didn't "roar" as the guidebook legend said, but maybe that was only
for nineteenth-century travelers like Victor Hugo.

The sun illuminated Titlis, Jungfrau, and Eiger. From the
back of Rigi, I looked down to parterres and the valley. The
houses were playschool toys, but the cowbell sounds floated up.
Like Gornergrat, the mountaintop was bare and uninteresting, but
the view was mind blasting. I sat a long time on a bench on the
summit, imbibing the view.

Two hundred years before we were there, Goethe visited the
mountain and commented in his diary on the 360-degree view: "All
around, the splendour of the world."

Kiko and I could have stayed several days on Rigi, but our male
companions wanted to shop in Lucerne. Before we left the hotel, I
bought a small book with Mark Twain's hilarious account of climbing
the Rigi. By dawdling and procrastination (and drinking), Twain and

his companion take days instead of hours to reach the summit. Twain
then blames Herr Baedeker for inaccurate information. Once at the
top, they manage to miss the sunrise by oversleeping. When they got
up to watch what they thought was the sunrise, they faced west and
actually saw the sun set. I imagined my grandmother laughing at
Twain's humor.

Johannes Brahms visited Rigi thirty years before Anna and
Edith. He wrote down a shepherd's horn melody, "High on the
Mountain." This Alpenhorn motif became the mournful French
horn theme in the last movement of his First Symphony. I wondered
if my grandmother knew that bit of music trivia. The music had
always moved me, but I now could layer the Rigi landscape under the
haunting sound.

When I read *Memories, Dreams, Reflections*, I identified with Carl
Jung's Rigi experience. Jung's father took him to Lucerne, then on a
steamship to Vitznau. The father could not afford the fare for two,
so he gave young Carl a ticket to ride up Rigi alone. Jung described
the wonder of the "strangest locomotive in the world, with the boiler
upright but tilted at a queer angle." The panorama from the peak of
Rigi overwhelmed the boy. He reported, "Yes, this is it, my world,
the real world, the secret, where there are no teachers, no schools,
no unanswerable questions, where one can be without having to ask
anything." He felt physically present in "God's world." Jung said this
was "the best and most precious gift my father had ever given me."

———⊗———

In 1987, Edith and I returned to Rigi on our forty-fifty birthday
trip. Waterfalls from melting snow accompanied our train ride up
the mountain from Arth-Goldau. A dozen hang gliders took off
from Rigi and stayed aloft up to four hours before landing in the
valley. The desk clerk gave us room fifty, saying it was the best room
in the hotel. To our list of life goals we added: Always ask for *das
beste Zimmer*. Room fifty had a spectacular view from the bidet and
bathtub. We watched the hang gliders for a long time then walked

EDITH ETHRIDGE

*Susan Harvey on Rigi 1987*

(slowly) to the summit. After the final trainload of tourists left, and the last hang glider sailed off, the mountain was pindrop quiet.

I watched the sunset from a bench outside; Kiko watched from the bathtub. The moonlight and stars were brilliant. I woke up every hour to see the mountains iced with seven-minute frosting. The lights in the valley were fairy dancers with lanterns. We could see the lights on Mt. Pilatus where, according to legend, the ghost of Pontius Pilate resides. We spun all night in a periscope bubble on top of the world.

Before dawn I again found my way through the bowling alley to a side door. In Mark Twain's day, the hotel woke guests with an Alpenhorn and gave them red blankets to wear to the summit. My sweater and windbreaker were inadequate. The frigid air stunned my lungs. I plodded to the summit just as the sun appeared.

Kiko and I ate our Mother's Day breakfast while a man raised the Swiss Flag, and two children sang the Swiss National Anthem. Even though the sky was blue, rain was due later so we left our *beste Zimmer*. During a day of train travel, we saw many families taking flowers to their mothers. From Zermatt that night, we called our mother in Rome. Mamie was the pipeline between Granny Harbin's Zermatt and ours.

August 7, 1998 Chapel Hill, North Carolina
*Dream: my back yard is full of people. In one bricked area, a woman does Reiki. I'm showing women the plants. There's a hybrid tree that's an unusual dogwood.*

On my mother's eighty-seventh birthday, the sun rose early on the far side of Grandfather and crept over to strike the tips of our trees. In our haven west of the mountain, morning arrived late. At breakfast, the Beavers, Kenums, and I sang, "Happy Birthday, Mamie."

While driving to Chapel Hill, Katherine and I talked of the Swiss Alps. When Sister Edith and I were on Rigi in 1987, Katherine had revisited Leysin, where she spent a summer school session. After we all joined David and Larry in Mürren, we learned that Katherine had also stayed in room fifty at the Rigi-Kulm hotel. The Rigi experience had passed to another generation. In twenty years, Harrison could continue the tradition and ask for *das beste Zimmer.*

We arrived at Ludie and Fred White's home in the woods in time to walk around their charming back yard. While Fred cooked shish-ke-bobs over dogwood logs, Ludie and I amused Katherine with stories about her Burney great-aunts. Alline Burney Harvey's sisters had grown up in strict formality on Lumpkin Hill. As adults, they mixed infectious laughter with imperialism: they made their own rules. Aunt Eloise refused to cut artichoke hearts in half for salads. When Alline sat at Huff's drugstore lunch counter, she made the soda jerk cut the crusts off her grilled cheese sandwich. Ninety-year-old Aunt Frances plowed her blue Cadillac down narrow Clark Drive like a Sherman tank. Trashcans swayed in her wake. Aunt Florence once tied towels on Uncle Gus's feet so he could mop the wet lawn before her garden club meeting. At night, Gus monogrammed towels for all her friends. Ludie inherited the Burney laugh. She and David both absorbed the concepts of proper behavior.

On the other side of the world, terrorists bombed our embassies in Kenya and Tanzania with much damage and loss of life. We had always thought that embassies were havens of order and American might, but they had become terrorist targets and scenes of anti-American protest.

August 8, 1998 Chapel Hill, North Carolina
*Dream: I go to my studio behind the City Auditorium. The back door is unlocked. There's not much sculpture there, some old pieces of junk. At a card table a committee is meeting to plan something.*

*Dream: In the City Auditorium, people sit in the balcony. I save a little girl from going over edge of balcony. I have a hotel room that's part of my deal with the studio. It's similar to the old Forrest Hotel. The wallpaper is floral, but the room is mine and I've really enjoyed it.*

*Dream: I'm with a group of women at a retreat to build a labyrinth. One woman leads us in a snake line spiral dance. We wind around, then the line dissolves. I was an observer on the outskirts. We may have been near Granny Harbin's spring.*

These were dreams to ponder. A committee of women was meeting in my studio in the auditory space of my city. I had my own private room in the General Forrest Hotel, a landmark of downtown Rome. I missed dancing in labyrinths with groups of women. The French word for spring is *la source*. These women were helping me find my source from Granny's spring.

———— ◦ ————

August 10, 1898 Meiringen AML journal
This morning we went to the [Aareshlucht] Gorge then to the Falls. Reichenbach Falls, I mean. Both were enjoyed very much. We then had lunch, went to Brienz, then across the lake to Giessbach. At Giessbach we saw the falls and they were beautiful as well as the woods around. At 7.20 we started for Interlaken

August 11, 1898 Interlaken AML journal
Took a carriage to Grindelwald—the drive there and back
was so charming—but the Ice Grotto was a failure according
to my notion.

August 11, 1998 Rome, Georgia
*Dream: David calls and says the bomb was going off. THE bomb or a*
*war or the end of the world, and I should immediately get the kids and*
*drive to a location on Highway 53 where we'd go underground. I grab*
*things. This emergency focused my mind like a tornado warning; the*
*Cuttino silver was incidental.*

*Dream: On a train. A woman gives me a remote control for the restroom*
*door. The code is 2-2 (my nickname). We have to run up to the train to*
*get back on. Some people are left behind. Are we on our way to the safe*
*place? On the train we overhear people talking about offers and deals they*
*got in the mail for safe millennium trips. We could pay a travel agent*
*$2000 to escape the millennium.*

After the trip to North Carolina, I looked forward to
catching up with my ladies in Meiringen, a mountain town south
of Lucerne. Here, an eighteenth-century Italian chef invented
a whipped egg white and sugar dessert, perhaps inspired by the
snowcapped Alps. Members of the French court translated the
name as *meringue.*

Sir Arthur Conan Doyle placed the death of Sherlock Holmes
at the nearby Reichenbach waterfalls. I didn't know if Anna and
Edith had read Doyle's short story, "The Final Problem," before
they went to see the falls. After protests from Sherlock fans, Doyle
reconsidered the death of his popular hero. He later wrote that
Holmes survived by grabbing a clump of grass on his way down.
A Sherlock Holmes museum in Meiringen honors Doyle and his
work, and at the falls, a plaque marks the fictional death place of the
master detective.

The Atlanta newspaper described the heat wave in Europe. One hundred degrees in Paris, and people were leaping into fountains to cool down. Waiters put ice in the red wine. *Quelle horreur!* The weather had cooled a little in Rome, and being outside was bearable. The evening news told of the Russian market collapse. Monica Lewinsky news saturated television. Bill Clinton would testify on Monday. We heard the word "impeachment."

———◆———

I forced myself to go to the nursing home. I arrived in time for "Primp and Pamper Day." Pillows supported my mother in a wheelchair. With rouge circles on her emaciated cheeks, Mamie was a marionette with no strings. The fastidious Mary Gilbert always had a standing appointment with Ruth at the Shop for Beauty. Her thin hair was now bundled into a spout on top of her head. She was Pebbles Flintstone, minus the bone. Attendants wheeled the residents to the "wreck" room to watch the Little Cloggers flap and tap. Fellini could have cast a movie in that room.

Outside, I gulped fresh air and walked to my car. A crow circled.

"Mamie's all dressed up, Doc," I yelled to my father's poltergeist. "Why in hell don't you rescue her from this purgatory?"

With a caw, he lofted skyward, a hanglider on an updraft at Rigi.

———◆———

August 12, 1898 Lake of Thun AML journal
Got a few pictures then had dinner and left going by boat across the Lake of Thun. That is charming too. Was sorry not to visit St. Beatenberg as Mr. Hunter told me not to miss seeing the view.

On the end pages of her 1898 journal, Anna made lists of the summer route and the sights she had seen. Mr. Hunter at Madame Bazin's pension had recommended St. Beatenberg. Anna would have to return to Paris without a check mark by this view.

I understood shrine regret. In 1957, I did not have the fifty dollars to go from Italy to Constantinople, so I had to tell Miss

Niederer at Hollins that I'd missed Haggia Sophia. In Japan in 1962, we couldn't extend David's leave to visit the Shinto shrine at Ise. In England in 1997, Edith and I overlooked one Neolithic chambered long barrow, but on our return, no one accused us: What? You didn't see Hetty Peglar's Tump?

> August 13, 1898 Lake of Constance AML journal
> Spent last night in Zürich—this A.M. went to Mary
> [Young's]. She had gone but the madame gave me my glasses
> and mail. Got letters from the P.O. then left for Munich.

Unable to see their Rome friend, Mary Young, Anna and Edith took a train from Zurich to Romanshorn on the south bank of Lake Constance (Bodensee). On the north side of the lake, they traveled from Lindau to Munich, their next-to-last city.

August 13, 1998 Rome, Georgia
*Dream: I'm doubled-parked in front of Esserman's store on Broad Street. I go in to look for clothes. A woman comes in, thinking it is a store for old ladies. I'd like to look, but I'm double-parked in a VW. I try to back up for a parking place, but I can't control the car.*

My massage therapist said he felt a band around my throat; something couldn't get up past my collar. I knew its name, and so did Edvard Munch: a silent scream of grief, anger, and frustration. Depression sat next to me and waited to pounce. Hep Hep! Hep me! I echoed the nursing home inmates.

> August 14, 1898 arrived in Munich AML journal
> Today we went to two churches and got tickets for the
> Opera—and sat in the Park for a while—have had dinner
> now and will go out late this afternoon I suppose.

August 14, 1898, Munich, Germany
My dear Mother and Father,
    I believe we left off telling you in Lucerne and we expected to go away from there early the next morning.

Well it was rainy when I looked out at 5.30 so we did not leave until noon. Went as far as Meiringen—stayed all night then the next morning went to the [Aareshlucht] Gorge. This is the most beautiful one in Europe and a long one too. We walked along a board path built from the rock over the rushing water. In one place the rocks almost meet and the width of the path between—I could touch both sides. Then we came round the hill and went to the falls. Reichenbach Falls. It was beautiful! After staying as long as we wanted we got our postals, had lunch, then got on the train for Brienz. We only had a few miles to go, then took a steamer across the lake to Giessbach to see the falls there. These I believe are the best in Switzerland. They take 7 leaps down the side of the mountain. Bridges go across in places. Edith walked under the falls in one place but I did not as my shoes were out at the toes and down at the heels—and no Mr. Cobbler to mend them.

The mountains and woods were beautiful—I could have stayed a week—but we had to go on, as our time was getting short. We went down the Lake of Brienz to Interlaken, got there at 9.30. The next day we took a carriage to Grindelwald, and rode within two miles of the Jungfrau. The views all along that way were beautiful. These snow mountains are charming and stand out so clear.

It was a perfect day, not a cloud anywhere. We got to Grindelwald at twelve, then walked to the foot of the Glacier to the Ice Grotto. I was disappointed in that. It is *made* you see, cut out of the ice at the foot of the Glacier. Nature is best. We then came back and on the way we met *a lady* among a number of threes (crowds go each way all the time). She asked in German if it was much further. We told her 50 minutes more of walking. And by the way—these walks are awfully rough—and most of it was in the sun. In a few minutes I saw she had turned to come back. Then she and Edith talked a while. I told Edith to tell her if she had ever seen a Glacier she need not regret not going on. She then said she had been three weeks in Chamonix and in her answer we saw she spoke English. Of course she did for she was an American! And she had taken Edith for a German and we thought she was German—so we had a good laugh.

She met her father in a few minutes sitting under a tree. He had not gotten near as far as she had, and had decided not to go on. He was a funny old fellow and kept on saying all sorts of things that shocked his daughter—but I laughed. Their name was Cooper, from near New York. We called "our carriage" and I wish you could have seen the old driver. He had taken just a little too much to quench his thirst and seeing 3 ladies and one gentleman said no sir, that was not *his* party and drove off. I went after him and then he stopped and we got in and came to Interlaken at a gallop, only he would put on the brakes going down hill and I do not like that.

After dinner when we came back from a walk on the main street seeing all the pretty things, that we had no money to buy. We were tired so got to bed in a hurry. I was just starting to say my prayers when a girl knocked at the door and handed in a card. I'll send it to you: Mr. Cooper and Daughter had called! So I wrote a note. Next morning we went to see her at St. George Hotel. She was in and seemed very pleased to see us. On leaving gave us her card and invited us to pay her a visit in New York. Think of that. *Somebody* made a mark on that little woman and I think it was Edith. We then got a few photos of places we had been and seen, then had dinner and started for Zürich, as we knew it would take more than one day to come here [Munich].

Think of the Lakes we have seen—Geneva— Maggiore—Como—Lugano—Lake of four cantons (Lucerne)—Brienz—Thun—Constance—been on and crossed all!

Then the places we have seen and stayed at least one
night and day—Köln, Bonn, Rhine River, Mainz, Frankfurt,
Heidelberg, Rastatt, Forbach, Zwickgabel, Strassburg,
Berne, Lausanne, Geneva, Chamonix, Territet, Zermatt,
Brig, Simplon Pass, Pallanza, Como, Lucerne, Meiringen,
Interlaken, Zürich, Munich, and we will go to Nürnberg.

I will have to digest all this, this winter. Munich is a
big place and lots to see—but the sun is warm and we are a
little tired now. At least it makes us tired to look at pictures
in a warm close gallery—we are hoping the windows will be
open here.

Yesterday we were in Zürich and got our letters. You
may be sure we enjoyed them immensely. Our papers did
not come. I guess they reached Geneva after these but had
been sent to Zürich, or Cook is waiting for me to tell him
the next place. After that mine will go to Paris and Edith's
to Berlin. I have decided to go to Madame Grégoire's but
I cannot quite make out her street—it looks like 9 rue
St. Beuve but I will be sure—I know it is opposite where
she was last spring, 142 Boulevard Raspail—but to be
certain send your second letter to Cook and Son, 1 Place
de l'Opéra, as I said last Sunday. I will go there for it and
as soon as I reach Paris will see how that word ought to be
spelled. It looks like Beuve—but I do not want to run the
risk of losing any letters. I will have to tell Madame Bazin
I have changed. That is the only thing I hate about it—for
here [at Madame Grégoire's] I will have a room where the
sun comes in and for much less, enough less to pay for quite
a number of lessons.

You ask what to give Bubber [for a wedding gift]—that
is just what has been puzzling our brains. I want to send
something nice and have no money to get it with. I wish we
did know. If he gets a good wife I will be satisfied.

What fun it would be to have you both come over next
spring, and spend two months, then all go home together!

Madame Bazin would be delighted to see you I am sure, and if you wanted to I could get rooms for you there, it is pleasant there in the spring.

Check came all right, I will get it cashed here, then you need not send me one until I tell you.

Many good wishes for a happy birthday and many pleasant returns. A heart full of love and kisses for you both.

Your own little daughter,
Anna

August 14, 1898 Munich, Germany
My dear Papa and Mama,

Sister has written such a rigamarole and used up so much paper, that only four pages are left for me. I believe I am to tell you about Interlaken and Zürich. After supper of the day we went to Grindelwald, we went for a walk to see the shops. They are much prettier I thought than at Lucerne. Interlaken is near the principal wood-carving place of Switzerland and the things displayed were lovely. The tiny animals were beautifully done. I wanted some but they were too expensive. We also passed the carved ivory store that took the first prize at the [Chicago] World's Fair. I think I remember seeing the things there [in 1893], but I enjoyed them more this time.

I would have liked to have a purse full of gold pieces for that store. The carved lampshades, exquisite things, are about all Sister has seen that she wanted, but they cost about three hundred francs. You see our tastes and purses are not in the right proportion. The embroideries too were lovely.

The next day we decided it was best to leave that day for Münich or else we would have to travel on Sunday. After dinner we crossed the Lake of Thun. That is a lovely lake for the view of the snow-covered Alps is so good. A long row with the Jungfrau in the middle could be seen. I was sorry to say good-bye to them.

We got to Zürich at about ten o'clock and gave our things to a hotel man at the station. We had to try at several hotels before he found one with a spare room. We went right to bed and here's a good joke on Sister. There were two nice rolls and some peaches left from our lunch. I ate my roll and the two softest peaches and did my best to make Sister eat hers while it was fresh, but she would not.

After I had been to sleep awhile she waked me up and told me to listen to those great big rats racing around over the floor and where did I put her roll. I certainly did not hear a thing, but she declares until now they waked her up. Anyway, she got up and got the roll to keep the rats from eating it. Mice even are very scarce over here, I haven't see more than two the whole time, but Sister will not believe that she had the nightmare. She talks and goes on ridiculously almost every night but the rats and roll story is the best so far.

Next morning we went to the station and found out all about the trains, then to the post office for our mail. We bought some more rolls etc, got our baggage from the hotel and left at 10.38 for Munich. We came as far as Romanshorn on the train then crossed the Lake of Constance to Lindau then straight here. From Lindau there were no third class carriages much to our regret for second class is awfully hot in summer. We were on that train from a little after two until seven-thirty, so arrived here roasted and covered with dirt, like a potato cooked in the ashes.

The lady served us with a very nice dinner in our rooms and I tell you what, it tasted good. My appetite is uncomfortably large at present and I am forever wanting something to eat.

We are not quite certain if we have a lunatic asylum or a school of oratory next us. From early this morning great big men have been walking up and down in the garden or sitting at windows reading aloud and reciting. It is really most peculiar.

It is nearly suppertime but I must tell you about a commotion we had in the train between Meiringen and Interlaken. The train was crowded so I got on with some baggage to reserve two seats. While I was reaching a strap in through the window a horrid old German tried to take my seat. I told him, please, these are taken and he said he had them and I would have to get out. That provoked me for his tone was so very impolite. I told him I was there first and I would not move, and then he said I could not sit in two places. I told him I did not want to do that, but one was for my sister. Finally he and the woman with him sat down with their baggage spread all around, but he did not want me to put my little satchel on the floor by *my side* because it was in the way at his feet. He made such a racket that I stood up and put the satchel on the bench to see if there was a place in the next car.

Just then a nice old man across the way took it and put it into his rack. Then he gave the man a lecture on politeness at which he got hotter and hotter. Then another man and a woman blessed him out and everybody, even in the next car, were taking up for me and my satchel. I didn't say much but Sister says I certainly *looked* at that man. I was furious! The other people were indignant and whenever they met me afterward for several days had something nice to say. I'll *show* you next summer how he did, it really makes me die laughing to think of it, for he looked so ridiculous.

My paper is up so must say goodbye. Love to all and oceans of it for you two.

Devotedly,
E.Lester

August 14, 1998 Rome, Georgia
*Dream fragment: I'm at a house where Evelyn Harle or Aunt Joy used to live. A man is either appraising things or getting ready for an estate sale. I look at everything like I do in my junk store forays: lacquer boxes grouped*

*together and some Fiestaware pottery. I spend a lot of time looking at all
this. Finally turn on a light to see better.*

Even in my dreams, I was going through things. Evelyn Torrence
Harle was a singer who directed the Rome Women's Chorus. Perhaps
my dream represented the chorus of women I had heard during
the summer. Joy Harper (my grandmother's "Jill") was an interior
decorator, antiques dealer, and an active woman of travel and art. Her
life modeled my fantasies. She earned her living in New York, and she
traveled with friends on steamships to Europe and Asia.

In the shower, I had a flash. I had to live my life to the fullest—
within my *own* parameters. I had appropriated the accomplishments
of other people as goals. I *ought* to have a full speaking calendar, full
social calendar, full exhibition calendar, multiple books published, a
fixed-up home, a functional family and marriage. I had to let go of
my summer pantheon. I was not speaker Patricia Fripp, artist Louise
Nevelson, or writer-artist Anne Truitt. I could only live from *my* own
center out to *my* parameters.

In *Daybook: the journal of an artist*, Anne Truitt discusses
ambition and aspiration in women, how we dismiss our creative urges
as unseemly or unwomanly. Truitt describes the physical hardship of
art production and the mental challenge of museum exhibitions. She
knew she could always retreat to the "woman cave" as homemaker
and mother, but her work urged her on.

Louise Nevelson chose an art career over motherhood. She said
that, with either choice, you pay a price.

Elizabeth Hardwick made a statement about women's creative
work. I wrote it in my journal before my first solo show in 1979.
Hardwick said: "It's not an easy step for a woman, no one cares
whether you do it or not, it's up to you."

Truitt, Nevelson, Hardwick, and I came to the same conclusion:
you make your art for yourself. To prove you can do it. To incarnate
your ideas in words or three dimensions.

I liked changing media and learning new things for my own pleasure, but I didn't have enough lifetimes to refine the skills of construction, welding, writing, printing, and performance. The word "dilettante" is a pejorative term for fickle artists. I looked it up.

Dilettante comes from the Italian: *delittare*, to delight. Well, that was better. I did what delighted me and what gave me pleasure. A butterfly is the quintessential dilettante. She lights and delights on successive blossoms. So be it. I contrasted the butterfly to a pileated woodpecker who knocks his beak against a hollow tree. The world values the woodpecker's obsessive-compulsion more than the butterfly's skittering.

My art career had been a combination of butterfly flit and woodpecker hit. When an idea infected me, I bored the nectar from the trumpet vine: research on the Cherokee Indians, Princess Nicketti, women's foot fashions. Then I became the gold miner's great-granddaughter and went down the mineshaft with a pickaxe and lantern to find appropriate materials. I exhausted one vein of ore, had closure, and then moved on. I liked the finality of words in

print, collages in frames, and sculpture on gallery stands—when the work could no longer demand that I change "just one little thing."

I was a sequential-focus dilettante, but one of my costumed archetypes was a huntress. "Clara Bow and Arrow" never appeared in public in her Greek tunic, but like the Goddess Diana, she wielded golden arrows as she scoped fresh elk to shoot.

*Clara Bow and Arrow*

DAVID HARVEY

Ding! Ding! Ding! The closing bell on Wall Street rang from the television. Ding! Ding! Ding! Cheerleaders announced the winners and losers. The Russian market collapse could affect our financial portfolio. Our retirement funds and my mother's income were at risk.

Coffins arrived from the American Embassy bombings in Africa. Americans had served their country and died for it. No one had heeded the pleas for beefed up security.

We had dinner with Harvey and Don Keiser. They described their retirement experiences, and we tried on scenarios for David's retirement. Nothing fit. The transition was coming too soon for me.

August 15, 1898 Munich AML journal
Went to the Old Pinakothek this morning then down town and got tickets to the Flying Dutchman. Did not go out in the afternoon.

August 15, 1998 Rome to Atlanta
At seven o'clock, I drove in heavy rain to the Georgia Power Building in downtown Atlanta for the Georgia Speakers Association meeting. These energetic sessions stretched my introverted skin. Women wore red suits with brass buttons. Male and female speakers had equally coiffed hair. Featured speakers bounded up the center aisle to the podium. I lacked a power suit, power hair, platform skills, and speaking topics. I needed a fax number, a press kit, a headshot, and high heels.

The featured speaker was Terry Paulsen, president of the national organization. He told us how to give our audiences "keeper notes." Ideas to retain and file.

My inherited letters from 1898 were the ultimate keeper notes. First, my great-grandmother read them and tied them with ribbons, then my grandmother put them in a trunk for sixty years, and then my mother moved the trunk to two other attics for thirty years. As the millennium approached, an obsessive granddaughter found the letters in a hatbox. She plastered the letters with sticky notes, zipped them into plastic bags, and stashed them in new plastic boxes. She challenged her eyesight by transposing the faint handwriting into a computer file. Now, that wasn't hard, was it?

After the meeting, I drove around Atlanta while the radio played *Die Fledermaus* in German. Anna and Edith Lester were in the opera house in Munich that day. If I'd heard *The Flying Dutchman*, the coincidence might have run me into a lamppost on Peachtree Street. Later I heard Beethoven's Ninth and the overture to *Tannhauser*. Granny and Sister Anna were disc jockettes controlling my airwaves as I headed for antique shops on Cheshire Bridge Road to look for Russell Wright china. I wanted a tall water pitcher in granite gray. I was building inventory for my own estate sale. I could hear my children groan, "Oh, no. Not more Russell Wright!"

At Harry's Farmers Market, my taste buds demanded haricots verts, fresh chives, watercress, pine nuts, macadamia nuts, and prosciutto. I bought sweet fresh shrimp for David and a pound of organic butter to spread on my rye crackers.

In my kitchen, I wrapped the translucent ham around cantaloupe wedges and pretended I was in Italy. I boiled David's shrimp, and we watched television news. When he switched to a football game, the referee's piercing whistle recalled decades of football seasons. Conversation was postponed until spring.

From David's CD library I chose *Wagner's Greatest Hits* and figured out how to play it on my computer. The disc didn't have *The Flying Dutchman*, but from my speaker came *Die Meistersinger*. Thrilling. Just in time for Nuremberg. The speaker quality was not great, but the control was at my elbow. I changed tracks. The Mormon Tabernacle Choir squeezed through the tiny speaker with the "Bridal Chorus" from *Lohengrin*.

While the pilgrims marched in *Tannhäuser*, I found the sixty-cent error in my checkbook. I blessed the metrics of Wagner.

August 16, 1898 Munich AML journal
This morning we went to the Crystal Palace and saw the pictures. To the bank and other places. It is too warm to enjoy going very much.

August 16, 1998 Rome, Georgia
*Dream: I'm on a big white Ferris wheel that doesn't have the weight balanced.*

My Ferris wheel was askew; I wobbled on a stalled life wheel. While one part of me was in Rome, Georgia, another part wanted to be in Münich with the ladies. A third magnet pulled me to the Alternate ROOTS annual meeting. From all over the South, artists were traveling to Black Mountain, North Carolina.

I looked up Ferris. The encyclopedia led me back to the Lester women. George Washington Gale Ferris invented his giant wheel for the World's Columbian Exposition of 1893; his Chicago wheel would rival Eiffel's tower at the 1889 Paris Exhibition. Anna Lester had taken Edith, aged 17, to Chicago for the World's Fair. I didn't know if they rode on the Ferris wheel, but they did visit the Women's Building.

Sophia Hayden, the first American woman to receive an architecture degree, designed the Women's Building at age twenty-one. Her "nervous collapse" before the building's opening reinforced some men's belief that women should not be architects. High on an arched wall, Mary Cassat's mural depicted *Modern Women*. The left panel portrayed *Girls Pursuing Fame*. The center panel was *Young Women Plucking the Fruits of Knowledge or Science*. The right panel showed *Arts, Music, Dancing*. Cassatt's vision of female ambition and education in the arts could subtitle the lives of Anna and Edith Lester.

On August 17, Anna wrote her mother a birthday postcard from Munich. An elfin monk wears a hooded black cape over his brown belted robe. He holds a large stein, and radishes spill out of his pockets. The little Munich monks may have been the inspiration for the Munchkins of Oz.

I calculated Eliza Mary Lester's age; she turned sixty-two on August 18, 1898. I had pictured my great-grandmother as an old lady in a shawl, but she was only a year older than I was when I found the card in 1998.

August 17, 1898 Munich, Germany
My dear Mother,

    Tomorrow will be your birthday, and I
send this jolly little München boy to make
you laugh and be young and wish you many
happy returns. We have seen a good deal and
been to the opera twice. It is fine here you know. Tomorrow
we go to Nürnberg where we part for the winter. I shall
remain there a few days longer as my ticket is good 3 days
more. I hope Paris will be cool so I can work hard. I want
to do so much this year. Keep well all of you and rest. Much
love from us both. I am your loving child,

Anna

Anna's little München boy had a postal adventure on its way
to Eliza Mary Lester. First postmarked 17 August in München, the
postcard was in Roma (Italy) on August 19 and 20. Faint purple
letters say, "Missent to Dead Letter Office and forwarded." A post
official had underlined the word "Georgia" in blue and added enough
Italian postage to get the card to Rome, Georgia.

August 17, 1998 Rome, Georgia
    My eyelids itched and my bones ached. The ragweed had hit.
Daughter Mary woke me up to say she received the fax from my new
faxmodem but with some glitches. She was e-mailing her new "nanny"
who was due to arrive from Colombia, South America, the next week.
    The morning news told me that Russia had devalued the ruble
and the Latin American stock and bond markets had plunged. Our
junior college's satellite link gave me news from France, and I tried to
understand the newscaster's bullet-speed French. I watched the Spanish
news in honor of Mary's new nanny. All I understood was "Beel
Cleenton" and *La Casa Blanca*. The White House. Of course. To me,
*Casablanca* was a movie title. I'd never dissected the Spanish words.
    I had just learned that Munich was the city of monks. I needed
to unpack all the names: Strassburg, Heidelberg, Nuremberg,

Grindelwald. I knew *burg* was castle, *berg* was mountain, and *wald* was forest. These root fibers were rhizomes under the written page. They sprouted in my notebook garden and on my computer. I wanted to turn over the soil, let the language roots breathe.

---

Thinking about roots transported me to Camp Rockmont in North Carolina. That morning the Alternate ROOTS group was in the camp lodge to begin a week of art, music, and theater. I was not there, but I heard the scrape of chair legs on the wooden floor. I felt the harmonic vibrations of song and the shuffling of sandals and bare feet. Artists encouraged each other to persevere despite muddy roads and hard times. I sang alone in my living room.

The lakeside camp complex had once housed the seminal Black Mountain College where Merce Cunningham danced, Robert Rauschenberg made innovative art, and John Cage staged the first multi-media "happenings." During the ROOTS meeting in 1995, I had conducted a labyrinth workshop on land made sacred by these artistic giants.

On a hot August afternoon, a costumed group of artists processed to the soccer field on the edge of Lake Eden. After I demonstrated how to draw the labyrinth seed, the nucleus from which the pathways expand, we began to construct the design. In a Scandinavian tradition, fishermen marked labyrinths with white stones. I had chosen a lighter-weight material. We used 250 recyclable white Styrofoam soup bowls anchored with wire marking flags. The marshy land accepted the colorful wire flags, and we accepted that our feet would squish pellets dropped by geese. The design fanned out from the seed and grew to about sixty feet in diameter. Before the nighttime program, the dancer Heitzo and I placed 250 votive candles on the lines. By dusk, the Styrofoam bowls mimicked white stones in moonlight.

ROOTS pilgrims assembled, and Heitzo swooped and flapped around the periphery in my spotted Dotty Bird wings. Wearing my hooded black cape, I directed participants into the labyrinth entrance with my golden apple baton. Dancers circled the pathways in their own rhythms and tempos. Drummers sent hypnotic thrumming into the moist mountain night. Singing erupted. The damp black earth smelled of crushed grass blades mixed with tang of goose. In the center, the circling rings coalesced male and female energy. One couple slept all night in the labyrinth's goal.

Since that event, I had seen a documentary on Buckminster Fuller's experimental work at Black Mountain College. In 1948, Fuller constructed an early geodesic dome on the same field where we built our labyrinth. His dome had collapsed, and my Lake Eden labyrinth candles were extinguished, but we shared the pulsing power of that charged setting.

In August 1998, I wanted to stand again by Lake Eden and watch mock funeral barges float at midnight and hear half-naked performers sing, "Wade in the Water." I wanted to see men with flaming guitars jump from the diving board. I craved bongo drums. I remembered the grace of Jim Grimsley and Kenneth Raphael as they navigated the group through race and gender confrontations.

*Black Mountain Labyrinth 1995*

Only the handcuffs of willpower kept me from leaping into my car and heading for North Carolina—a swallow to Capistrano, a bat to the steeple light.

————⊷————

August 18, 1898 Munich AML journal
Mother's birthday, our letters came.

August 18, 1998 Rome, Georgia
*Dream: A Steinway piano has a plaque designating whose it was. Someone was to play it, perhaps me, or my son David.*

Artifacts continued to surface from the boxes in my basement. I either had selective blindness, or the Universe augmented my diet when my digestion was ready. Anna's railroad ticket book (*Zusammengestelltes Fahrscheinheft*) was the equivalent of a Eurail Pass. Pinholes pierced the paper with the sisters' departure date: 27-6-98, the twenty-seventh of June. They spelled the word Köln as Koeln, although one would think the *umlaut* would have been an easy task for pinholes. When Anna signed the small gray book, she knew she had to return to Köln before her ticket expired on the twenty-fifth of August at *Mitternach*. Anna said they "jumped the track" of their predicted itinerary in order to visit Chamonix and Zermatt. If she had known how little time remained in her life, she might have jumped more tracks and stayed in her favorite places for "a week" or "a month."

————⊷————

Our Hollins Abroad group drove to Munich in July 1957. We passed medieval villages where men and women cut and stacked hay. I wanted to run in the wheat fields, not only for pleasure, but also to escape our capsule of thirty bus-crazed young women. We ate lunch in Dinkelsburg. I sent Granny Harbin a postcard of the medieval Rothenberg town gate. In Munich, we toured the city in a cold rain. At the Deutches Museum, we saw a collection of pianos.

After supper, Nina Terry, Sally Ordway, and I went to the Hofbräuhaus where we met some American soldiers who stood on chairs, stomped

their feet, and sang drinking songs. I noted in my journal: Lord help
the western world if this is the U.S. Army in Germany.

———•———

I picked up the quarter-liter beer stein that
Anna and Edith brought home. A Munich monk in a
smudged blue robe spreads his arms to bless or welcome.
He holds a book with a cross on the clasp. From a
library book, I learned the definition of stein: a handled
drinking container designed to hold beer and covered by a hinged lid.
Stein means stone and stoneware comes from the German *Steingut*.
A beer holder is a *Bierkrug* unless it's stoneware. Beer connoisseurs
believe that stoneware tankards preserve and enhance flavor. A
sixteenth-century health law dictated lids to keep out flies. Bannester
Lester, the sanitary grocer, would have approved.

During the summer, I had dreamed about Steinway pianos, but
I had never cracked the word: the stone way. I was on the Stein Way
as the ladies drank from steins in Munich and their cobblestoned way
together ended. One of the postcards in their *Album für Postkarten*
depicted the exterior of the Germanic baroque Hofbräuhaus. From
angled windows, those inside could watch neighbors walking in the
street. An interior view showed a vaulted room with a painted ceiling.
Men sat at tables filled with steins. One man talked to a uniformed
soldier. A crown over the HB initials on the Hofbräuhaus shield
indicated royal patronage.

I remembered a story from the European trip of Rena Patton
and her mother-in-law. Lila Bowie Patton was matriarchal in
stature, dress, and conduct. She was one of our tradition-keeping
ladies at St. Peter's Church in Rome. In Munich, Rena and Lila had
the obligatory beer at the Hofbräuhaus. When Lila did not drink
fast enough, some German men at the next table yelled, "Trink!
Trink! It's good for your *titties!*"

———•———

August 19, 1898 Nürnberg AML journal
We got to Nürnberg last night at 12. This is a *dear* place and
we have been *all* round the old part of the town.

August 19, 1998 Rome, Georgia
*Dream: I'm in a museum building like the Guggenheim, full of paintings
and art. We're moving all the art and re-building and re-arranging.
I'm proud about how fast we've rebuilt. One building has exposed
underpinnings. What is the basement equivalent of rafters? Studs? Struts?*

*Dream: I'm at my childhood home on Westmore Road, where someone is
messing with the foundation. Is she a female saboteur? I call the police to
catch this saboteuse. I'm showing people around the museum. The walls
are concave, covered with gray flannel or carpet.*

Anna and Edith were in their last city. Each day I had put their
trip first, followed by a mad dash to clean, wash, swim, get food,
and do errands. The Princess decreed that the "Mad Dash" was a
new punctuation mark showing rampant anger or craziness. My
skin tingled, my face had a rash, and I had sweats and chills, perhaps
punctuation revenge from the Mad Dash or the Hormonal Period.

On Channel 99, a program on Ernest Hemingway gave good
advice to the Mad Dasher: Never mistake Motion for Action.

August 20, 1898 Nürnberg, Germany
Dear Mother and Father,
        Monday first thing [in Munich] we went to see the
pictures in the old Pinakothek (that is an awful word to
pronounce). I wanted to call it Moses and let it pass. You
see these Galleries are so close it is almost impossible to stay
more than two hours and not have a headache. Then we
went downtown to get tickets to the Opera—for Munich
is a fine place for music—and I, you know, have heard
only one concert since last summer. Went to Cosi fan tutte
and the Flying Dutchman, first by Mozart and the last
by Wagner. You know we go so early—while the sun is

shining—that at ten o'clock we are out—and ready to go to bed at a reasonable time.

Tuesday we went to see the modern pictures in the Crystal Palace and in another building there. Some of these were beautiful and the Palace is such a beautiful place for an exhibition. Gardens and fountains inside and so cool and lovely. Pictures without number! I could not see or remember a third. One ought to stay in Munich months to see all the art. It is next to Paris you know in that line. We then went to the Bank and I got my check cashed—and do let me tell you, this is the first time my Pass Port has been of use. He asked if I had anything to identify myself, so I produced that and got my money.

Wednesday morning we went to see the Glyptothek—the place where casts are—and a few marble statues. Some are beautiful. Then we went down town to get some pictures [photographs]. In the afternoon went to the English garden.

Thursday morning first thing went out to the cemetery. This is one of the finest they say in Germany. It looks more like a French one though. Whole families are buried in the space of one grave. Each time one dies the others have to be dug up! Horrors.

We walked down the wide aisle to the arches in the end. I was making for that because I had heard that back of the arches was a room where the dead people are kept three days—before putting them in the grave—to see if they come to life. The coffins are partly standing and all covered with flowers. There, an electric wire is attached to the left hand of the dead body and in case they should move—a bell will ring. I did not want to see them but I wanted to know how it looked. Edith said at first she was not going near and I shuddered, too, but after seeing a few minutes it was not so bad. They looked just as if they were sleep—only four were there—each one numbered—but we could see where some four or five coffins had been removed that day. I would not want to see it at night when it is all lighted up.

It is a splendid place only it seems horrible to have one's friends there on exhibition where everybody can see. Women and children go. I saw women holding up little bits of tots to look in the windows. One old woman spoke to us and as near as we could understand her, she said one did not look as if she were dead. All looked as if they were asleep to me except one, and I would be sure she was dead. The women were in black with orange blossoms on their head and a small white veil. Funny idea, I think.

From there we went to a live place: the Hofbräuhaus— and had some of the famous München Beer! I took some just to say I had. I did not want to leave Munich without drinking any but I *made a face* and disgusted Edith. I do not like the stuff—it makes cold chills run down my back—but I drank half of my mug full. This is the first I have tasted since last summer and it will be the last. I want *cider*—good home made sweet cider—ice cold out of our own little refrigerator in Rome, Ga!

Glad the time is on the downgrade? Well, I should think I was. I would come tomorrow and stay two months if I could. Then work in Paris all winter with a will. There are a *few* people I *love* in America and only one over here and I cannot have her anymore now until next summer!

Anna M. Lester

———— ✦ ————

Nuremberg (Nürnberg), located on the Pegnitz River, had preserved its Roman walls and its Renaissance reputation of artistic and intellectual freedom. Part of the romantic European tour for Americans, the city attracted Henry Wadsworth Longfellow in 1844. I had found two copies of Longfellow's *Nuremberg* in my grandmother's collection of books.

As Anna and Edith prepared to part, I went back through their postcard book, looking at each card. I saw the towers, gates, and stone walls of Nuremberg as well as clothes drying on balconies. Albrecht Dürer's timbered house had five stories, topped with a red tile roof. I noticed a vertical sundial on the wall of the house next door.

In my basement, I dug into a box of Anna's books and found a series of biographies of famous artists: Raphael, Murillo, Correggio. I wiped off the small gray volume on Albrecht Dürer. Below Anna's inked signature is the date 1888; she had studied Dürer's life for ten years before she visited his city. Many of Dürer's engravings depict Bible events, but they are set in the half-timbered architecture of Germany. To give Mary and Jesus a drink, Joseph draws water from a well in the basement of a Germanic house topped with the Dürer monogram. In a Bavarian forest near a fairytale castle, a stag and whippet dogs observe the Conversion of St. Eustace. Dürer's drawing of praying hands was a perennial cover on the Southern Baptist service bulletins of my childhood. His plump hare could have inspired Beatrix Potter or a Meissen ceramic artist.

A quotation on the book's title page came from Tiziano Vecelli (Titian). *The whole world without Art would be one great wilderness.*

I doubted that Anna had her Dürer textbook in Nuremberg, but I knew she had Longfellow's slim booklet. Only an eighth of an inch thick, the gilt-edged book would have slipped comfortably into her skirt pocket. The port wine cover felt like waxed linen. Below the title, an embossed gold crest showed a winged figure with claw feet, a pageboy hairdo, a crown, and a breastplate.

Visitors to Nuremberg bought this souvenir book to see the German city through the eyes of an admiring American poet. Between engravings of Nuremberg, Longfellow describes the town in rhyming, singsong couplets. He calls Dürer the "Evangelist of Art," and the frontispiece is an engraving of Nuremberg's most famous son.

When I visited Dürer's grave in 1957, I sketched his monogram in my journal. At that time I had not seen *torii*, the large wooden portals leading to Japanese shrines. Dürer's capital "A" resembles one of these Shinto gates; his "D" sits beneath the high crossbar. Dürer branded all his work with his woodcut logo.

Dürer's gravestone inscription is in Latin. Longfellow notes the word *Emigravit* (he emigrated) and insists: "Dead he is not,—but departed,—for the artist never dies." The word "emigrate" comes from the Latin *emigrare*, which means to depart from a place, to leave one country or region to settle in another. Some people say that a dead person has been "translated." At death we get a final stamp in our passport. We cross the border into a new language with celestial syntax.

The Longfellow book has an engraving of Hans Sachs. His furry collar melds with his bushy beard and wavy hair. Sachs, a shoemaker, was the most famous Nuremberg mastersinger. These German poet-musicians treated literary art as a craft or trade. In the late Middle Ages, they revived the fading art of the minnesingers, the wandering poet-musicians. Song competitions had rules, and song schools were organized like medieval guilds. The mastersingers' popularity peaked in the early 1500s, but the tradition continued into the 1800s. The poets did not produce great literature, but they achieved lasting fame through Wagner's opera, *Die Meistersinger von Nürnberg*.

I slid the Wagner compact disc into my computer, and the prelude to *Die Meistersinger* came through the little holes in my Power Macintosh G3. Wagner's music had moved from his brain to written score to orchestra to records to tapes, and it now emigrated from the CD into my Georgia morning.

As Longfellow "paced the streets and courtyards" he muses to Nuremberg:

*Not thy Councils, not thy Kaisers, win for thee the world's regard;*
*But thy painter, Albrecht Dürer, and Hans Sachs, thy cobbler-bard.*

Longfellow teaches a lesson for all communities: Municipal sewers, perimeter highways, and mass transit systems are fleeting. Artists and poets make the lasting work.

August 20, 1898—Nürnberg.

Dear Mama,

This place is charming! I leave in a little while for Dresden. But Sister stays here until Wednesday. Enjoyed your letter of August 2 very much. Good Bye. Will write when I reach Berlin.

Lovingly,

E. Lester

August 20, 1898—Nürnberg AML journal

Went round walls. Edith had to leave a little sooner than she expected. Now I am all by myself! Took a long walk after it got cool—and came back and went right to bed. I got a Longfellow's Nürnberg for myself but gave it to Edith—Did not know she cared for it until the last minute.

After two months of travel, my kinswomen were ready to work. Edith's piano pulled her to Berlin. Anna's charcoal and paper waited in Paris. In a final generous act, Anna gave Edith her copy of Longfellow's Nuremberg poem. She later bought another copy for herself. As Anna walked the city walls alone, Edith took the train to Dresden and on to Berlin. A few days later, Anna would return to Paris and stay until December 1898. The sisters would not see each other until Edith returned from Europe in July 1899. Anna was Edith's senior by fourteen years. Logic decreed that the older sister would die first, but I doubt that either sister thought that Anna would only live two years past their happy summer.

August 20, 1898 Nürnberg

My dear Mother and Father,

Here I am alone again. Edith left at noon for Dresden where she will spend tomorrow then go on to Berlin on Monday. Nürnberg is the dearest old place we have been. The old Roman Walls are still around the old part of the town and very picturesque in color and form. Albert Dürer, the artist, and Hans Sachs, the shoemaker and poet, lived

here. Their houses are to be seen also statues, etc. Everything hangs around these two and all manner of mementoes.
I have gotten pictures of the places of interest, also Longfellow's Nürnberg, a little poem bringing in these two. Longfellow was most fond of Nürnberg and Heidelberg so wrote of these beautifully. I wish I could paint these as well, but it is not in me. I wonder I ever tried to paint at all. Some of the fountains over here are very striking. I have to tell you of these when I come.

Friday afternoon we went out to this lovely park and had our supper. And by the way, have been eating my breakfast picnic style under a grape vine since I came here until this A.M.—it rained so had to go inside. It is fine. Let's have ours outside when we come home.

I suppose Edith is seeing the lovely [Sistine] Madonna in Dresden today. I am glad she is going to move and have a larger room this winter and I hope will have better fare, too. She has enjoyed the eating this summer and has a good live appetite now. I too am better in that way and if I do not have enough when I go back to Paris I am going to make a fuss! I shall be glad to get back to work and also to the little chapel. It does not seem like Sunday when I do not go to church once.

I think I have done up Nürnberg pretty well and I am going in the morning. I would not know what to do with myself here all day so will be in Paris one day sooner. I trust God will keep you well and happy all these months to come and you will not be any older than when I left I am sure.

Must I get old or young?

With a heart full of love for you both, your loving child,

Anna M. Lester

August 20, 1998 Rome, Georgia

I thought of Anna's last question as I did the morning assignment from *The Artist's Way*. In describing my childhood room, I found my own mixture of "old" and "young."

When we lived on Westmore Road, my parents enclosed a porch for my bedroom. A large picture window had bookshelves on either side. At my built-in desk I worked on my Girl Scout merit badges. I sewed the round embroidered patches on my uniform sleeve to signify accomplishment and deserved merit. The Girl Scout uniform had survived in my mother's attic. I retrieved it from my upstairs linen closet.

When I touched the green fabric, my days in Troop Six returned. My childhood stitches held the badges in place, and the primary colors had not faded. One circle had a row of books. Other badges showed a palette, a musical staff, flowers, cooking, sewing, and nutritious food. The Parthenon represented architecture. One badge had a cup of steaming tea. The prophetic Scout badges had grown into my adult passions. The patch with a Swiss chalet and snow-capped mountains reflected my summer's research. The only badge I didn't relate to was the gavel of parliamentary procedure. I didn't want to be president of any organization, but I did like to call things to order.

In my journal I drew circles and listed my summer badges: good mother, good wife, good granny, good friend, good writer, good exerciser, good computer novice, good basement excavator, good family memorabilia sorter. My good daughter badge was a one-way exercise in duty, as my mother could no longer reward my accomplishments.

My good artist badge was in limbo. I needed sales to pay my studio rent, but I was not in a marketing mood. Clearing my studio would make room for the next life stage, but when I gave away something, I often wanted it back. Some people call that Indian Giving, but the American Indians considered a gift a loan to someone in need; when the need was over, they expected the item to be returned. I, child of Great Depression parents and WWII rationing, wanted to hoard it all.

Which items in my studio sizzled with current energy? Could I jettison those whose potential I had seen twenty years before? Off with their heads! Make them walk the plank. In my studio, of course,

I had planks. I also had Junk Woman's sword to nudge malingering objects overboard.

———— ———— ————

Anna walked the walls of Nuremberg in cadence with Longfellow's hypnotic verse. I had another battlement wall to walk: an appointment with my husband at his office. David and I filled out questionnaires for the pre-retirement seminar we would attend in Milwaukee in October. As we compared our answers, we saw our parallel paths of transition. We were both shedding snake skins. David could retire but what would he do? Would he be bored by endless golf and television? I wondered if he would alphabetize my spices and reload the dishwasher in concentric rows. I no longer found energy in making sculpture, but if I abandoned my messy studio, I would have no identity. Who would I be if Junk Woman died?

———— ———— ————

Perhaps I feared David's retirement because my father's retirement had coincided with Mamie's early days of dementia. We had thought our dad's Colorado mountain climbing was a guarantee of longevity, but he had the first strokes in the family. Doc's presence at home curtailed the things Mamie loved. She gave up her garden club, the Music Lovers' Club, and historic preservation conferences in Georgia towns.

If left alone, Doc opened all the kitchen drawers and cabinets and forgot to turn off the sink faucets. We took away lethal items. The pistol came out of the hall closet. We confiscated the keys to the Buick. We flushed the pill samples we found in Doc's dresser drawer.

When he could no longer play golf, our father sat in his green leather chair and watched videos. He never acknowledged Mamie's declining mental state.

"Doc, how do you think Mamie is doing?" I asked, when I took him on drives in the afternoon sun.

"Mamie? Oh, she's just fine. Why do you ask?"

Mamie hung her cane on the refrigerator door handle and forgot where it was. She put her clothes on backwards. I assembled pills in individual envelopes for each day. This method worked until she forgot what day it was, or if it were morning or night. We then hired caretakers to supervise meals, medicines, the house, and the yard.

---

One summer day, our father slipped out of the house and hitched a ride downtown to Broad Street. A salesman at Owens-King called me.

"Susan, Dr. Gilbert has just bought a good-looking suit and some shirts. He's ready to go home."

"What? My dad? How did he get to town?"

"Some nice people dropped him off."

"I'll be right there." I abandoned the artwork I was gluing for an exhibit, picked up my dad, and took him home. Velma, the caretaker, was searching the nearby woods.

"I thought I could find him before I called you," she said. "I didn't want to bother Doctor Peter at work."

Doc was pleased with his afternoon. All he wanted was a new suit. And a bit of adventure.

When I got home, it was too late to resume my art project. I recognized the diabolical force that sabotages women's creative work. I liked the sneaky Irish blessing: "May you be in Heaven five minutes before the Devil knows you're dead."

Quick, Artist, make something before the Anti-Creator sees you in your studio.

---

The newspapers blared news of Bill Clinton's confession. The president ordered the bombing of terrorist sites in Afghanistan and Sudan to retaliate for the bombings of American embassies in Africa and to pre-empt further terrorist strikes. When the news conference was called, the press corps was watching the movie *Wag the Dog*. The lines blurred between truth and fiction.

After Clinton's speech and seeing the Washington Monument on television, I dreamed I was walking across fields and woods carrying an obelisk. I hoped it was my own power tool.

August 22, 1898 Nürnberg
My dear Edith,

    Does my little girl know how much I hated to have her leave me? I just wonder if she does. After dinner on Saturday it stormed then cleared off and we had a pleasant afternoon. I walked half way round the old walls then came back here and had my rolls and pears and went to bed. Yesterday morning I went to the museum. I think there must have been 777 rooms instead of 77. I saw what I could, then left. Got some soft bread on the way back. After writing home and taking a nap, I went out to walk the other half of the way round. That side was not interesting, as so much had been taken down. So instead of *retracing* my steps as I did Saturday, I kept on and completed the whole town, got here fifteen minuets of eight. I went to bed at 8.30 expecting to get up early this morning, but slept until 7.30! Think of that.

    I got ready and took my hat down to breakfast, so started out at 9.30. First went to the Depot and asked that other man about my ticket. He could not speak English but said the train left here at 7.11 and I did not have to "*aufsteigen*" [*umsteigen* means to change] between here and Mainz. I did the whole town over again, going to Hans Sach's statue, too. It was only two steps around the corner from his house.

    I went for a Longfellow [book] and the other man waited on me and said he had no more *red* ones so I had to

take an ugly blue one. I was mad and kept thinking he did
not know, so on my way back I went in to see if I could get a
photo of a picture I had seen in Dürer's house and knabbed
the other fellow and told him to *look* for one like I got
Saturday. He said we have a plenty and changed mine. So
much for going back, you see. I then got a good photo but
not of the picture I wanted, they had none. Then could not
find our bread place, though I saw it on my way out. Sun
was too hot to look.

Dürer's house is interesting. I am sorry you did not
go in. At twelve I was in front of that clock and *nothing*
happened. Had started to go off as everyone else did when
a feeble strike came and those little figures walked round
three times, then the two other figures attempted to lift their
trumpets but they were too heavy so their hands fell. It was
not worth waiting to see.

I am going in the morning. I have seen this town twice
and half again, and am lonesome. So will arrive in Paris
Thursday I guess instead of Friday.

I hope you did not melt on the way to Dresden. Going
north it may have been cooler. Will write when I reach Paris
and know the name of the street.

With much love, your own Sister,
Anna M. Lester

Forgot to say that I have sat through 3 "tobble dotes"
*[tables d'hôte]* without a word. The English fellow has
not turned up. All German and French yesterday. Today
American boys sat in front of me so I had amusement.

August 22, 1998 Rome, Georgia
Even though Anna missed Edith, I related to her solitude
as she walked the walls and read Longfellow. Solitary eyes give a
concentrated vision, and I craved some time alone. Daughter Mary
had said I could go to their Grandfather Mountain house during

the first week of September. My solo time there in 1997 had been rich after the intensity of the Alternate ROOTS annual meeting. I wanted to observe myself when I was alone. How much quiet could I take? How long could I sleep? When would I need to drive down the mountain in search of grilled fish?

---

I decreed a finish-in-the-basement day. David gave me the morning, and Anthony showed up. From the dirt crawl space under our bedroom they pulled out fragments from demolished Rome buildings. My archifrags were a scrapbook of Rome's history. I had limestone keystones from the Harbin Hospital, gable brackets from Madeline Kuttner's house, the iron fence from Miss Carrie Beysiegel's house, and a wooden column and bricks from the demolished Broad Street depot.

In the red dirt of the side basement crawl space, I unearthed remnants of dioramic scenes I had constructed in deep dresser drawers. These small stage sets were my first installation artwork, but even in the 1970s, the Lester ladies were present. Glued to the wood were postcards from Paris, Sister Anna's Clarence Eddy concert ticket, German newspapers, Edith Lester's opera scores, and a mother-of-pearl inlaid calling card case from Aunt Joy Harper.

I had photographed these theatrical vignettes when they were new, but later I cannibalized them for other boxes. After twenty years in the basement, the glued papers were fused to the wood, but the boxes were too depleted to save. I hushed the voice that whispered: But, what about your retrospective at the Guggenheim?

Anthony, the undertaker, took the wooden boxes to the gutter, and then we sat down in the shade with cold drinks. Anthony told David about his preacher's dire warnings about the Y2K bug. David decided he had time for nine holes of golf before dark. After they left, I went to the Gilberts' pool to cool off. I took Pete and Suzy a fireplace grate, a bell, a grapple hook, and enameled bedpans and stainless canisters for a future Harbin Clinic Museum. I planned to call yardmen to cut the shrubbery, antique dealers to appraise leftover furniture, and painters for the basement. We would begin in our catacombs and work up to the gutters and roof.

All summer I'd looked for a sign that I was not destined to follow Anna and Edith around in Europe. Validation came from news reports. All the airports in Europe and America were on high alert due to terrorist threats from Osama bin Laden. I might have been so immersed in Nuremberg that I would have missed the alerts from America.

I confessed my summer addiction to live television. I had watched Clinton's *mea*(almost)*culpa* and his subsequent show of force. I had waited for the president to come out for his press conferences. I liked the immediate talking head analysis. I watched the closing bells on Wall Street. I craved a solitary capsule, but I wanted to know what was going on.

> August 23, 1898 Mainz, Germany AML journal
> Came to Mainz today. Two Americans were on the train and
> came to this Hotel. They say they are going down the Rhine
> tomorrow. I am too if it is a good day.

August 23, 1998 Rome, Georgia
*Dream: It is Thanksgiving; I'm worried because I have no money in the bank in either account. I go to my studio. Parts are empty. One part has a big piano in it. I didn't know I had a second piano. The door is ajar and other people are in it. No art, just a big room with a few tables of academic people.*

The gray August day and my fuzzy brain demanded caffeine. I took Sister Anna's teacups and pot from Granny's secretary. I stirred lump sugar into my *café au lait*. I didn't know where in Paris Anna had bought the tea set, but I knew her fingers had rubbed the art nouveau blue and white flowers tipped with gold.

When I rattled my cup on its saucer, I heard the ghosts of other women. Grandmother Gilbert told me that, even in the wilds of a Colorado mining camp, her English mother liked to drink her tea from "thin china." I clinked my wafer-thin spoon on the side of my cup. Granny Harbin said that silversmiths fashioned the Cuttino spoons from molten metal salvaged from the ashes of Peter Cuttino's home in Georgetown.

The grandmother ghosts rested while I looked around my living room at my treasures. Having ignored them during the summer, I ignited their spirits in a roll call: Heidi, Iron Man, Ludwig, Peter, Spring Frog, Venus. All answered: Present.

Heidi is a German doll given me by my grandmother. She has the apple Alpine cheeks of the storybook character.

Iron Man is a cast-iron Japanese figure in a gilded kimono. His silver topknot seduced me on Okinawa in 1960.

Ludwig von Beethoven's copper bust from Berlin once sat in my grandmother's music studio. Ludwig watched little Harbins and Gilberts toil through five-finger exercises and scales.

Peter Cuttino, my great-great-great-grandfather, looked down from his gold-framed portrait over the sofa. One finger marks his place in a small red book. His blood links me to France and Ile de Ré.

Spring Frog came from a book of lithographs of Native Americans. He wears a yellow tunic and a blue print head scarf. My siblings owned portraits of our local Cherokee luminaries: Chief John Ross, John Ridge, and Major Ridge. The portraits were valuable, although the Cherokee people had not been deemed worth saving. My mother had one of the land lottery deeds that granted Cherokee property to white occupiers. I could not hang it on my wall. The deed was the equivalent of a Nazi inventory of seized Jewish possessions.

Venus de Milo was a plaster cast statue from Anna Lester's drawing classes at Mary Baldwin College. Venus stood inside a six-foot obelisk made from gilded steel rods. Standing in the corner of our living room, next to the French doors, the obelisk frame was a pointed reminder of my Nexus Gallery installation in Atlanta in 1985.

* * *

When I wrote the press release for the Nexus Gallery show, I exited the role of polite Parenthetical Wife. In the 1960s, the U. S. Navy had labeled me a Wife in Parentheses. In Rome's Junior Service

League, the term was literal: I had signed the roster as Mrs. David (Susan Gilbert) Harvey, Jr. Even though David did not use Junior after his name, in social correspondence, I had to distinguish myself from my mother-in-law who was Mrs. David Harvey, Senior.

Social tradition said that women's names should be in the newspaper only three times: at birth, marriage, and death. Our status could be daughter, granddaughter, mother, or spouse. A modest Victorian woman would have fainted at the thought of writing a press release about herself.

The first time I used the unadorned "Susan Harvey" as my professional name in a press release for a Rome exhibit, a news reporter added, "wife of former Rome City Commissioner, David Harvey." My female friends were livid. I was the current artist; he was a past commissioner. By tradition, the press demanded a link to an established male. At my show in Washington in 1979, my enlightened husband walked up the steps from Dupont Circle and signed the guest book as "Mister Susan Harvey."

<hr />

The opening of the Nexus show was February 22, 1985. The date was George Washington's Birthday and the one-hundredth anniversary of the Washington Monument dedication. The coincidental date demanded a show about monuments, but could I name the show whatever I wanted? I predicted that the Nexus exhibit might be my last large exhibit, so I refused to censor my title. In an earlier show about women's constrictive clothing and shoes, my working title had been *Chastity Belts and Other Restraints.* I had softened it to *Silver Shackles and Gilded Cages.* For the Nexus show, I chose: *Monumental Erections.* An Atlanta newspaper renamed it: "A Feminist Installation."

In our mock jousting with the patriarchy, Junk Woman and I had measured the Washington Monument and Dr. Robert Battey's monument on Rome's City Hall lawn. I couldn't replicate the Washington Monument, so I hired metal artist Ham Dixon, Jr. to construct a proportional steel version of Dr. Battey's shaft.

When President Washington died, some grieving women painted their mantelpieces black as a sign of mourning. I took the black mantelpiece from my portrait of *The Gynecologist* and mounted it on boxes to form a birth passage. Viewers walked through the female gateway to confront the

OWEN RILEY, JR.

*Nexus Gallery 1985*

golden male obelisk rising from George Washington's "bed." A white iron throne in the distance represented the Apotheosis of our first president, grounded by his size thirteen footprints.

To balance the male monument theme, I created a *Memorial Fountain to the Mother of Atlas.* Around a spherical orb, I placed golden cylinders from a dairy milking machine. Lactic symbols were appropriate for the nurturing role of mothers. Even mythical figures like Atlas, Romulus, and Remus needed the sustenance of a mother's milk.

After the Nexus show closed, I placed the Venus de Milo statue inside the obelisk frame in my living room. A Jungian analyst might have pontificated about "the resolution of the male-female conflicts in the work of Susan Harvey." David was more direct. He named the arrangement, "Venus in the Penis."

———◆———

From my living room in 1998, I remembered the stubborn determination it took to get Washington's bed and Battey's obelisk to the third floor of the old Nexus gallery. The "Hallelujah Van" from my housekeeper's church had died in an Atlanta intersection during morning rush hour. While I waited in a repair shop, a radio program discussed the connection between Egyptian obelisks and Pharaoh's semen. The synchronicity startled me, but the morning was wasted for installation.

At Nexus, the pulley ropes broke as we hoisted my black piano crates through the third floor window to the gallery. Julia Fenton went to get more rope. Lisa Tuttle climbed ladders up to the rafters to light the exhibition. Because of the automotive delays, and because I did not have the fifty dollar fee, I could not rent a fog machine to shroud *Monumental Erections* in the mists of patriarchy.

Owen Riley, Jr. photographed the Nexus show, and David made a grainy video of the opening, but no documentation could substitute for walking in and around my work. I spent one afternoon in the gallery alone. I climbed to the balcony for an overview. I crouched under the vaginal mantelpiece for the underview. My work gave me an erotic high, but there was always the refrain of "if only." With every show, there was one thing I didn't get to do or make. After Nexus, I harbored fog machine regret.

A phase ended. I had several more small exhibits, but I never worked on that theatrical scale again.

---

Because we were in the Celtic fall ingathering of fruits and livestock, I clustered my possessions in vignettes. Decorators call them tablescapes. I renamed them "tablescapegoats." The Alpine animals had grown fat and sassy on high pasture summer greens, and I led the bell-ringing goats into my barn for the winter. I gathered some Rome, Georgia, memorabilia. I had a brass door handle that my dad and I had salvaged from the Harbin Hospital ruins in 1979. I had a framed magnolia leaf that someone in David's family picked up and marked "Mrs. Wilson's Funeral." David had given me a treasure after the General Forrest Hotel closed. In a rare Junk Husband act, he went through a trash pile in the former hotel lobby. He found a brass key, marked for room number 322. Neither of us knew the brass key was a prophetic sign of our future.

I wished Eliza Mary Cuttino McNulty Lester a happy August birthday as I spread one of her shawls over my mother's piano. I took Aunt Joy's ceramic green vase and combined it with my mother–in-law's Rookwood vase on a forest green lacquer tray. I unfolded a set of miniature Japanese screens. I gathered Sister Anna's miniature paintings from Paris: a delicate portrait of my grandmother, a baby, and a French model. I no longer arranged piano crates and oxygen tanks in galleries, but I could pose objects in vignettes.

I picked up Sister Anna's cup and saucer, and my tongue found one last drop of sugared coffee milk. As I left my brown living room, I looked back at Tommy Mew's 1978 *Prometheus* painting over the piano. The "X" markings coordinated with my coral and brown Dhurrie rug. The orange paint picked up the rust tone of the sprig of bittersweet in an onyx-green Japanese vase. One phrase on the Mew canvas was leitmotif for my transitional summer: *ma jeunesse est finie.*

August 24, 1898 Down the Rhine AML journal
The sun struggled through the clouds at 8.30 so I left on the
first boat for Köln. It proved to be a charming day. I enjoyed
it all except the conversation going on around me!

August 24, 1998 Rome, Georgia
*Dream: I'm touring the home of an opera singer. Her house is fascinating,
like a storybook cottage with painted colors, words are written on walls.
I go up the staircase to look out from an upstairs window over a formal
back yard. This woman has the freedom to paint and draw on the walls
with colors and words.*

August 25, 1898—Back in Paris! AML journal
Reached Paris at 8.30 this morning. Was pretty tired and could
not sleep. Rested then went straight to Cooks. Paid Mme Bazin
a visit—she had my home letter. I then wrote to Cook's here and
in Geneva to see if I could hurry up my *own* letter.

August 25, 1998 Rome, Georgia
*Dream in heavy sleep: I'm at a mountain house with the Beavers and lots
of kids and people. Out back the water starts to rise. The kids have written*

*all over the stairwell: names, initials, sayings. Then on up in the hall, adults*
*have also gotten into writing on the walls. In some bedrooms Mary has let*
*them glue Cheerios and macaroni on the walls and ceilings in patterns.*

Hurricane Bonnie was coming and my sadness rose with the
water. I called the House Doctor. He sent his P.A. to assess and
diagnose our problems. I hired him to paint the basement with
waterproof paint and repair the back steps.

The basement was almost cleared. The residue from Mamie's
house sat in plastic boxes: sheet music, old art journals, files of
Rome medical history, family photos from East Third Street,
Westmore Road, and Fieldwood. Harbin cousins would come to
take what they wanted.

> August 26, 1898, Paris, France
> My dear Mother,
>
> I got here yesterday A.M. about 8.30 and came right to
> Mme Grégoire, then after lunch went to Cook's for my mail.
> I then went to the bank. I told them to send my trunk this
> A.M.(it has come) then I paid Mme Bazin a visit—there I
> found your letter. She enjoyed yours to her. I was sorry not
> to go back to her and she seemed to be sorry too. Both she
> and her mother sent their best greetings to you and father.
> And Edith.
>
> My address is 9 rue Sainte Beuve, c/o Mme V. Grégoire.
> Will write you a letter on Sunday. This leaves on the French
> line. Am so glad you are all well. Hope you will not have any
> more very warm weather now before *I come home!* Think of
> that. It is too good to say so. Love to all—Have a lot of cider
> cool ready for me. *I am thirsty!*
>
> Your loving child,
> Anna

August 26, 1998 Rome, Georgia
*Dream: I'm in a new nightclub opened by some Alternate ROOTS people.*
*It's a large space with interesting things hanging from walls and ceilings,*

*like Cirque du Soleil. I tell someone I've always wanted to design a*
*restaurant on Broad Street.*

Even though I was divesting myself of things and not making
large sculpture, I dreamed of arranging objects in space. Grandpa
from Grandpa's Attic picked up a cabinet, a rack, and some other
junk. I gave Mrs. Skelton the old hand plow that I had bought at her
antique shop. The trash truck brakes squealed on East Fourth Street
near the back gate. I saw my wood scraps jounce down the street on
top of yard trash. My maternal wisdom said a clean house would
make me feel better, but my petulant child still wanted her *stuff*.

August 27, 1998 Rome, Georgia
*Dream: I look in my studio window from outside and there are green*
*plants growing out the window like huge chives or vines. Something is*
*growing in there.*

*Dream: I'm with a group of women out past West Rome near some*
*monoliths, some covered with vines. A woman uncovers a huge menhir*
*with carvings like those at New Grange in Ireland: lozenges, spirals, and*
*crosses. I'm amazed. Right here in Floyd County.*

*Dream: Sister Edith and I are in a taxi going to a hotel. We tell the driver*
*that we've traveled in Europe, and now we are exploring our own country.*

Some of my dreams were enigmatic, but I saw the truth in that
day's crop. A green form of life was growing from my studio window.
During the summer, I had been in Europe with the sisters, but I
was also anchored in my hometown. Through letters, I'd heard my
grandmother's youthful excitement. I'd met my great-aunt and seen
her determination, ambition, and feisty spirit.

I wanted to explore Sister Anna's Paris life.

*Whatever you do in life will be insignificant.*
*What is important, is that you do it.*
Gandhi

# Interlude in the Hammock

*Every day is a journey, and the journey itself is home.*
Matsuo Bashō

September 1998
Grandfather Mountain
Day One

My dual summers are over. Edith and Anna Lester are back at work in Berlin and Paris. Having lived in the past all summer, I want to move into the present. To ground myself, I have a new journal. I will record my thoughts and make notes during a few solo days at the Beavers' mountain house.

On the way to North Carolina, I look for ways to enhance the six-hour trip. I remind myself that life is not about the destination; it's about the journey. Who said that? Bashō? I open my windows as I twist through the Nantahala Gorge. The river's roar and cool air fill my car with mountain zest. In Asheville's Biltmore Village, I visit the Bellagio shop and covet every cape, silk scarf, and dangling earring. If I won the lottery, I'd come here to wrap myself in Japanese jackets with sleeves like wings.

On the radio, a man says, "It's not the destination, it's the journey."

I shout at the dashboard: "I just said that!"

After passing through the village of Linville, I mount the hillside to Mary and Walt's house. The hot weight of summer dissolves

behind me as the temperature drops at each curve in the road. Our
family is sad that the Beavers have put their house on the market,
but I recall other arrivals for good times. I pull into the driveway and
decide to use my car as storage. I unload only the necessities: food,
sweatshirts, books, pens, and paper.

I watch the sunset from the hammock near the boulder field.
With my glasses off, the pointillist green leaf dots are myopic gifts
from Pissaro or Seurat. The sound of the forest is the Sound of God,
a swish through the branches. Hardwood forest tempos differ from
the pine forests of my childhood. Oaks and hickories quiver and chat
gently; pine woods whisper and moan. The woodpecker drill could be
one of my cousins tapping Granny Harbin's wood block. Small birds
tweet in the grasses. A rabbit freezes when he sees me. I say hello. He
is Albrecht Dürer's hare from Nuremberg.

I fall asleep in an upstairs bedroom overlooking the valley. During
the night I sit up, startled to hear a car motor on the steep driveway.
I run to the playroom window, open it, and call out "Hello?" The
car lights go off. They probably thought the house was empty. Now
they've seen my car. I race back to my room, throw on clothes, and
call Mary in Charlotte to see if the guards patrol at night. She is out.
I get the security gate phone number from the fire department, and
Gate Guy drives up to investigate. The mystery car is gone. Perhaps
the intruders turned around and rolled back down the hill with their
headlights lights off. A shaky way to start the night alone.

Day Two
*Dreams: A nice old man is looking at some of my artwork. I have a
contraption like a fat broom made out of blue turkey feathers. I say I'll
take twenty dollars. He's built a playhouse for my grandson Burns. I help
Burns get turned around to come down the slide feet first. David pulls
out some Darth Vader masks or heads, wants to sell them, too. I may have
some new hedge clippers.*

At nine o'clock a real estate agent calls. He wants to show the
house at ten. I hide my stuff in a closet, grab a sausage biscuit, and
wait. At ten-thirty he calls to say the client has not shown up. I walk

out onto the deck. The mid-morning sunlight has come over the mountain and filtered through the trees.

The crows hold a raucous caucus in the woods. My father, that old crow, floats in nonchalance on the rising mountain currents. Hard to pin down, my father. He caws a greeting in passing. He is unconcerned about his bride, who lies oblivious under a pink velour blanket. Doc the Crow prefers hillsides, rocks, and cruising on the Sunday skies with his golf buddies.

From my dad I inherited a love of language, mountain solitude, and the full moon. His non-conformity, corny humor, and word play infected my artwork. Doc loved comfortable clothes, art, opera, and Walt Whitman. He liked to sketch, whittle, and pick up driftwood on the beach. I believe he had no regrets.

The wind rises and a cloud gathers—a cotton ball dipped in lead-gray water. The coleus plants on the deck had retracted into parched stems, but my water last night gave them purple hope. The ruby coleus is the color of my mother's corduroy beret. Old ladies love the garnet tones, as well as the raw beef of begonia leaves. One lone white petunia trumpets in the stick planter box, a pretender to Easter lily royalty. A hummingbird thunders by, flying sideways on frenetic wings. There is peace on the mountainside, peace in the valley.

A small brown leaf lands in my coffee cup and floats in the cream residue. The leaf is two-toned, one side beige, one side dark mocha. The dark veins make a batik pattern. The edges curl like the butterballs we ate at the Peninsula Hotel in Hong Kong on our first trip away from baby Mary on Okinawa.

I water grownup Mary's moss-filled planter boxes. I wonder why God didn't make hydrangea stems strong enough to support their blossoms, probably a procreative necessity. The puffballs curtsy to the ground, a mass of wedding dress pearls.

My lunch is hydroponic Bibb lettuce, ham, snow peas, and Alouette cheese with basil and sun dried tomatoes. I nap—maybe hours. Time is liquid. I ignore clocks. I wake up when I think I hear voices, but the conversation comes from golfers on the course below. Solitude magnifies routine sounds.

*Heavy nap dreams: There's to be an art show in my studio complex. It's an old warehouse or store. I go down an alley to get there. I go to the opening of my studios. I may control five or six of these converted schoolhouse rooms. The rooms are all installations, not much saleable art. Some young women are helping me. Too much space for me. I think I should get some of my work out, get some writerblocks and postcards for display. Ludie and Fred White come in. They don't get it. I tell them this is not like art you see in galleries. It's non-representational and non-objective. They say, "It sure is!"*

The sun approaches the horizon. I emigrate from the bed to the hammock. I take an envelope with me. Last October, Mary Hood told our writing class at Berry College to seal the envelope and mark it "not to be opened until…." I've forgotten what I wrote inside, but I've reached the moment of "until." My finger unseals the flap.

Mary Hood had given us three instructions. Write down our deepest dream for five minutes. Then condense it for three minutes, then for one minute. I had written: I want breathing room, freedom of movement, mountain air, research adventures, solitude with paper, and good food. I wanted to shake an idea from all directions. Mary Hood then had us reduce our dream to one word. I chose the word, "process." I love to take a single idea from fertilized seed to fruition and harvest. Perhaps that's the same as choosing journey over destination.

———※———

David calls. Uncle Tom Harbin has died after his long struggle with Alzheimer's disease. Aunt Margie got to the nursing home in time to say "Stop!" as they were resuscitating him. My siblings and I fear that, in spite of our signs on the wall, notes in our mother's chart, and the blue No Code sticker on the door, a well-meaning night nurse will call 911 and prolong our mother's non-life with machines.

I talk to Aunt Margie. Having just settled after the long drive, I will not return to Rome for the funeral. I remember Uncle Tom's laugh, his competitive spirit, and a postcard he sent me when I was six. The card photo showed Tom in Venice. Seated in a gondola, he was debonair, suave, and Valentino handsome.

Day Three
*Dream: I'm coming out of my house with a project due. I am meeting with the new executive director of the arts council. My new role may be to direct the council of artists within me.*

Before walking to the deck to greet the birds, I fix a cup of coffee from the small bag I bought in a Linville store. Mocha Java should wake me up. I sweeten it artificially, but add a splash of heavy cream. I like my *café au lait* heavy on the *lait* or *crème*. The cream has monodyglicerides, the label states, to help it stay whipped: Viagra for heavy cream.

Caffeine makes my fibrocystic breasts hurt. They want to know why I start my day with a drug and chemicals. I tell them I'm on vacation, and I want the hot creamy real coffee taste. At home I drink hot water in a Tesa DuPré mug, followed by Kashi and skim milk or Ryvita and all-fruit jelly. Now the coffee tastes machine-oily. The dialogue has tainted it, but the mocha will tap a java beat all day.

In this week of *The Artist's Way,* Julia Cameron tells us to puncture denial. She says to stop saying "It's OK" and start saying what it really is. So, do I feel "OK" about cleaning out my basement? Could I give up my artwork, my studio? No one can steal my memories. I loved the search and the excitement of combining disparate objects. Working in space satisfied me in more than three dimensions. To height, width, and depth, I added time and spirit.

I never intended to make commercial work. For my exhibits I made what I wanted and dared people to like it. Sometimes I ruffled the feathers of polite society. I could, however, put on a silk print dress and go the Coosa Country Club with David for a Chamber of Commerce banquet. They introduced the head table: David Harvey (and his lovely wife, Susan). I chuckled. "Lovely Wife Susan" was, in reality, the mighty Junk Woman, seen that afternoon at the Anniston Scrap Yard on lower East Third Street.

The year 1999 will mark twenty years since my first solo show at the Berry College Moon Gallery. I'd like to get an overview of what I've created and find justification that my work mattered. In the 1960s, I made burlap pillows and hooked tapestries. I still love texture, fiber, and fabric, but I moved into the hard stuff in the 1970s. My heavy metal pieces slipped men's discs and tortured my legs and spine. Because I used gears, wheels, and rusty tools, some gallery visitors assumed I was a male artist. Most people think that female artists make fiber nests, organic pouches, diaphanous wall hangings, or, if you're Judy Chicago, ruffled pink plates.

I have photographs, videos, and sound recordings of my site sculpture and performances. I'd like to see everything in a gallery space arranged by decade. To me, it's all one work. I'd make a scrapbook, give work to family and friends, close my studio, and walk free of it. I want visual closure, but the saboteuse whispers in a husky southern drawl: Honey, why in the world do you think *you* deserve a retrospective?

———————

At sunset, I break my news fast. The television echoes in my house of one. The Dow Jones Industrial average plunged 512 points, the second worst point loss in Dow's history. I squelch panic and switch to a biography of Princess Diana, one year after her death. On the day of her funeral, I got up before dawn to cry with the world as Sir Elton John sang, "Goodbye England's Rose." Later that morning, I hosted one of my Pissed Princess workshops. We women honored Diana as a prototype of the syndrome we were exploring.

A design show from Paris incites longing for that city. I want to walk those narrow streets. I crave the cadence of the French language. Paris lust is insatiable, but even a *soupçon* requires funds. I think about pitching the summer of 1898 story to a publisher, but the book industry systems are convoluted and arcane. Do I have time to perfect and edit a manuscript, find an agent who will submit the work, and wait for rejection and more rejection? I'd have to put the Pissed Princess on hold, but she's used to that.

Sister Edith and I talk. We can't believe Mamie is the last of her Harbin siblings to survive. Uncle Tom is free from his withered body. Our mother is not. We are virtual orphans without the funeral.

I describe the fragile joy of focused aloneness. After the hot summer, I need this retreat with unlimited sleep, no clocks, just listening to my body and tracking my mind. I tell Edith about my speaking tour in Louisiana, when I drove from one performance to another, stopping to tour antebellum houses along the back roads. On a country highway in West Feliciana Parish, I saw a road sign pointing to Solitude. Solitude, Louisiana. One arm jerked the steering wheel toward the side road. Hunger pulled me toward the State Line Café. I regret missing Solitude. What was the population? One? Sounds about right.

I had written a poem about the Postmistress of Solitude. She has no mail to deliver and plays solo tic-tac-toe in the dust on the post office counter. Post-mistress. Is that like post-modern? Beyond or past mistress? A widow or divorcée in a post-marital state? Post-office would be the retirement stage for David. Post-man might be at the other end of a spectrum that started with Pre-man. When *homo* got up off his *sapiens*, looked around, and said, "Wow! Solitude."

My wandering back road days had surreal moments. At one sold-out retreat center, they rented me a room already prepared for a honeymoon couple due the next day. They didn't mind changing the sheets on the canopied bed, but would I please not drink the champagne in the goody basket? I agreed. I slept with the tall French doors open to the cool swampy night. Birds that Audubon had painted scuffled in the leaves. The next morning a snow-white peacock stood on my doorstep with its tail extended in an opera fan. A stunning gift from James Whistler.

Day Four

*Dream: there's a garden behind a house. The descent is steep. The outside rocks of the path start to crumble down. I'm on the middle rocks, which seem more solid. There are architectural elements, maybe men working in the garden.*

I wake up earlier, ready for coffee and porch. The shock of being here has worn off. Even paradise loses its edge. I take for granted the cool air, the breeze, but I hear hammers down the hill. The mountains are full of new houses, and I'm sitting in one. The Princess prefers to have her kingdom all to herself.

I ponder the plunge of the Dow. I know David is worried about our retirement funds, and Mamie's portfolio lost more money, but I can't visualize these paper losses. If my house burned, I'd know which Cuttino silver spoons melted. When the stock market crashes, I have to calculate the financial loss in trip-to-Europe units. How many trans-Atlantic plane flights dissolved today? How many hotel rooms, how many *coquilles Saint Jacques?*

The sun hits the treetops overhead. I am in the shadow of the mountain. Coolish. In the kitchen, I eat my oatmeal and listen to President Clinton speak political mush in Moscow. Outside, the crows caw about something. Perhaps their Crow Dow went down. I ask them what the crow stock exchange is like. Who are the winners, the crow blue chips?

After a few days, my messiness creeps out, though I must be ready to let realtors show the house. A drawer is not quite shut. My one plate sits in the sink. I can be neat, but it's not my natural bent. I want my things spread out around me: stacks of books, journals, new pens, rice paper, and sumi ink. I see that I would need two weeks—or a lifetime—to play with all the projects I've brought. I want to reread Anna and Edith Lester's summer letters and review my summer journals. I need to change the point of view and voice in *The Pissed Princess*. I also would like to read and write some poetry, sketch, and cut paper squares for folded ornaments to sell at my Christmas studio sale. I'll start with *The Summers of '98* because fall is a time of new beginnings.

David calls to report that our weekend houseguests are not coming. I can stay another day. He has a golf game planned and a football game to attend, so wife-guilt is assuaged. I inhale a deep breath. I have a reprieve from the governor.

I go out onto the driveway and walk an imaginary labyrinth from memory. I step into the woods and gather small sticks. I am a hunched Black Forest peasant woman gathering kindling for a fire. I arrange my sticks in lines to mark the labyrinth pattern. Back into the woods for longer branches. I find a black crow feather, a brilliant yellow leaf, and a blue bead in the mulch beside the house. I place them in a birch-bark barge in the center goal of my construction. For the first time, I have a private labyrinth to walk.

After years of labyrinth walking, I know the rhythm of the circuits. When I penetrate from the entrance onto path number three, I know I will be spun out to path numbers two and one before the coil tightens to the center goal. I'm free as a seagull on the outer rims. Even though I'm moving away from my goal, this expansion prepares me for the compression of paths four to seven. I approach the tightness of level eight, the goal.

Standing in the center of the nautilus shell, I see my summer's work. I have been traversing the outer circuits, at times feeling lost, disjointed, and far from home. Reaching the inner goal of a labyrinth is half the journey. I have ended my three-month sojourn with Anna and Edith Lester. To continue my own story, I must re-coil Ariadne's golden cord as I spin from the vortex, step by step.

> *Whatever you can do, or dream you can, begin it.*
> *Boldness has genius, power, and magic in it.*
> Goethe

# Life in the Forrest

September 2008
Forrest Place, Rome, Georgia

On a blue morning in early September, I stand on the corner of
Broad Street and East Fifth Avenue. These intersecting streets are
my home coordinates. For five years, David and I have lived in the
former General Forrest Hotel, now named Forrest Place. When our
son Dave and his family moved to Rome in 2003, they bought and
renovated our East Third Avenue home. Husband David and I sorted
the accumulations of forty-four years of marriage. We pitched books,
papers, and outgrown clothes, but we moved the best family furniture
to our new residence on Broad Street.

I transferred the Anna and Edith Lester archives to my small
new office. One large expandable file held the rough manuscript of
*The Summers of '98*. I moved Anna Lester's Paris journal, her letters
and address book, and boxes of Lester mcmorabilia. I now had my
own Paris journal. In November 1998, I spent nine days at Hotel le
Sainte-Beuve in Anna Lester's room. In June 2005, I founded Golden
Apple Press and published *Tea with Sister Anna: a Paris Journal.*

At night, bikers park their hogs at the curb below our apartment
windows, but David and I say "Sooey!" and sleep through the gnarled
roar. As nouveau-urban pioneers, we have returned to the Broad
Street of Albert Sidney Burney and Bannester Smith Lester, our
store-owning ancestors. We gave up patio, pine straw mulch, and leaf
blowers for the no-maintenance convenience of downtown living.

From the rear parking lot of our apartment building, David can see his childhood home on East First Street. He has not retired. His office is one block away, on East Sixth Avenue.

The Forrest Hotel building is a large cube of yellow bricks. The roof cornice dentils are the size of dinosaur teeth. The architect, A. Ten Eyck, also built Rome's City Hall. The hotel's builders named it for Confederate General Nathan Bedford Forrest, the "Wizard of the Saddle." During the Civil War, Forrest saved the city of Rome. After Union Colonel Abel Streight's Lightning Mule Brigade surrendered in 1863, General Forrest made a triumphal entry into Rome.

The Nathan Bedford Forrest Chapter of the United Daughters of the Confederacy raised funds for a memorial statue of Forrest. In 1908, they broke ground in the middle of Broad Street, but the first location was too close to the streetcar lines. A year later, the statue stood near the intersection of Broad and East Second Avenue. We Rome High School students perched on the stepped base of General Forrest's statue during football game parades. In 1952, the Forrest Monument hopscotched again, to the base of Myrtle Hill Cemetery. There it joined another statue-in-exile from Broad Street, a Memorial to the Women of the Confederacy.

After the Civil War, Confederate veterans honored their women with a marble obelisk. At the base of the monument, a stone woman tends a wounded soldier. This woman represents the nurses admired by grateful patients (in gray *and* blue) in Rome's Civil War hospitals. She personifies the "ministering angel" described by the Reverend Dr. Wills in his 1881 graduation address to the Rome Female College students. At least two young women from his audience rest nearby. Ellen Lou Axson Wilson has a small plaza near her grave. President Woodrow Wilson chose the words for his wife's memorial stone. Anna McNulty Lester is on the top of the hill with the Lester family.

An early autumn breeze rounds the corner next to Forrest Place. At the base of the steep Fifth Avenue hill, a round medallion plaque honors ironworker Karl Dance. Before long, three (male) gingko trees will drop golden leaves over the narrow park tended by the Town View Garden Club. I remember the fourth ginkgo, the martyred Jeanne d'Arc tree of Fifth Avenue. I'm glad that her offspring took root in my former back yard on East Third Avenue.

Although I am seventy-one years old, my mother's Broad Street Rules are indelible taboos. Never wear shorts into Wyatt's Bookstore to shop. Never eat or chew gum while walking on Broad Street. Never go out with pincurls or curlers. Always wear heels and a girdle—and maybe a hat and gloves—when shopping for clothes at Kuttner's, Fahy's, or Esserman's.

If you were a teenaged girl in the 1950s, you knew that the Forrest Hotel corner had two forbidden places of business. No self-respecting young lady would glance down the cement alley beside the hotel. She might see the Camel-smoking boys who leaned on their cue sticks at the Hill City Pool Hall. My mother told me never to look in a barbershop, where barbers wrapped men in neck aprons, washed their hair, and shaved their beards.

This fall morning, I consider hair legends. Delilah betrayed Samson by having his head shaved. Adoring Rome women snipped ringlets of General Forrest's hair to appropriate his warrior charisma. Victorians made earrings from the woven hair of loved ones. Willing to tempt fate, I peek inside the Forrest Barber Shop, to see if lightning, the Philistines—or my mother—will strike me dead.

The Forrest Hotel was once home to many elderly ladies who had moved from their larger houses. As I pull open the glass doors to Forrest Place, I speak to the spirit of Miss Edna Sulzbacher. Every afternoon, Miss Edna rocked in the sunshine outside the hotel entrance. I would like to sit and compare my life to hers. Instead of silk stockings from Esserman's, I wear Mediven support hose under my socks and walking shoes. My cane has no gold handle. For wildflower walks, I have telescoping trekking poles from REI.

My casual attire might not meet Miss Edna's standards, but my dowager personality grows daily. Miss Myrtle Crêpe de Chine emerges when people don't *do right*. She rails at the evening news anchors when they use the collective noun "troop" to describe a single soldier. Miss Myrtle hates wimpy silverware in restaurants. In church, she likes the "old" hymn tunes. She corrects her physical therapists when they say, "Lay down on the table."

Miss Edna and Miss Myrtle might raise their lorgnettes at the raven-haired girls in gothic-black tee shirts at the Body Canvas tattoo parlor next door to the Forrest. They smoke on the sidewalk and expose their thonged derrières on a window bench. They contemplate serpents, hearts, and Confederate flags for their exposed skin.

Compared to these young women, my Junk Woman costume and my monument measuring of thirty years ago were a quaint form of "acting out."

The former lobby and dining room of the General Forrest Hotel are now gracious spaces for wedding receptions and parties. The tile floor border is a Greek key design in red, green, and black. The chandeliers and sconces once illuminated an elegant lobby with comfortable leather chairs. If you squint, you might see traveling salesmen reading newspapers, tapping cigars into ashtrays, spitting into brass cuspidors. The Forrest Hotel advertisements boasted: "best food in the South." In the Blue Room, white cloths covered individual tables set with green stemware, green ceramic water pitchers, and roses from Mr. Leo Hackett's garden. Sunday lunch found churchgoers savoring an iceberg lettuce wedge drenched with Thousand Island dressing, roast beef au jus, mashed potatoes, and yeast rolls. The vanilla ice cream served in footed metal cups owed its richness to pure whipping cream. Your sundae toppings could be maple or chocolate. If you spilled a drop, the fastidious Mrs. Hackett had to send the linen cloth to Memphis for laundering.

Mr. Leo Hackett forbade his bellhops to walk down the center of the hotel corridors. To preserve the carpets, they tiptoed along the edges while guests strolled down the middle. When David and I return from a trip, we roll our suitcases down the side of our third floor hall carpet in tribute to Mr. Hackett.

The hotel elevator may have the ghost of a former bellhop permanently at the controls. When the elevator got stuck between floors in 1966, Clarence Smith pried open the third floor door and tried to reach the stranded elevator. Clarence fell down the shaft to his death in the basement.

When our current elevator runs non-stop for twenty-four hours, I suspect that Clarence may be on a spree. He may be listening to rock and roll on the radio show of another bellhop character, "Horace of the Forrest."

With the help of our landlord, David and I joined two apartments to make double master suites on the third floor. After years in a three-story house, we like our one-level space. With two apartments, we can choose proximity or privacy. I can close three doors between us when David plays torpedo movies.

In the Imperial Suite, King David rules in his black leather reclining throne in front of his sovereign television set. His Oriental rug fringe is always raked straight. His books with black and red covers sit aligned on shelves, arranged by author, sub-categorized by publication date. To fit the 1840 Burney secretary under our nine-foot ceilings, we removed the top cornice. David's office desk sits below the gold-framed portrait of Peter Cuttino, my Huguenot ancestor. We call David's kitchen the Aperitif Kitchen because it only contains wine for our guests. Overhead cabinets store his orange marshmallow peanuts, popcorn, and chips. The ledge above the kitchen cabinets is a display space for my small iron sculptures and my brick collection from defunct Rome brickyards.

On sunny days, David rides his red Vespa to his office in a clapboard house a block away. His office was once the apartment of Miss Isabel Gammon, Rome's legendary Society Editor. I'm sure she keeps her reporter's notebook poised to describe David's highly-polished Queen Anne conference table. He has no sconces or epergnes, but the stamps on his envelopes are precisely aligned. Miss Isabel could write one of her convoluted columns about how high school sweethearts David and Susan (née Gilbert) Harvey live immersed in their history.

———— ⧫ ————

The Historic Floyd County Courthouse dominates the central view from our apartment windows. The towering red brick building is the scale of a Romanesque cathedral rising in the center of a French town. The rounded arches of the tower have sculpted terra cotta friezes. The human faces that extend from the intricate brick borders are not from Floyd County. One pudgy face could be Nubian; another resembles the vegetative Green Man of pagan Celtic mythology. A few stick out their tongues like Notre Dame gargoyles. In the second floor courtroom, a plaque lists the judges of Floyd County, including David's great-grandfather who served the Rome Circuit from 1870-1873. Judge R.D. Harvey fell from his horse when a passing train spooked the animal on the Cave Spring Bridge. The judge died following the amputation of his leg. He rests, perhaps with his lost leg, in Myrtle Hill Cemetery.

I like to sit on my grandmother's piano stool by our bay window and look west down Broad Street toward the South Broad Bridge. Myrtle Hill could be the terraced Glastonbury Tor rising above Salisbury Plain. After I climbed the Tor in 1994, I saw that our cemetery has similar labyrinthine paths. With binoculars, I can locate the stone wall beside the Burney family lot where Alline Burney Harvey lies beside her husband, David Donaldson Harvey, Senior.

After the Civil War, the Ladies Memorial Association raised funds for a Confederate soldier monument on the crown point of Myrtle Hill. When their nest egg vanished in a bank failure in 1873, they started over. By 1887 they could afford a pedestal base. They added the Confederate figure in 1909, after an embarrassing gaffe. In the sculptor's first version, the soldier wore a Spanish-American War uniform.

During the annual Heritage Holidays tour of Myrtle Hill, storytellers dress in period costumes to portray dead Romans. Our notables range from college founder Alfred Shorter to a woman who died of banana ice cream poisoning. For one Heritage Holidays tour,

I dressed as Edith Lester Harbin beside her grave. Another year, just back from Paris, I wore Anna Lester's gold art medal and posed by her easel. When I planted my feet beside these women's graves, the moist October air connected me with the Lester spirits who hover on the hill. I thanked my ladies for sharing their adventures during the summer of 1998 and in Paris the following fall. Anna's headstone says *Aufwiedersehen*. I take the German word as a promise because I plan to be buried in a plot next to Sister Anna.

We buried Warren Gilbert in the Harbin lot in 1991. Mary Harbin Gilbert ended her long travail in 1999. All of my Harbin aunts and uncles are now there, except our stalwart Aunt Margie. Margie's ancestor, Dr. Robert Battey, has a huge mausoleum on the river side of the cemetery. A large stone fleur-de-lis tops the Battey family's mortuary cave. The flower is a blatant reproductive symbol, but I don't know if it is a pistil or a stamen.

America's Known Soldier rests at the foot of Myrtle Hill. Private Charles W. Graves, in his third burial place, occupies the center of our Veterans Plaza. A World War I Doughboy looks down on his grave. The South Broad Bridge is now the Charles W. Graves Memorial Bridge.

The D.A.R. monument that commemorates the 1793 Battle of Hightower has been moved from behind Myrtle Hill to a more prominent location next to the bridge over the Etowah River.

I once saw a Native-American feathered spear at the base of General John Sevier's monument. If you listen, you may hear drumbeats from Chief King Fisher and the defeated Cherokees.

———— ◦⊰⊰⊱⊱◦ ————

From the east-facing window of David's apartment I can see City Hall. Just over the left shoulder of City Hall, the Days Inn sign marks Lumpkin Hill, where the Rome Female College and the Albert Sidney Burney house once stood.

I need to warn you that the City Hall monuments are restless. In our continuing monument chess game, a committee plans to honor Admiral William Towers, a Rome native who was a pioneer in naval aviation. The proposed Towers memorial site is the City Hall corner now occupied by Dr. Robert Battey's obelisk. Dr. Battey's granite shaft will sashay to the right of City Hall. The Spanish-American War Veterans monument will then hop over to the Carnegie Building lawn. The oak tree behind Dr. Battey's "scapel" will be sacrificed and its mistletoe returned to the Druids. To give better visibility to Admiral Towers, the large white pine in front of City Hall may be cut down. An annual "temp" tree may be hired as our "Holiday" tree.

The Capitoline She-Wolf will remain as the only female between the father of naval aviation and the father of gynecology. Having spent World War II in protective custody in the basement of City Hall, the wolf and Romulus and Remus are secure, unless their nudity and trans-species familiarity offend a later generation of Puritans.

---

A hallway joins David's apartment to my Queen Suite. In my small kitchen, I assemble our simple meals. If we walk to a downtown restaurant, we'll stop to speak to L.D. Raines, who has retired from yard work in our old neighborhood. Since his wife died, L.D. sits in the twilight on a Broad Street bench, too depressed to go home. Anthony Raines might be talking to his father. If it's June, Anthony will want a birthday gift.

When my Harbin cousins come to town, we gather at the Forrest. Miss Isabel would call them a "feminine visiting contingent." We don't eat in the Chinese Room where Miss Edna entertained guests, and where John Philip Sousa hosted a luncheon for our grandmother. We buy our lunch at the downstairs coffee shop and take our sandwiches and salads upstairs to my apartment. We may use paper napkins, but I unwrap the silver forks of Anna Susan Cuttino McNulty, our great-great grandmother.

We have laughing memories of our mothers. Aunt Jane insisted on the correct pronunciation of "buffet" and "niche." Boofie only drank Coca-Colas from six-ounce bottles. She once wrote a thank you note to a gentleman who held a door open for her. Many of the treasures around us date to Mamie's love of family history: a wooden box from the Lester grocery store, Sister Anna's watercolors, Edith Lester's framed music.

David and I eat breakfast at the Burney dining room table in the uncomfortable Burney chairs. From the window we see the pyramid-roofed courthouse tower. Floodlights on the tower serve as our nightlights. During the day, the tower clock is our wall clock.

When we read the ever-shrinking morning newspapers, David clips sale coupons and his clients' obituaries. I rip out articles for my Omen File: the feng shui McDonald's, the renaming of Crayola crayon colors, the endangered watercress snail darter, and the demise of the objective case. We are annoyed to look up from our papers and see that the County Courthouse clock has stopped. After breakfast, David will notify the county. He will then call the cable company, because we don't yet receive the promised (and paid for) Opera Channel. If he retires, he'll report every burned out streetlight on Broad Street. Some neighbors call him "Mr. Mayor."

My office holds my computer and files for speaking engagements and book sales. Crowded closet shelves hold Anna and Edith Lester's letters, their memorabilia, and my manuscript drafts. Hundreds of slides and tapes from my exhibits and lectures wait to be put onto discs. I use a gynecological examining table from my dad's office to hold paper and computer supplies. In a jab at Dr. Battey, I've placed wooden shoe molds in the brass stirrups; my dad's stainless steel speculum grasps a white egg.

I had discarded some of my art work fragments in the great summer purge of 1998, but I kept enough sculpture for a 1999 retrospective exhibit at Berry College. I closed my studio and gave away my black piano crates. Small key pieces remain. Winged angel feet stand on my office bookcase. A well pulley wheel with feathers recalls the Trail of Tears. The seminal piece of my career sits on a pedestal. The wooden assemblage dates to my design classes at Shorter College. When I arranged those wood scraps in 1970, my mind and spirit snapped into three dimensions. *Cantilever* symbolizes living outside the rectangular frame of two-dimensions, just as David and I now live outside the norm of a house on a lot.

When I drink my morning coffee, I look out at the former
Esserman's store, now the Peach Palace nightclub. The Essermans, like
the Kuttners, were successful Jewish merchants. I admire the art deco
frieze and incised letters on Esserman's façade. The architect placed an
Egyptian lotus above the stylized pilasters. Hebrew slaves might have
waved such palm-shaped fans over the pharaohs of Egypt.

A few doors down Broad Street, the classical G.C. Murphy
building was the site of lunch counter sit-ins during Civil Rights
demonstrations in March 1963. Today, a pickup truck out front
might have a rifle in the gun rack and a Confederate flag on the
bumper with the slogan, "Fergit, Hell!"

On summer nights since our move to Broad Street, son Dave
and his family call us as they approach El Zarape restaurant across
the street. We open a window and wave. Ryan, May, and Wesleigh
Harvey yell, "Hey Moo Moo!" "Hey Datee!" When the entire
Harvey clan gathers for holidays in Rome, we fill half of Schroeder's
New Deli with Beavers, Kenums, and Harveys.

From my living room, when the willow oak trees are bare, I can
see the lantern lights on the new Chief John Ross Pedestrian Bridge,
which spans the Oostanaula River. The bridge connects downtown
to the former Cherokee Chief's land. The lights of Shorter College
twinkle on its hill in West Rome. The original downtown Shorter was
alma mater to my grandmother; Mary Harbin studied on the West
Rome hill. A bookcase from Granny's farm holds the ceramic cup I
made in 1949 in the Shorter art department with Martha Griffin.
Behind white Ionic columns (salvaged by Son of Junk Woman from
an Atlanta office building) I've propped the seven-foot hooked
tapestry panel I made in 1969 in Virginia Dudley's class. My coffee
table is a Carnegie Library catalog case with small vignettes in the
drawers. I named it *Woman's Work is Never Done.*

My living room combines my art career with Anna Lester's. Sister
Anna's Paris trunk sits under the windows next to a cabinet holding
her palette, paint-mixing tray, horsehair brushes, charcoal fragments,
and her Paris miniatures. Three of her still life paintings lean against

the wall. Two wicker baskets on the floor hold my Writerblocks from the summer of 1998. My grandchildren dump the blocks on the rug to build towers and towns with the word-covered blocks. One day they will get the joke: "Oh! Moo Moo made Writers' Blocks!"

On a corner table, I display a book by Amy Steedman, Anna Lester's Scottish friend in Paris. After living at 9, rue Sainte-Beuve in November 1898, Steedman became a well-known author and artist. Amy's roommate, Frances Blaikie illustrated many children's books.

These Scottish women lured me to Edinburgh in 2000. Using notations from Anna Lester's 1898 address book, I located their former homes. Dr. Tom Barron and Dr. Jim Strachan, the current residents of Amy Steedman's house, invited me to spend the night. In an Edinburgh library, I found an obituary for Frances Blaikie, who died in 1915 at the age of forty-six:

> "[She was] at her best illustrating nursery rhymes, benefitting from her gift of benevolent caricature. Immensely popular and widely loved, sadly she died just after an important contract had been signed. Wherever she went—the various Art Schools, in Paris, at the Club in London, at the Flats-her wonderful gift of kindly caricature made her widely known, and those who were admitted to her inner circle give thanks for having known the most helpful, loyal, and true friend that ever lived."

Tom Barron and Jim Strachan joined me in a late afternoon search for Holydean, the former Blaikie family house in the Scottish Borders south of Edinburgh. When we appeared on their doorstep, Alison and Charles Melville invited us into Holydean, their lovely country home. In a small church near Melrose, we found a memorial plaque to Frances Margaret Brunton Blaikie. When I stood by her grave at dusk in the quiet cemetery, I thanked "Miss Blaikie" for extending my adventure with Anna Lester. Her "benevolent caricatures" became illustrations for *Tea with Sister Anna: a Paris journal.* The incandescent spirits of Amy Steedman and Frances Blaikie are as powerful to me as those of my kinswomen.

*F. Blaikie 1898*

My bedroom continues my layered mini-museum. Like my entire apartment, the walls are painted Susan Harvey Taupe. I have hung Anna Lester's nude charcoal drawings on two walls. Anna predicted that Romans would be too modest to look at her nude studies from Paris. I am pleased to have them in my space, even if they distract workmen and embarrass young grandchildren. More nudes are in my bathroom: Anna's plaster statue of Venus overlooks my bathtub. A nude photograph by Owen Riley, Jr. reflects in the vanity mirror. Virginia Dudley's metal fish sits on my windowsill. His nudity offends no one.

Some of my scavenged archifrags made the move from East Third Avenue. A wooden panel from Madeline Kuttner's Fourth Avenue house stands in one bedroom corner, next to ventilation grates found in the Harbin Hospital debris. Miss Carrie Beysiegel's iron fence became the welded headboard for my bed. Because Miss Carrie's stubborn tenacity frustrated my grandfather's hospital expansion on Third Avenue, I call my fence headboard "FaFa's Revenge."

Behind the glass doors of my grandmother's secretary, Sister Anna's Paris teapot sits beside the Newcomb Pottery vase my mother bought on her New Orleans honeymoon. On top of the secretary, the Fahy Store hat rack holds my black hat from Bon Marché and an original creation by Rome's Mildred Galloway. Eliza Mary Lester's paisley shawl drapes over Granny's ladder-back desk chair. My mother's Chinese-orange Parson's table supports my lacquer collection and the burnished clay pots I bought from "Pale Moon" on the Pamunkey Reservation in Virginia in 1996.

Bookcase shelves hold my research books on labyrinths, sundials, Neolithic stone circles, and Jungian symbols. A Carnegie Library catalog case supports my travel journals and dozens of Paris books. Under the back window, I have covered Granny's gate-leg table with a black and taupe Charles Rennie Mackintosh cloth from Glasgow. The tablescape includes Alline Harvey's after-dinner coffee service, Mary Gilbert's stacked silver coffee pot, and the small silver teapot I bought on my last Paris day with Sister Anna in November 1998.

The back window of my apartment puts me at eye-level with the yellow cottage where David grew up. As she declined, his mother sat on the front porch and counted the cars that passed in the street. If she thought the number was too high, she called the City Manager. After many people stepped on the struggling ivy plants in the parkway instead of using her stone steps, Alline made the city erect a sign: Please Use Steps. When lightning stops the City Clock, I think of David's mother before I complain.

Our brother-in-law, Fred White, planted the magnolia tree that now obscures Alline's house. Sixty years ago, David helped his mother graft a pink dogwood stem onto a white dogwood tree in the parkway. Each spring, the hybrid dogwood sprouts limbs of winter-white blossoms followed by pink afterthoughts. The tree encapsulates Alline: she grafted pink ladyhood onto every facet of her life.

From my bed I watch the morning sun hit the white latticework of the City Clock. Lit by the first rays of sun, the balustrades remind me of a New England widow's walk. Pink clouds by Magritte might spatter a Tiffany blue sky behind the tower, three church steeples, and the synagogue's Greek temple façade. Crows often caw past my window: my dad is on patrol. Once a month, a full moon rises behind Clocktower Hill, traverses the sky, and sets outside my western window behind Myrtle Hill Cemetery.

＝—＜◇＞—＝

As I stare out my window, the City Clock strikes twelve elegant bongs. A Sno-Cone cart putters down East First Street. "Turkey in the Straw" blares from its honky-tonk speakers, followed by "When the saints go marching in." Which message should subtitle my morning? When the First Baptist Church carillon chimes a sermonette, I choose its optimistic refrain: "In hope that sends a shining ray, far down the future's broadening way."

＝—＜◇＞—＝

In September 2008, the world rocks with earthquakes, cyclones, and floods. An unresolved war in Iraq, a jittery stock market, a deflated housing market, and talk of recession fill the evening news. We will break either a gender or racial barrier for our next Democratic presidential nominee.

Edith and Anna Lester hiked across the Mer de Glace near Chamonix in the summer of 1898. This year, while the euro trampled the dollar, that Alpine glacier receded a few more inches up its rocky valley. I'm glad my sister Edith and I visited the shrinking glacier in 2002.

On September the eighth, David and I will fly to Paris for nine days. We will celebrate our Golden Anniversary, a year early, in room nine of the Hotel le Sainte-Beuve. We will play tourist at the Paris Opera, on the roof of Galleries Lafayette, and on the upper deck of a Seine River *vedette*. After a picnic in the Jardin du Luxembourg, we will eat pistachio macaroons from the Gérard Mulot bakery.

Each morning, I will wake up in Sister Anna's room on the *troisième étage*. Christian (*le petit*) will pour my *café au lait* as he did in November 1998. I will step out onto the damp cobblestones of Anna Lester's Montparnasse streets. I now claim them as my own.

I'll send you a postcard.

Postmarked Paris.

*Dream of Paris!*
*SGH*

# ACKNOWLEDGMENTS

My primary thank you goes to Edith Lester Harbin and Anna McNulty Lester for their inspiring lives. Mary Harbin Gilbert's trove of family history provided archival materials, but she did not live to see the golden apples from her orchard. Margie Troutman Harbin and Sherrie Lanier Bacon died in 2009. I miss their enthusiastic support for my art and writing.

My gifted editor, Mindy Wilson, used her pruning shears to shape my life as an espaliered fruit tree against the garden wall of Rome, Georgia. I am grateful to dozens of Romans who contributed anecdotes, names, dates, and bits of town lore. For longer interviews, I thank Elizabeth Chisholm, Jody Selman, Ben Lucas, Larry Osborn, Frances Dent, Villa Heizer, Mary Tipple Cobb, Frances Davis, Elaine Smith, and Mary Jervis Hayes. Lynn Maddox brought gifts from Nuremberg. Anne Culpepper, the Queen of Myrtle Hill, gave an immediate response to every question.

Sutton Bacon supplied valuable technical support in 1998. In 2005, Page Skinner Thomas transcribed many 1898 letters. I thank Mary Hood and Rosemary Daniell for writing classes in 1997 and 1998. Snowbird Mountain Lodge was my occasional refuge for writing and editing this book.

I'm grateful to Hans and Mary Rogers and the talented team at Caldwell Printing Company. Tracy Cole did the layout and typesetting. Debbie Stubbs made the maps and line drawings. Their patience and skill made book production a joy.

The WHIM group has been my writing family for over two decades. Bambi Berry, Mildred Greear, Nancy Griffin, and Rena Patton are valued friends and mentors.

I thank my brother and sister-in-law, Peter and Suzy Gilbert, for their love and for the use of their pool during the hot summer of 1998. Edith Gilbert Ethridge has been the perfect companion on our sister travels in England, France, and Switzerland. She and Larry Ethridge were our travel partners in Switzerland in 1985 and 1987. My Harbin cousins shared their family memories and treasures from our grandmother's attic.

For over fifty years, David Harvey has given me his love and wisdom. His bedrock support makes my creative life possible. Our children, Mary and Walt Beaver, Katherine and Tim Kenum, and David and Jaynee Harvey, have been cheerleaders for their mother. This book is for all of them and for our wonderful grandchildren: Christopher, Drew, Clay, Burns, Harrison, Carson, Ryan, May, and Wesleigh.